Revelation and Reconciliation

Revelation and Reconciliation

An Angle on Modernity

Stephen N. Williams

ⓒ
James Clarke & Co

JAMES CLARKE & CO

P.O. Box 60
Cambridge
CB1 2NT
United Kingdom

www.jamesclarke.co
publishing@jamesclarke.co

Hardback ISBN: 978 0 227 17738 9
Paperback ISBN: 978 0 227 17739 6
PDF ISBN: 978 0 227 90738 2
ePub ISBN: 978 0 227 90739 9

British Library Cataloguing in Publication Data
A record is available from the British Library

First published by Cambridge University Press, 1995
Second Edition by James Clarke & Co, 2021
Copyright © Stephen N. Williams, 1995, 2021

Contents

Introduction   vii

Chapter 1   1
Around and About Descartes

Chapter 2   33
Restoring a Measure of Faith in Locke

Chapter 3   63
Troubled Giant

Chapter 4   91
The Verdict of Nietzsche

Chapter 5   122
From a Theological Point of View

Chapter 6   151
Towards Reconciliation

Bibliography   179

Index   187

Introduction

Towards the end of the last millennium, I published a relatively brief volume on *Revelation and Reconciliation: a Window on Modernity*.[1] It was both a polemical and a constructive attempt to consider modernity from a specific and limited point of view. Although it did not deal with postmodernity, it did note that postmodernity could be regarded as late modernity.[2] Its polemic was directed against those who highlighted epistemological issues in the intellectual breakdown of Western Christianity. Conversely and constructively, I argued that underlying the surface contrast and collision between reason and revelation was the contrast and collision between what may loosely be called moral self-sufficiency and the Christian claim that God has acted in history for our reconciliation. According to Nietzsche, who featured quite prominently in my account, 'the moral (or immoral) intentions in every philosophy have every time constituted the real germ of life out of which the entire plant has grown. . . . I accordingly do not believe a "drive to knowledge" to be the father of philosophy.'[3] The argument in my volume did not amount

---

1. Stephen N. Williams, *Revelation and Reconciliation: a Window on Modernity* (Cambridge: Cambridge University Press, 1995).
2. Colin Gunton, whose work came in for much consideration, drew no sharp lines between modernity and postmodernity in this respect in *The One, The Three and the Many: God, Creation and the Culture of Modernity* (Cambridge: Cambridge University Press, 1993) 5, 12.
3. I quote from the translation of Nietzsche's *Beyond Good and Evil* (London: Penguin, 1990), section 6, used in my 1995 volume. From now on, this work is

to a direct endorsement of Nietzsche's claim; had that been its aim, it would have flopped badly, for I made no pretence to an engagement with philosophy. Further, my argument was no more indebted to Nietzsche's thought in general than it was overtly committed to this far-reaching categorical judgement of his in particular. Nevertheless, the argument that I ran clearly resonated with Nietzsche's judgement and constituted a proposal for the primacy of the moral over the epistemological in a way consonant with it.

The reason for turning the searchlight on the question of epistemology was that some theologians had appropriated and endorsed observations by Michael Polanyi that called for critical interrogation. What polemically drove the first edition were largely, though not solely, the contributions of two of them, Lesslie Newbigin and Colin Gunton, to discussions of the Enlightenment and modernity. They highlighted the significance of the epistemological shift effected by Descartes and Locke, which, they opined, disastrously overthrew the theologically and philosophically correct way of ordering the relations of reason and revelation. In the first chapter of the volume, I described Newbigin's and Gunton's arguments, voiced preliminary doubts about them and then briefly looked at Descartes from a different point of view. The second chapter dealt more rigorously with Locke. A third chapter enlisted Barth in the service of the argument that epistemological shifts in the eighteenth century, while most certainly significant, were nonetheless less basic than and were at the service of developing pretensions to autonomy in contrast to the Christian tradition. This chapter, like the previous one, also touched on deism. Nietzsche was the subject of the fourth and Don Cupitt of the fifth chapter before a final chapter concluded with brief reflections on a dogmatic, as opposed to an historical, approach to the theological question of reconciliation in history. Gunton's Bampton Lectures, *The One, the Three and the Many*, appeared just too late for me to integrate discussion of it satisfactorily into the main body of the book but, as it dealt with relevant matters, an 'Appendix' was devoted to it.

This second edition, which now sees the light of day, is very substantially revised to the point of being largely re-written; witness a one-word adjustment in the title to signal the difference. It sees the light of day because of the kind encouragement of theological friends to produce it, and special thanks in that regard go to Dr Andrew Moore in Oxford, Professor Bradley Green of Union University, Tennessee and

---

abbreviated as *BGE* and Adrian Del Carro's translation, *Beyond Good and Evil/ On the Genealogy of Morality* [*OGM*] (Stanford, CA: Stanford University Press, 2014) is used.

Professor Daniel Treier of Wheaton College, Illinois. Its production has taken longer than it should have done because it initially seemed to me that there were only two ways of realistically going about it, each of which had a drawback. On the one hand, an edition that was only slightly altered would be unsatisfactory, failing to reckon with the passage of time since the first. On the other hand, a completely new volume would confound the purpose of re-launching the old. *Tertium non datur* (there is no third way) seemed to be writ large over the project by a scowling Muse. However, I have now defied her with all the boldness of a Classical hero and attempted a middle way. I trust that this resulting second edition is neither a lame compromise between the two rejected alternatives nor an unsightly dialectical attempt to transcend antitheses but, on the contrary, a felicitous re-writing.

What is going on now, in this second edition, is as follows. Lesslie Newbigin's work continues to command attention in missiological circles. Yet, without implying that there is no value today in what he said on the subject with which *Revelation and Reconciliation* originally dealt and deals now, I have re-oriented the discussion in this book so that he is ungraciously airbrushed out of its main body. By way of compensation, it well serves my purpose to recapitulate below, in this introduction, the substance of my original engagement with him. I have treated Colin Gunton with greater dignity. Rather than compel him either to carry the burden Newbiginlessly from the beginning of the book or virtually disappear Newbiginly in the course of it, the level of academic interest in his work since the first edition has warranted my expanding and strengthening what was originally the 'Appendix', re-writing it so as to form a chapter in the main body of the book. I have also kept him in the frame before that by way of occasional allusion. [4] In arguing my thesis, then, in this second edition, I have formally distanced it somewhat from some of the contributions that goaded me into it in the first place, but the concerns and substance of my argument remain exactly what they were in the first edition.

In this revised edition, the material arising from a consideration of Descartes has been expanded in the first chapter at the expense of our two theologians, though the chapter is not just about Descartes. The second chapter, on Locke, and the third, on Barth, are slightly altered

---

4. Michael Polanyi, whose critique of Locke steered Newbigin and Gunton's analyses and who correspondingly occupied an important place in the early chapters of the first edition, has attained the via media in relation to these two. I enlarge his profile in this edition, but he does not attain the Guntonian heights of a dedicated chapter.

here and there, but they remain substantially the same. The first half of this volume, then, has been revised and somewhat expanded overall, but most of it is not substantially re-written. It is otherwise with the second half. The (fourth) chapter on Nietzsche has been entirely re-written. [5] The chapter on Don Cupitt, which originally followed it, has simply been dropped and Colin Gunton is now substituted for Cupitt in the fifth chapter. The final chapter has been largely re-written, while retaining a key argument from the original. None of this will matter much to anyone except the author, but remnants of a once noble, if rather shallow, professional conscience oblige me to square accounts with the (doubtless equally noble) reader.

THE NATURE OF THE ENQUIRY

Explaining how Lesslie Newbigin and Colin Gunton set me on the trail followed in the first edition is not an exercise in wandering down memory lane.[6] It explains the concerns that lay and lie behind this work. A generation ago, there was a significant movement in the United Kingdom to proclaim the gospel as 'public truth'. No one was more prominent in it than Lesslie Newbigin, perhaps the most influential missiologist of that generation in the English-speaking world. In his Osterhaven Lectures, published under the title *Truth to Tell: The Gospel as Public Truth*, Newbigin declared the need 'to affirm the gospel not only as an invitation to a private and personal decision but as public truth which ought to be acknowledged as true for the whole life of society'.[7] He urgently advocated a cultural renewal comparable to what Augustine strove to accomplish in and in relation to a decaying Classical world. What Augustine did was to establish publicly the main elements of a Christian world-view by unashamedly starting with dogma, specifically Christian dogma. Following Augustine's act of intellectual creation came intellectual transgression, featuring Descartes, who led the way in persuading us to start our intellectual constructions with doubt rather than with dogma. 'I hope', said Newbigin, that it is 'not overdramatizing'

---

5. I had the opportunity of pursuing Nietzsche in greater depth in the interval between the first and the present editions. See Stephen N. Williams, *The Shadow of the Antichrist: Nietzsche's Critique of Christianity* (Grand Rapids: Baker Academic Press, 2006). In this work, I cite quite extensively secondary literature on Nietzsche along with the primary literature, whereas in this volume, relatively little secondary literature is cited.

6. I repeat here some of the material found on pages 1-12 of the first edition.

7. *Truth to Tell: The Gospel as Public Truth* (London: SPCK, 1991) 2.

to 'say that the new Cartesian starting-point, which has been so foundational for all that has followed, was a small-scale repetition of the Fall'.[8] From then on, the critical method expanded, eventually to implode under the pressure of its own logic, leaving the stark and sinister Nietzschean will as the source of understanding. Responding to this state of affairs, Newbigin offered a rationale for a new Augustinianism, making belief again the starting-point of knowledge. His modern mentor in this project was Michael Polanyi.

In identifying Polanyi as the most prominent of his aides or guides in the task of epistemological renewal, Newbigin was recycling an argument developed with some passion and force in at least three previous works.[9] Jointly considered, these works constituted a proposal for intellectual reconstruction built on a critique of the legacy of the Enlightenment. The passion for the restoration of meaning and hope exhibited in these works was suited to the high social, religious and cultural significance of their author's aims. Newbigin did not doubt that the Enlightenment brought great gains, which must be preserved. However, he opined that their salutary preservation required a Christian frame of life and thought. The Enlightenment framework turned out to be catastrophic. On account of its problematic epistemology, it led culturally to the loss of both meaning and hope. Doubt was given epistemic primacy over belief. This found its most prominent expression in the scientific world-view. Speaking of faith – which, in this context, meant the same as 'belief' – in its relationship to doubt, Newbigin said: 'The reversal of roles between these two words was at the heart of the experience which ushered in the modern scientific world-view. . . . At the centre of the movement which created our modern culture was a shift in the balance between faith and doubt.'[10]

If Descartes was responsible for the fall, it was John Locke who merited the stick at the particular point where these words were written. As far as Newbigin was concerned, Polanyi neatly and precisely

---

8.   In light of Newbigin's vocabulary, we note that belief 'that the task of Cartesian philosophy is to make good what we lost with the Fall' was present early; see, e.g., Nicholas Joseph Poisson in 1671, quoted in Stephen Gaukroger, *The Emergence of a Scientific Culture: Science and the Shaping of Modernity, 1210 – 1685* (Oxford: Clarendon, 2006) 337. Had Newbigin made reference to Francis Bacon, he would have been referring to a project explicitly dedicated to that task.

9.   *The Other Side of 1984* (London: World Council of Churches, 1983); *Foolishness to the Greeks* (London: SPCK, 1986); *The Gospel in a Pluralist Society* (London: SPCK, 1989).

10. *The Other Side*, 20.

identified the problem bequeathed by Locke. This was the elevation
of demonstrative reason over faith, and it constituted the hallmark of
the critical mind at its modern cultural advent. In the round, Newbigin
was pitting Augustine and Polanyi against Descartes and Locke in the
enterprise of restoring faith as the ground of knowing. What made
Polanyi's contribution particularly weighty was that it issued from a
philosopher of science. Science is 'the intellectual core', the 'mental and
spiritual heart' of our culture. Its abandonment of teleology is the key to
the way it understands nature, and its generalized philosophy contains
the epistemological poison that entered the bloodstream of Western
thought. While Polanyi did not espouse Augustine's Christian faith
in particular, he made room for and gave support to a contemporary
repristination of Augustine's basic epistemological approach, viz., the
grounding of knowledge in faith and the presentation of truth on a
foundation of dogma.

Newbigin's main theological ally in advancing this line of thought
shared the limelight with him in my original enquiry. That was Colin
Gunton, who engaged in rather more detail than did Newbigin with the
aforesaid epistemological issues. In an essay exploring the 'epistemology
of the concrete', Gunton claimed that 'the Gospel's unique contribution
to epistemology is best illustrated by means of an instance of creative
and imaginative rationality, which is still essentially grounded in the
concrete and the particular'.[11] It is vital that we promote this in light of
the 'baneful legacy which Enlightenment epistemology has bequeathed
to our culture'.[12] The personalistic theology that Gunton sketched in
order to counter that legacy was associated with Polanyi's brand of *fides
quaerens intellectum*. Like Newbigin, Gunton was here sustaining a line
that he had taken for some years. Epistemology is not just *an* issue.
Newbigin wrote the foreword to Gunton's *Enlightenment and Alienation*,
a volume that set out a thesis parallel to his own, albeit developed
differently.[13] Gunton argued here that the Enlightenment produced
a variety of alienations whose first mark 'is the tearing apart of belief
and knowledge'.[14] Tackling this theme in three parts, Gunton duly dealt

---

11.   See 'Knowledge and Culture: towards an epistemology of the concrete' in Hugh
        Montefiore, ed., *The Gospel and Contemporary Culture* (London: Mowbray,
        1992) 84-102, quotation from p. 94.
12.   'Knowledge and Culture', 85.
13.   *Enlightenment and Alienation: An Essay towards a Trinitarian Theology*
        (Basingstoke: Marshall, Morgan & Scott, 1985). In this work, Gunton picked out
        for commendation *The Other Side of 1984* from amongst Newbigin's works, ix.
14.   *Enlightenment and Alienation*, 5.

with epistemology first.[15] Descartes lies at the bottom of our problems. He succeeded in dividing the world dualistically into a world of senses and a world of intellect, an operation that results in the alienation of mind from the world. By forging a lamentably skewed philosophy of perception, Descartes promoted intellectual error, eventually generating a conceptual incapacity for epistemological realism. The religious outcome of this was that claims essential to any sound theological epistemology were outlawed. In this context, Immanuel Kant was able to spin out a philosophical anthropology and a moral philosophy that featured an autonomous moral subject, separated in freedom from the external world of causal order and convinced that any external authority, supremely God, was an interference with autonomy and, thus, with moral agency. Gunton perceived that the sad end of all this is that we are alienated from our world, our true selves and our God.

'The sad end' – but if epistemology was the beginning, what exactly was the end? Moving in a general direction similar to that of Newbigin on nihilism, but limning the contours of his account a bit differently, Gunton remarked on the atheistic telos of the trends he was concerned to expose. With Newbigin, he followed Polanyi in his indictment of Locke and with Eberhard Jüngel he indicted Descartes. Descartes is a significant source of atheism. Jüngel judged Western atheism to be eminently a reaction to a God whose predominant attribute is power. Descartes' methodological doubt had two relevant consequences in this respect. Firstly, in the process of his deductions, by the time Descartes had worked his way out of the *cogito* through to the demonstration of divine existence, God turned out to be necessary for human identity. If God is necessary, we are dependent, and it is the notion of such dependence, such a relation to power, that largely fuelled atheistic revolution. Secondly, Descartes' conclusion could be up-ended. God was so positioned in the intellectual scheme of things that, in effect, he was dependent on us humans, for he emerged at the end of human logical operations. Conceivably, then, he is the product of my thought. Ontological power turns out to be perched precariously on a highly suspect appearance of logical necessity. Enter Fichte, Feuerbach and finally Nietzsche, who will topple the deity by razing the foundations on which deity was mounted.[16]

---

15. While Gunton appears to accord priority to the epistemological question, describing 'the tearing apart of belief and knowledge' as the 'first *mark* of alienation' (my italics) is not the same as saying that it is the first *cause* of alienation.

16. See especially chapter 10 of the work to which Gunton is indebted here,

Like Newbigin, Gunton offered a rich and positive contribution to the theological resolution of these problems, his own being of a studiously Trinitarian nature. Saluting their fruitfulness and force, I did not in the original edition interest myself in the substantive and worthy doctrinal proposals of either author, nor in that of Jüngel for that matter. My interest lay in their report on the past. Two questions troubled me on that score. The first applied to Gunton's work and was then, and remains now, of lesser importance, though not unimportant. If Gunton agreed with Newbigin's positive account of Augustine, as far as it went, he showed little sign of it; it was to the negative and not to the positive features of Augustine's intellectual effort that he persistently drew attention. My interest was not then, and is not now, in adjudicating Gunton's critique of Augustine's substantive theology, but in his reading of the influence of Augustine on intellectual history. Overtly, it was entirely different from Newbigin's, yet they both agreed with Polanyi's appeal to Augustine. Moreover, my interest in his reading of the influence of Augustine on intellectual history included an interest in the general principles of Gunton's reading of intellectual history.

The second question, by far the chief, that exercised me in connection with our two authors provides us with an entrée into the present volume. In *The Other Side of 1984* and *Foolishness to the Greeks*, Newbigin made much of the rise of modern science and scientific method. The success of scientific explanation led to a wider, if not imperialistic, ideal of explanation in the form of generalisation from science and this disabled people from accepting forms of explanation other than the narrowly scientific. Scientific knowledge became a paradigm for knowledge. Then, in *The Gospel in a Pluralist Society*, we encounter an interesting admission. In *The Other Side of 1984*, Newbigin had fleetingly referred to the influence of the Renaissance on the eventual outcome for theology of the seventeenth-century scientific method. Now, in *The Gospel in a Pluralist Society*, he observed that Reventlow's detailed study of *The Authority of the Bible and the Rise of the Modern World* had led him to see that broad currents of humanistic spirituality and rationality flowed even deeper than the stream of scientific movement under the surface of modern culture.

'Spirituality' is the more interesting and telling word in this pair. Well might Newbigin use it alongside 'rationality' in his account of Reventlow's work. Reventlow documented the way in which the notion of Christianity as a scheme of moral action dominated the beginnings and development

Eberhard Jüngel's *God as the Mystery of the World* (Edinburgh: T & T Clark, 1983).

of biblical criticism up until the eighteenth century, and he did it so as to give clear prominence to the place of broadly moral considerations in the formation of modernity. On Reventlow's account, a humanistic religious outlook, of which Stoicism is a significant component, undergirds the form of post-Reformation rationalism that bears fruit in the deistic turn against traditional Christianity and its claims to revelation. [17] What made Newbigin's acknowledgement of Reventlow's influence interesting and telling is that it led him to no perceptible modification of his historical thesis on the role of epistemology in either this or in the succeeding volume, *Truth to Tell*. Why not? Reventlow places epistemological and scientific questions in a wider context. This should surely have affected or challenged Newbigin's diagnosis of modernity. Apparently it did not.

A little probing unearthed more questions. When, under the influence of Basil Willey, Newbigin claimed that the Enlightenment was characterized by a shift towards celebrating the general sufficiency of the scientific mode of explanation, he picked out the familiar fact that Newton taught the Enlightenment to start with and work from what is observable. Do this, however, and you just end up with a bloated version of the observable with which you started. So Newbigin thought:

> The totality of all observable phenomena is 'Nature'. 'Nature' in effect replaces the concept of God, which is no longer necessary. The characteristic position of the eighteenth century, known as 'Deism', did indeed retain the concept of God as a sort of Prime Mover standing behind the processes of nature. But even in that century there were plenty of critics who defined a deist as 'a person who is not weak enough to be a Christian and not strong enough to be an atheist'. The nineteenth century drew the obvious conclusion: there was no place for 'God'.[18]

These words indicate a hiatus in explanation. Leaving aside the questions of whether the characteristic position of the eighteenth century should be identified with deism and then deism identified with this notion of God, something was obviously missing from Newbigin's

---

17. E.g., Reventlow uses the phrase 'moralistic-spiritualistic religious humanism' to describe this outlook, H. G. Reventlow, *The Authority of the Bible and the Rise of the Modern World* (London: SCM, 1984) 72. See his discussion of Herbert of Cherbury in part 2, chapter 2.

18. I had made much of these words in a brief article on 'Theologians in Pursuit of the Enlightenment', *Theology* LXXXIX, September, 1986, which included discussion of the work of Andrew Louth.

summary account. If the concept of God in the eighteenth century merely fulfilled a role that, logically, 'Nature' was equipped to fulfill, then we might indeed understand the logic of the atheistic outcome as described here by Newbigin. That is, God retreats with the advance of Nature. However, there was significantly more to nineteenth-century atheism than one would gather from this account. Take Kant. On Newbigin's account, replacing God with Nature recasts the whole understanding of law, reason and conscience, a fact to which Kant's philosophy is something of a monument. Yet, as far as Kant was concerned, whatever happens to God when you are talking science, cosmological and even teleological arguments, you require at least some kind of God in some kind of way when you talk morality through to its end. Morality blocks atheism. Granted, the survival of God on Kant's moral understanding may be adjudged extremely tenuous and the surviving God theistically thin. Nonetheless, Kant's insistence on God's regulative presence in this domain of moral discourse testifies to the way in which the concept of God had provided the foundation for morality in Western Christianity hitherto. God had been intellectually required to account for human moral agency as well as for the physical cosmos. This is where questions arose about Newbigin's account. In light of Kant, what was Newbigin proposing? Was he implying that the trajectory in the breakdown of revelation that eventually led to the denial of God *began* by acquitting God of responsibility for creation and *proceeded* from there to his suspension from office as moral judge? If this was the historical claim about the course of intellectual history, could it possibly be right? Newbigin was scarcely making such a detailed historical claim, but how could he arrive at his conclusions about atheism by limiting his attention to science?

It was not only his reference to Reventlow that generated my questions about Newbigin's account. In *The Other Side of 1984*, Newbigin drew on Charles Norris Cochrane's celebrated study of *Christianity and Classical Culture* for his interpretation of Augustine's philosophy of cultural renewal, and in *Truth to Tell* he confessed how much this work had influenced him.[19] It is as important to ask why Newbigin, influenced by Cochrane's work, followed the epistemological trajectory that he did as it is to ask why, influenced by Reventlow's work, he did not follow the moral trajectory that Reventlow did. While Cochrane certainly made much of Augustine's reconstruction of epistemology, he also made clear that Augustine located the error of Classical culture morally in the realm of self-will even more fundamentally than in the intellectual realm of

---

19. *Truth to Tell*, 15.

epistemological method.[20] 'The conditions of wisdom are, at bottom, not so much intellectual as moral.'[21] Here, Cochrane shored up the familiar account of Augustine on the centrality of the human will and of pride in human thought and deed.

We know that, prior to the Enlightenment, such figures as Luther, Calvin and Pascal took this general line. After the Enlightenment, Kierkegaard observed in rather Augustinian vein:

> People try to persuade us that the objections against Christianity spring from doubt. The objections against Christianity spring from insubordination, the dislike of obedience, rebellion against all authority. As a result people have hitherto been beating the air in their struggle against objections, because they have fought intellectually with doubt instead of fighting morally with rebellion. [22]

How did Kierkegaard's analysis stand in relation to Newbigin's account, drawing deeply, as Newbigin did, on Augustine and proximately on Reventlow? The question could not be avoided of whether Newbigin had failed to integrate into his account a perspective or perspectives that would potentially have modified that account very significantly indeed.

So much for the literature that inspired the enquiry in the original edition of *Revelation and Reconciliation*. I have alluded to it both in order to explain what sparked my engagement with Descartes and Locke and as a prelude to what follows in the present volume. I shall now let Newbigin rest in peace and Gunton be content with an occasional appearance until he comes into his own the fifth chapter.

---

20. C.N. Cochrane, *Christianity and Classical Culture: a study of thought and action from Augustus to Augustine* (London: Oxford University Press, 1944). Although it is the discussion that closes the chapter on 'Nostra Philosophia' (446 – 455) that particularly brings this out, it is heralded in an earlier expository comment that, from the standpoint of the human subject conceived 'as a centre of radiant energy . . . the different so-called faculties may all be considered as functions of the will' (389).

21. *Christianity and Classical Culture*, 451.

22. Quoted in Howard and Edna Hong's translation of Kierkegaard's *Works of Love* (New York, NY etc; Harper & Row, 1962) 11. More poignantly: 'Everything essentially Christian must have in its presentation a resemblance to the way a physician speaks at the sickbed; even if only medical experts understand it, it must never be forgotten that the situation is the bedside of a sick person', Kierkegaard, *Sickness Unto Death: a psychological exposition for upbuilding and awakening*, tr. H.V and E.V. Hong (Princeton, NJ: Princeton University Press, 1980) 5.

In the first edition, I underlined the fact that the volume was not designed as a work of deep or comprehensive scholarship. Whether or not the scholarship was beyond my capacity, it was certainly beyond my ambition. So it is with this new edition. While I invariably enjoy and usually profit from comprehensive analyses of Western intellectual history relevant to my theme, I am not interested here either in offering anything comprehensive myself or even in citing the important works that do.[23] À propos of this second edition, I underline, now in bold, this scholarly limitation by adding to the original a confession about the present edition: I have no more tried to incorporate all the relevant scholarship of the intervening period between the editions than I did all the scholarship of the late twentieth century in the first edition. It goes without saying that this can no more be an excuse now than a corresponding excuse would have been then for making sloppy and indefensible judgements. In preparation for this present edition, I have consulted more recent scholarship to see whether something said in the earlier edition needed to be shored up, supplemented, modified, corrected or abandoned. However, like that princely and exemplary student who regarded every mark above the 40% required to pass the module as a sign of a corresponding number of hours wasted in the library, I have done the minimum in order to secure a pass. Whether or not I have succeeded is, of course, up to the examiners of this volume.[24]

23. However, three works that I have found instructive should be mentioned. One is Charles Taylor, *A Secular Age* (Cambridge, MA: Harvard University Press, 2007), which is particularly interesting in light of the use I make in chapter 1, below, of Taylor's *Sources of the Self: The Making of Modern Identity* (Cambridge: Cambridge University Press, 1989). A second is Bradley S. Gregory, *The Unintended Reformation: how a religious revolution secularized society* (Cambridge, MA: Harvard University Press, 2012). The third, to which I am much indebted beyond what I have learned from it of intellectual history, is Iain McGilchrist, *The Master and his Emissary: The Divided Brain and the Making of the Western World* (New Haven, CT/London: Yale University Press, 2012). There is a fourth and different kind of work that deserves mention. While written on a different subject from the one with which this book is concerned, and not a work on intellectual history, Shoshana Zuboff's devastatingly well-documented and chillingly sobering *The Age of Surveillance Capitalism: The Fight for the Future at the New Frontier of Power* [one of two alternative sub-titles] (London: Profile, 2019) confirmed my growing sense since the first edition of *Revelation and Reconciliation* that the absence of Max Weber from it was as regrettable as the absence of Hegel, which I acknowledged at the time (xiii). With regard to Hegel, this judgement was confirmed by my reading of a work that influenced Colin Gunton, namely, Edward Craig, *The Mind of God and the Works of Man* (Oxford: Clarendon, 1987). Zuboff's analysis of the 'second modernity' is sobering.

24. For a persuasive and properly scholarly account of a germane subject that shows how relatively slender is my own treatment, see Peter Harrison, *The*

In what follows I have quoted extensively from both primary and secondary sources. I confess that it is not my preferred way of writing nor, sometimes, of reading, but I have judged it helpful to the reader of this volume to quote freely and, indeed, I have found it useful to myself. I trust that the reader who shares my literary taste will indulge me in what I high-mindedly perceive to be the public interest and the greater good. In any case, absolutely no shadow of value-judgement attends my literary preference. Questions about epistemology and scientific culture inevitably float around in the background to this work, though they are not substantially treated in the course of it. On matters surrounding these questions, I am instructed by many people but want to pick out the work of the late Mary Midgley. Why gratuitously mention her name? Well, firstly, because she exemplifies that style of literary communication that, for myself, I find most congenial. And why gratuitously mention that fact? Because, secondly, it gives me an excuse to smuggle in reference to her support for the proposition that 'change of moral temper, and not any scientific discovery, seems . . . the root cause of the modern estrangement from traditional religion'.[25] Although a relatively brief study such as follows cannot hope even to get close to demonstrating that point, I hope that it contributes to grounding its plausibility.

Fall of Man and the Foundations of Science (Cambridge: Cambridge University Press, 2007).

25. *Science as Salvation: A modern myth and its meaning* (London; New York: Routledge, 1992) 118. Cf. 125.

Chapter 1

Around and About Descartes

In his *Third Letter on Toleration*, John Locke wrote:

> For whatever is not capable of demonstration . . . is not,
> unless it be self-evident, capable to produce knowledge, how
> well-grounded and great soever the assurance of faith may be
> wherewith it is received; but faith it is still, and not knowledge;
> persuasion, and not certainty. This is the highest the nature of
> the thing will permit us to go in matters of revealed religion,
> which are therefore called matters of faith; a persuasion of our
> own minds, short of knowledge, is the last result that determines
> us in such truths.[1]

Michael Polanyi commented as follows on these words:

> Belief is here . . . no longer a higher power that reveals to us
> knowledge lying beyond the range of observation and reason,
> but a mere personal acceptance which falls short of empirical

---

1.   In the next chapter, I turn directly to Locke's writings; at this juncture, I lift the
      quotation from Michael Polanyi, *Personal Knowledge: Towards a Post-Critical
      Philosophy* (London: Routledge & Kegan Paul, 1958) 266. References are not
      always specified below if they are on or proximate to that page. Polanyi's words
      begin with Locke's 'how well-grounded', to which I have added the preliminary
      words from Locke's text as found in any of the editions that Polanyi would
      have used, such as *Works* (London, 1824) vol. v.

and rational demonstrability. The mutual position of the two Augustinian levels is inverted. If divine revelation continues to be venerated, its functions . . . are gradually reduced to that of being honoured on ceremonial occasions.

Here lies the break by which the critical mind repudiated one of its two cognitive faculties and tried completely to rely on the remainder. Belief was so thoroughly discredited that, apart from specially privileged opportunities, such as may still be granted to the holding and profession of religious beliefs, modern man lost his capacity to accept any explicit statement as his own belief. All belief was reduced to the status of subjectivity: to that of an imperfection by which knowledge fell short of university.

These are the observations that both directly and indirectly generated this present essay; that is, they are of interest both in their own right and on account of their persuasive influence on theologians. Theologians who refer appreciatively to this passage have not always interpreted it in quite the same ways. Two who have made noteworthy contributions to theology in the English-speaking world deserve special mention. Without citing Locke directly, Colin Gunton apparently took Polanyi to imply that the reduction of belief to subjectivity is an historical *development* of Locke's position. [2] On the other hand, in an essay on 'The Framework of Belief', Thomas Torrance appeared to endorse a putative claim by Polanyi to the effect that the aforesaid reduction is a summary *interpretation* of that position. [3] Gunton took Polanyi to be saying that Locke holds that 'faith or belief is simply an inferior form of knowledge'.[4] This interpretation of Polanyi was presumably accounted for by Polanyi's reference to belief as an 'imperfection by which knowledge fell short of university'. Yet, according to the actual wording of the passage cited from Locke, faith is presented as something epistemologically *inferior* to knowledge and not a *form* of it.

Principles of exegetical and philosophical strictness should constrain a commentator to sort out (a) what Locke said (b) what Polanyi said that

---

2.   *Enlightenment and Alienation*, 4-5.
3.   'The Framework of Belief' in Thomas F. Torrance, ed., *Belief in Science and in Christian Life: The Relevance of Michael Polanyi's Thought For Christian Faith and Life* (Edinburgh: Handsel, 1980) 1-27, especially 8-9. For Torrance on Polanyi's philosophy of science, see his *Transformation and Convergence in the Frame of Knowledge* (Belfast: Christian Journals, 1984) chapter 3. Descartes and Locke are discussed in the first essay in that volume, 'The Making of the "Modern" Mind from Descartes and Newton to Kant'.
4.   *Enlightenment and Alienation*, 5.

Locke said and (c) what both Torrance and Gunton said that Locke and/
or Polanyi said. Instead of engaging in this exercise, let us cut to the chase
by formulating on behalf of Locke's critical interpreters a unifying charge
sufficient to orient and launch an investigation. It goes like this: Locke
so discredited belief that it either tended towards or attained subjectivity.
Although Polanyi noted that Locke allowed for exceptions to be made
in the case of religion, he judged this concession to be epistemologically
barren because the foundations of Locke's general epistemology are too
weak to give birth to and sustain an epistemology that warrants religious
belief. The upshot of Locke's endeavour is that demonstrative knowledge
rules the roost and belief is demoted. The various participants in this
discussion make no relevant distinction between faith and belief; they
have in view simply the cognitive dimension of faith.

What Polanyi said in *Personal Knowledge* on the subject of faith, reason
and Locke occurred in the course of his attack on the Enlightenment
for spawning an erroneous set of epistemological convictions, which left
'modern man' largely incapable of insight into what truly happens in
cognition. If you lack that capability, the outcome is the loss of a grip on
important substantive beliefs. When modernity succeeded its predecessor
culture, it produced a scientism that fettered thought 'as cruelly as ever
the churches had done. It offers no scope for our most vital beliefs'. What
we need instead is an enhanced view of personal judgement, rooted
within a 'fiduciary framework' that breaks with the preceding critical
framework, the latter of whose monument is the philosophy of Locke
and which had itself broken with the earlier Augustinian framework,
according to which *nisi credititis, non intelligitis* ('unless you will believe,
you will not understand'). Adumbrating a thesis in the philosophy of
science, Polanyi strenuously defended not just the propriety but also the
necessity of rooting thought in faith, though not necessarily in religious
faith, Augustinian or otherwise. 'We must now recognize belief once
more as the source of all knowledge'. Polanyi integrated this judgement
into his account of personal knowledge and thus into the chief goal of
his book, which was to achieve 'a frame of mind in which I may hold
firmly to what I believe to be true, even though I know that it might
conceivably be false'.[5]

This is not the only place where Locke's epistemology lands him
in trouble with Polanyi, and in the next chapter I shall indicate that
his seminal description of Locke's thought, both in *Personal Knowledge*
and elsewhere, is very misleading.[6] The reason for quoting Polanyi on

---

5.   *Personal Knowledge*, 214.
6.   With respect to *Personal Knowledge* itself, see Polanyi's early comments on the

Locke in the introduction to this present chapter is not only and not principally to set the scene for my alternative description of Locke's thought in the next chapter, but in order to note how much more Polanyi is doing than describing Locke's epistemology. He is describing its momentous historical significance. This gives us our bearings for the argument that proceeds in this volume. Our interest will be not only in Polanyi's claim about what Locke believed but, more than this, in his claim about the historic significance and place of that belief. In highlighting the importance of the epistemological question in the formation of modernity, Polanyi pulled some theologians in his train, at least when it was rumbling along Locke's track. While the next chapter is devoted to the correct interpretation of Locke's thought, the aim of expounding it is to contribute to an assessment of Polanyi's claims, and those of theologians indebted to him, about epistemology and modernity. Examination of Polanyi's constructive substantive thought as such on the question of epistemology is not on our agenda. It is his reading of intellectual history and its theological appropriation that are of interest.

As far as Polanyi was concerned, it is well-nigh impossible to exaggerate what was at stake in his reading of the place and role of epistemology in history. Mark Mitchell puts it straightforwardly: 'For Polanyi, the horrors of twentieth-century totalitarianism resulted directly from a critical framework that precludes at the outset any possibility of making meaningful moral claims.'[7] Nothing thwarts good morality more than does bad epistemology. Whatever Locke himself did with moral claims and moral thought, the broad epistemological framework that he established for their treatment was devastatingly wrong.[8] 'Having recognized the moral vacuum at the heart of twentieth-

---

constraints imposed by experience on scientific theory (9). See too Polanyi, *The Logic of Liberty: Reflections and Rejoinders* (Chicago: University of Chicago Press, 1951) 94-97 and pertinent remarks in Polanyi with Harry Prosch, *Meaning* (Chicago: University of Chicago Press, 1975) 145. See too Mark T. Mitchell, *Michael Polanyi: The Art of Knowing* (Wilmington, Delaware: ISI Books, 2006) 157. However, Polanyi does not oppose everything in Locke's thought: see his remarks on Locke's political doctrines in 'Beyond Nihilism' in M. Grene, ed., *Knowing and Being: Essays by Michael Polanyi* (London: Routledge & Kegan Paul, 1969) 3-23, specifically 22. Even Locke's empiricism seems to have a limited, contextual justification inasmuch as it liberated contemporaries from established authority, for which see *Science, Faith and Society* (Chicago: University of Chicago Press, 1964) 75-76.

7.   Mitchell, *Michael Polanyi*, 106.

8.   See Polanyi, *The Logic of Liberty*, 97. Locke kicked off the train of thought

century totalitarianism, he [Polanyi] dedicated himself to articulating an approach to knowing that would once again make belief in moral and religious truth possible.'[9] In this connection, Mitchell offers a telling contrast between Michael Polanyi and the political philosopher, Eric Voegelin. 'Polanyi argues that the moral and political chaos of moral inversion results from an errant view of knowledge. . . . Thus . . . a proper view of knowledge will open the door to a restoration of balance. For Voegelin, on the other hand, a properly balanced consciousness will, among other things, result in a proper approach to knowing.'[10] This contrast neatly accords with or even broadly reflects the general nature of the concerns that underlie my engagement with Polanyi on Locke and theologians who take their lead from him in this area. Roughly speaking, I could wish that they had paid to heed to Voegelin's contrasting emphasis. However, it is not the comparative positions of epistemology and 'consciousness' (a term that is technical as well as key in Voegelin's writings) that will be in view. Instead, my interest centres on the relations of epistemology and soteriology, the latter of which embraces the question of moral and religious consciousness. Should we really be looking in the direction of 'an errant view' of knowledge in order to discern the roots of the discrediting of the claims of Christian revelation in the intellectual history of the West, a discrediting whose extreme issue was explicit atheism?

It is important to underline that not only is substantive discussion of Polanyi's epistemology off the agenda, the same is true of Polanyi's wider counsel as expressed, for example, in the following statement: 'Moral judgments cut much deeper than intellectual valuations.'[11] This is most congenial to the argument that I pursue in this volume. An attempt to do justice to Polanyi's work as a whole would seek to integrate what he says about Locke and epistemology into this remark about moral judgements, whether or not that is easily done. It may well be that Polanyi ultimately agrees that epistemological moves are morally driven. If so, he is a welcome ally. However, the exercise of

---

that pretended that ethical principles could be scientifically demonstrated, by saying that good and evil could be identified with pleasure and pain, and that ideals of good behaviour are maxims of prudence.

9.   Mitchell, *Michael Polanyi*, 137.
10. Mitchell, *Michael Polanyi*, 148.
11. This statement comes from *Personal Knowledge* (214), which also contains, as do many of his writings, discussion of Marxism (e.g., 230-31). Polanyi's description of the moral passions of Marxism, across the range of his works, illustrate his point. Colin Gunton expressly takes this up in *Enlightenment and Alienation*, 77-85.

understanding the substance and coherence of Polanyi's work as such is no more my concern in this volume than is his epistemology, even when much in Polanyi's work may impinge on my sphere of interest.[12] To repeat: it is Polanyi on Locke in *Personal Knowledge* and the use to which his surrounding observations on epistemology have been put by theologians that is my quarry.

Stepping Back

Although Polanyi observed that '[t]he belief that philosophic doubt would appease religious fanaticism and bring about tolerance goes back to Locke', the *éminence grise* lurking behind all talk of doubt, epistemology and modernity is, of course, René Descartes, and he can scarcely be expected to mooch idly around the wings when knowledge, doubt and epistemology are under discussion and their modern histories placed under the spotlight.[13] Nor does Polanyi consign him to the wings. He is faithful to the truism that, before Locke, Descartes struck out on the fateful epistemological path by putting together his programme of universal doubt.[14] Descartes is unsurprisingly implicated in Polanyi's criticism of Locke on epistemological method.[15] According to Polanyi, '[m]odern totalitarianism' is 'a consummation of the conflict between religion and scepticism'.[16] This is strong, straight and sober talk. Polanyi's reference to totalitarianism surely jolts us out of any erstwhile inclination to demote thoughtlessly the cultural and social, along with the intellectual, significance of epistemological questions. Descartes was deeply implicated in the question of scepticism.[17] Polanyi implies that what Locke does is to state programmatically

---

12. Perhaps the historical direction in which we should look for an internal qualification of the burden of Polanyi's quoted remarks about Locke is his appreciation of the fact that 'science was a late child of the Renaissance' and that the spell of Augustine – that certainty of God came from a contrite heart and humility – was 'broken . . . by a gradual change in the balance of mental desires in the fifteenth century', *Science, Faith and Society*, 26.
13. For Polanyi's observation, see *Personal Knowledge*, 271.
14. *Personal Knowledge*, 269; see also *The Logic of Liberty*, 15.
15. Mitchell, *Michael Polanyi*, 157. See also Polanyi's comments on animals as machines in *The Study of Man* (Chicago: University of Chicago, 1958) 52, in the context of his critique of what sometimes goes under the label, 'machine thinking'.
16. *The Logic of Liberty*, 110; see too *Meaning*, 21.
17. For a challenge to the view that the question of scepticism motivated Descartes' epistemological enquiry, see Stephen Gaukroger's detailed *Descartes: An Intellectual Biography* (Oxford: Clarendon, 1995) 11-12.

what Descartes does not about the relation of faith to demonstration. It is certainly true that, whatever Descartes personally believed about their relation, he does not state matters as Locke does. He would have got into ecclesiastical and political trouble if he had. Polanyi's acknowledgement of Descartes' undeniable importance confirms the common sense of adverting to Descartes before turning to Locke when the epistemological question, in the form in which it has been introduced, is on the table.[18]

Descartes developed his methodological doubt and sought to pave a route out of it partly in response to a scepticism that turned out to be of the first order of magnitude on the scale of intellectual and cultural history. He was responding to an intellectual and social crisis in Europe in which philosophical scepticism was implicated along with religion and science. The last member of this trio (science) had a mighty beneficent social responsibility to fulfil because its second member (religion) had blood on its hands. In an influential work, Montaigne – who will shortly reappear in our account – remarked: 'Christians excel at hating enemies. . . . Our religion was made to root out vices: now it cloaks them, nurses them, stimulates them.'[19] The first member of our trio (philosophical scepticism) lured forth from its stable the pale Cartesian horse trailing the question of philosophical Doubt – harbinger, for some of Descartes' critics, of religious Death – in its wake, and sallying forth to sort out the mortal chaos on European earth.[20] Scepticism momentously took hold of the European scene with the re-publication of the work of Sextus Empiricus in 1562, which threw down the gauntlet of

---

18. Polanyi is not entirely unsympathetic to Cartesian doubt. With reference to Bacon and Descartes, he observed that '[w]hat these men said was true and important at the time', *The Tacit Dimension* (New York: New York, Anchor, 1967) 63. It is just, Polanyi continues, that 'once the adversaries they fought had been defeated, the repudiation of all authority or tradition by science became a misleading slogan'. Cartesian doubt, which, along with Locke's empiricism, became one of 'the two powerful levers of further liberation from established authority', has its value, *Science, Faith and Society*, 75. Polanyi gives credit to Descartes for being amongst those onto 'something profoundly true and important' in the challenge to authority, 'The Republic of Science: Its Political and Economic Theory' in *Knowing and Being*, 49-72, quotation from 65.

19. Michel de Montaigne, *An Apology for Raymond Sebond*, ed. Maurice Screech (London: Penguin, 1993) 7.

20. The reference is to Revelation 6:8. William Temple essayed the celebrated judgement that the moment of the Cartesian discovery of the *cogito* as an antidote to doubt was the worst moment in European history, *Nature, Man and God* (London: Macmillan, 1953) 57.

Pyrrhonism, that form of Classical scepticism that outdid Academic scepticism – the latter is too dogmatic because the Academic claim that nothing could be known is itself a knowledge claim and thus a species of dogmatism and not of authentic scepticism.[21] There was nothing either funny or philosophically idle about this discussion as long as rival claims to religious knowledge issued in a bloody Europe.

No figure on the European scene deserves more attention in connection with sixteenth-century scepticism, whether in his own historical right or in relation to our immediate interest in Descartes, from whom he elicited a response, than Michel de Montaigne (1533-1592). If getting Locke in perspective means stepping back to Descartes, getting Descartes in perspective means stepping back to Montaigne. In his account of the scepticism that spawned modern philosophy, Richard Popkin observed, with reference to Montaigne's *Apology of Raymond Sebond*, that 'Montaigne's genial "Apologie" became the coup de grâce to an entire intellectual world. It was also to be the womb of modern thought.'[22] Stephen Toulmin surmised that 'the opening gambit in the chess game of Modern Philosophy had been, not Descartes' method of philosophic doubt, but the sceptical arguments of Montaigne'.[23] One way or another, Montaigne's *Apology* put the sceptical fox amongst the religious chickens. Polanyi opined that scepticism was 'located in the prejudices and mental habits of objectivism', but that is most certainly not true of its historical and historic expression in Montaigne.[24]

---

21. Of course, Renaissance authors prior to 1562 were no strangers to scepticism.
22. Richard H. Popkin, *The History of Scepticism: From Savonarola to Bayle* (Oxford: Oxford University Press, 2003) 56. It was through Montaigne that Renaissance scepticism 'became crucial in the formation of modern philosophy' (43). Popkin's study of scepticism is allied to the belief that 'modern philosophy developed out of a sceptical crisis . . . that developed in the sixteenth century', viii. As he invites us to balance our interest in Descartes with an interest in Montaigne at the origins of modern philosophy, so he invites us to attend closely to Pierre Gassendi (1592-1655), the development of whose intellectual career 'perhaps more than that of René Descartes, indicates and illustrates what J.H. Randall called "the making of the modern mind"'(91). For Gassendi's response to Descartes' *Meditations*, see John Cottingham, Robert Stoothtoff and Dugald Murdoch, trans., *The Philosophical Writings of Descartes*, volume II (Cambridge: Cambridge University Press, 1984) 179-240. My use of Popkin does not entail disagreement with Harrison's criticisms of his analysis in *The Fall of Man*, 84-87.
23. *Cosmopolis: The Hidden Agenda of Modernity* (Chicago: University of Chicago, 1990) x.
24. Mitchell, *Michael Polanyi*, 165. Polanyi mentions Montaigne fleetingly in *Personal Knowledge*, 298, and in *The Logic of Liberty*, 8, he mentions the days of

What gives Montaigne's *Apology* its sceptical power is not simply the relentless positing of opinion and counter-opinion and his concluding destruction of trust in either reason or the senses. It is what he says about animals. Much of the first quarter of his *Apology* is taken up with a levelling operation pursued by exalting animal powers (Montaigne is often informed by Plutarch) so that a reader's sense of human superiority shrivels. 'We are neither above . . . nor below' most creatures.[25] Towards the end of his work, he returns to animals briefly in order to hammer home the sceptical point about human powers.[26] The effect of the *Apology* is that our wonder at and admiration for animals increases and humans emerge as, at best, humble creatures not in the virtuous but in the ontic sense, in comparison with animals.[27] God is there, at least *ex professo*, but his distinction or removal from the world of human frailty does nothing to elevate the human condition. In context, Montaigne's conclusion that it 'is not within our power to acquire a higher recommendation than to be favoured by God and Nature' sharply punctures human pretensions to knowledge.[28] That is Montaigne when he is being cool and not polemical about it all. He quotes Seneca (his 'favourite') at the end of the *Apology*: 'What a vile and abject thing is Man if he does not rise above humanity.'[29] Although his critics often thought that Descartes failed to make a successful conceptual distinction between humans and animals when it came to the machinery of thought, it is easy to see why Descartes would be worried about what was left distinctively of men and women after Montaigne had finished with them.[30]

Montaigne, along with those of Bacon and Descartes, as the beginning of the rebellion against the Christian churches.

25. *An Apology*, 24. '[W]e do not place ourselves above other animals and reject their condition and companionship by right reason but out of stubbornness and insane arrogance.'

26. 'If we want to judge the activities of the senses we should agree with the animals and then among ourselves', 183.

27. In his editorial introduction, Screech notes how the seventeenth-century appropriation of Montaigne's attitude to animals revealed how 'in its own way it even had something of the appeal of Darwin', *An Apology*, xxii.

28. *An Apology*, 25. It is doubtful whether we can be justifiably confident about Montaigne's religious beliefs. Although it would seem excessively sceptical to doubt the sincerity of his Catholic conviction, it is surely impossible to be sure how convinced he was.

29. *An Apology*, 189. For Seneca's favourable status, see 55. Threading his way through Classical authors, as he does throughout the work, Montaigne earlier pronounced on the 'mad Monster with all its many arms and legs . . . weak, miserable, wretched Man. An ant-hill disturbed and hot with rage!' (40).

30. Desmond M. Clarke observes that 'one factor in Descartes' decision to

You did not have to be sympathetic to Descartes to share his worry. Blaise Pascal was amongst the respondents to Montaigne and he also worried about Montaigne's view of humankind. However, his worries embraced a different set of concerns from those that chiefly occupied Descartes and they applied to what Montaigne made of humans' relationship with God. In his *Pensées*, Pascal had formulated a response to Montaigne suitable for those within the sphere of the latter's influence. The *mondain* circles in culturally progressive France in Pascal's day found in Montaigne the prototype of urbane scepticism.[31] Montaigne was the model of *honnêteté* in that world of *honnêtes hommes* too refined to attach themselves to – and far too refined to live by – Christian faith.[32] Montaigne, 'patron' as he was of 'every free man on earth', 'more than anyone else, created that public of *honnêtes gens* capable of judging and testing . . . [s]ouls regulated and created by themselves, not from without'.[33] As far as Pascal was concerned, Montaigne's plumb-line never got close to measuring life's true depths, but he fell short not as one who fails in a sincere search but as one less than entirely receptive to truth. Thus, 'Montaigne uses reason "diabolically" because of a certain *agrément* more satisfying to him than the truth itself.'[34] Montaigne's mistakes were not innocent;

---

structure the *Meditations* as he wrote them, with the First Meditation rehearsing the strongest possible sceptical arguments available, was the popularity of Montaigne's *Essays* and the fashionable scepticism that they endorsed', *Descartes: A Biography* (Cambridge: Cambridge University Press, 2006) 191. Descartes' critics were not convinced that he had successfully overthrown Montaigne's conclusion that 'animals employ the same method and the same reasoning as ourselves when we do anything', *An Apology*, 25. Descartes' dualism is actually expressed with rather less confidence than one would suppose from standard affirmations that he was a dualist and, for example, a slightly tentative note on animal free will is struck very early in his writings, John Cottingham, Robert Stoothoff and Dugald Murdoch, *The Philosophical Writings of Descartes*, volume I (Cambridge: Cambridge University Press, 1985) 5. Descartes' *Treatise on Man* is instructive in connection with the question of man as machine, *Philosophical Writings*, I, 99-108. On animals and machines, see part 5 of Descartes' *Discourse on the Method* in *Philosophical Writings*, I, 109-51. None of Descartes' major critics of the *Meditations* was satisfied that he had proved his distinction between humans and animals, even if they did not always say it pointedly, *Philosophical Writings*, II, 66-383.

31.   J.H. Broome, *Pascal* (London: Arnold, 1965) 81.
32.   J. Mesnard, *Pascal: His Life and Works* (London: Harvill, 1952) 48-49.
33.   We follow here the characterisations offered by Stefan Zweig and Thibaudet, quoted in Donald M. Frame, *Montaigne: A Biography* (London: Hamilton, 1965) 319 and 315.
34.   Broome, *Pascal*, 81. We might recall here Montaigne's citation of Varro's words:

they arose from trying to cut a good figure; consequently, an intolerable nonsense emerges.[35] 'What is good in Montaigne can only be acquired with difficulty. What is bad in him, I mean apart from morals, could have been corrected in a moment if someone had warned him that he was making too much of things and talking too much about himself' (649). It is not that Pascal is unsympathetic to everything that Montaigne says; his superficially comprehensive charges have to be carefully specified and weighed; and Montaigne's positive influence on him is often mentioned in the secondary literature.[36] However, it remains the case that Montaigne could strike at what Pascal most wanted to defend intellectually and spiritually. 'He inspires indifference regarding salvation: "without fear or repentance". As his book [presumably the *Apology*] was not written to encourage piety, he was under no obligation to do so, but we are always under an obligation not to discourage it (680).'[37]

Pascal's response to Montaigne is particularly instructive compared to Descartes' celebrated philosophical response to the scepticism that Montaigne promoted.[38] Perusal of Nietzsche's observations on Montaigne and Pascal suggests that pitting the one against the other would take us a long way in a cultural analysis of the tension between Christianity and early modernity. At one stage, Nietzsche was deeply under the spell

---

'Since man only wants to find such truth as sets him free, it can be thought expedient for him to be deceived', *An Apology*, 109.

35. Pascal, *Pensées*, trans. A.J. Krailsheimer (London: Penguin, 1966) paragraph 780. (Paragraph references to Pascal's work are placed in the text below.)

36. Maurice Screech wastes no time in highlighting Pascal's considerable indebtedness to Montaigne in his introduction to *An Apology*, ix. See too Krailsheimer's introduction to the *Pensées*, 23.

37. This paragraph includes further criticism. Montaigne is frequently mentioned in the *Pensées* either uncritically or without strenuous criticism (409; 525; 577) but the main burden of the *Pensées*' religious substance weighs against Montaigne. Although there is no explicit reference to Montaigne in Pascal's statement that 'what is nature in animals we call wretchedness in man' (117), there is implicit opposition to him in the statement that '[i]t is dangerous to explain too clearly to man how like he is to the animals without pointing out his greatness' (121). And when Pascal writes that '[p]ride counterbalances' human miseries and that 'man either hides or displays them, and glories in his awareness of them' (71), is Montaigne amongst those in view? Montaigne's *Apology* is specifically mentioned in 236.

38. Inasmuch as we can speak of Descartes' own scepticism, we must heed Heidegger's observation that 'Descartes does not doubt because he is a sceptic; rather, he must become a doubter because he posits the mathematical as the absolute ground and seeks for all knowledge on a foundation that will be in accord with it', quoted by Brian Brock, *Christian Ethics in a Technological Age* (Grand Rapids, MI/Cambridge: 2010) 47.

of Schopenhauer and, one way or another, the spell lingered somewhat after he had officially parted company with him, but even before Schopenhauer's star was slated to plummet, Nietzsche paid Montaigne a significant compliment. 'I know of only one other writer whom, as regards his honesty, I would set equal to or even above Schopenhauer: this is Montaigne . . . this freest, most energetic of spirits.'[39] Nietzsche identified Montaigne with the tradition of great French *moralistes* of whom six restored the spirit of antiquity, perpetuating the great heritage of the Renaissance.[40] Montaigne came first on the list as befits one who is greater than Shakespeare as a moralist (*HH*, I.176). Montaigne, the free spirit, and Montaigne, the moralist, receive higher acclaim from Nietzsche than does Descartes, the naïve.[41] Nietzsche's observations imply that the contrast between Montaigne and Pascal – the one post-biblical Christian who stood tall in the breach as a foe to Nietzsche, the one who stands for everything that Nietzsche strives to avoid – gives us a window on the spiritual alternatives in early modernity. Nietzsche judged that Pascal could be vanquished only by the spirit of wantonness displayed by Montaigne.[42] Descartes is not immediately visible on this battle-front.

Nietzsche admired Pascal. Like Montaigne, Pascal was a good moralist, one whom you could rank with the great moralists of antiquity – Epictetus, Seneca, Plutarch (*HH* I. 282). Pascal had a soul and not just a mind.[43] Nietzsche dubbed him '*der Erste aller Christen*' ('the first of all Christians'; *D* 159; cf. 549). He could see through your attempts to flee from yourself. More than admire, Nietzsche tells us in the section contrasting him with Montaigne that he *loved* Pascal (*EH*, 'Why I Am So Clever', 3). This makes it an unbelievably sad business, as far as Nietzsche is concerned, that Pascal was firmly in the clutches of

---

39. 'Schopenhauer as Educator' in Nietzsche, *Unfashionable Observations* [*UO*], trans. Richard Gray (Stanford: Stanford University Press, 1995) 181. (Where possible, after the first reference to one of Nietzsche's works, I place paragraph or section references along with the abbreviated title in the text.)

40. *Human, All Too Human: A Book for Free Spirits* [*HH*], trans. R.J. Hollingdale, intro. Richard Schacht (Cambridge: Cambridge University Press, 1996) II. 2, paragraph 214.

41. *Writings from the Late Notebooks* [*W*], ed. Rüdiger Bittner (Cambridge: Cambridge University Press, 2003) 9 [26].

42. *Ecce Homo: How One Becomes What One Is* [*EH*], trans. R.J. Hollingdale (London: Penguin, 1979), 'Why I Am So Clever', 3.

43. Nietzsche, *Daybreak: Thoughts on the Prejudices of Morality* [*D*], trans. R.J. Hollingdale, eds. Maudemarie Clark and Brian Leiter (Cambridge: Cambridge University Press, 1997) paragraph 481.

Christianity. Here, with Pascal, not just as a Christian representative, but with the man himself, we encounter 'the most instructive of all sacrifices of Christianity, slowly murdered first physically then psychologically'. Pascal exhibits 'the whole logic of this most horrible form of inhuman cruelty'. He bears the penalty for the sin of Christianity. It is a sordid destiny and only by the Montaignian spirit can you avoid it. Christianity has its trophy: it depraved Pascal.[44] You will find no better proof of its destructive strength.

In seeing Montaigne and Pascal as locked in the struggle between the free spirit and Christianity, Nietzsche is not merely setting up type against antitype and foisting combat on ideal combatants. He is talking history. Descartes, stirred by Montaigne's scepticism, responded with that exercise in intellectual purgation which yielded the *cogito*. Nietzsche was vitally involved in the spiritual tussle between Pascal and Montaigne. He knew that the former held that inability to know the truth proceeded from moral decay.[45] For his part, Pascal was stirred by both Montaigne and Descartes. On the subject of indifference, Pascal writes with anything but indifference.[46] What troubles him is the cool distance from eternal matters, the careless heart where sober searching should fire its thermal flesh.

Herein lies the contrast with Descartes' approach to Montaigne. Certainly, we can describe the contrast between Descartes and Pascal in terms of conflicting epistemologies. In this regard, Pascal would appear to be closer to Montaignian 'fideism' than to Cartesian rationalism if we have to measure comparative distances, although 'fideist' does not suit Pascal at all.[47] However, the literary contrast between Descartes and Pascal is also characterized by their respective selection of themes. Their constituencies overlapped. Both wanted to reach those reached

---

44. Nietzsche, *The Antichrist* in *Twilight of the Idols and The Antichrist* [*A*], trans. R.J. Hollingdale (London: Penguin, 1990) section 5.
45. Nietzsche, *The Will to Power* [*WP*], trans. Walter Kaufmann and R.J. Hollingdale (New York, NY: Vintage, 1968) I.83.
46. See *Pensées*, 427.
47. Williams, *The Shadow*, 134-37. Hence Allan Bloom is completely mistaken when he characterizes the opposition between Descartes and Pascal in terms of '*bon sens*', on the one hand, and 'faith against all odds', on the other, *The Closing of the American Mind* (New York, NY: Simon and Schuster, 1987) 52. It is extraordinary that he should further characterize the choice as one between reason and science, on the one hand and revelation and piety, on the other. See too 37. I mention Bloom because his discussion of figures who shall occupy us later – Rousseau, as well as Nietzsche – is both important and illuminating in adumbrating his important thesis.

by Montaigne. Yet where Descartes envisioned a philosophical task to be accomplished by means of an epistemological coup, Pascal envisioned a religious task to be accomplished by means of an existential theological anthropology. The French seventeenth-century ecclesiastic, Pierre-Daniel Huët, said that it is pride rather than Pyrrhonism that is dangerous to Christianity.[48] If Pascal would have modified his assent to this, it would only have been in order to observe that sixteenth-century Pyrrhonism could be a form of pride. Pascal contrasted the task of anthropological with the pursuit of scientific or mathematical study and Descartes is implicitly criticized in that connection (687). Correspondingly, Pascal, the last person in the world to exhibit scientific or mathematical indifference (or inferior talent!) invested his energies in an exploration of what is human, all too human, when he expounds Christianity.[49]

If the *Pensées* contain a programmatic statement, it is this: 'For the Christian faith consists almost wholly in establishing these two things: The corruption of nature and the redemption of Christ' (427). Alternatively: 'All that is important for us to know is that we are wretched, corrupt, separated from God but redeemed by Christ' (431). Or again: 'The whole of faith consists in Jesus Christ and Adam and the whole of morality in concupiscence and grace' (226). Pascal was Augustinian, believing that human corruption had its seat in the heart with its will and passions.[50] In his religious epistemology, Pascal set high store by the task of reorienting the will in humility. He never despised reason – on the contrary – nor strove to prevent its proper deployment, but he used it largely, though not solely, to expose the human condition and to testify to its own limitations. Its operations are located in relation to the *status hominis peccatoris* (the status of man as a sinner). The source of unbelief lies in the passions rather than in reason (410). The heart rather than reason is the organ of religious discernment (424). Error is produced by lack of love for the truth (176). 'Jesus Christ and St. Paul possess the order of charity, not of the mind, for they wished to humble, not to teach' (298). If we do speak of Jesus' teaching, then '[a]ll Jesus did was to teach men that they loved

---

48. Screech in Montaigne, *An Apology*, xxxi.
49. The phrase 'human, all too human' is borrowed from the title of Nietzsche's book of that name. Actually, although he can be cryptic and we cannot be certain that everything attributed to Pascal was actually said by him, he was negative about Descartes; see *Pensées*, 84; 887 and the second of the '[s]ayings attributed to Pascal' on p. 355.
50. Compare with Montaigne's appeal to Augustine, *An Apology*, 54, n. 115.

themselves, that they were slaves, blind, sick, unhappy and sinful, that he had to deliver, enlighten, sanctify and heal them, that this would be achieved by men hating themselves and following through his misery and death on the Cross' (271). According to Pascal, this is essentially what Montaigne needed to know.

Pascal believed that the fundamental religious crisis of his day was, from a theological point of view, a matter of anthropology and soteriology, into which the epistemological question was folded. As we shall see in a later chapter, Nietzsche also identified this as precisely the battle-ground where Christianity is at stake. Pascal detected a unity between moral and epistemological crises arising from scepticism in a form in which Descartes did not, even if Descartes does not separate moral questions and moral philosophy from the wider intellectual and cultural turbulence of his day.[51] What shall we make of Descartes in the light of this?

Descartes

Someone may lodge a protest at this point. Surely I am getting this volume off to an inauspicious beginning by implicitly or overtly casting Descartes in an unfavourable light, so as to sap the confidence of readers who rightly expect a dispassionate investigation. Why, it may be demanded, should Descartes share Pascal's agenda? Is my volume attended by an *a priori* religious and intellectual expectation that Descartes, with his mathematical and scientific interests, *ought* to be grappling with soteriological issues exactly as Pascal, alongside *his* mathematical and scientific interests, grappled – and ought to be doing so along the lines of and in the spirit of Pascal? If so, does such an expectation skew the overall analysis that will follow?

The question and the challenge are fair. If factual questions about Descartes' personal, as opposed to literary, preoccupations are to enter the picture, they can be treated only by trying to understand Descartes'

---

51. J.B. Schneewind's (edited) two-volume anthology of the history of modern moral philosophy begins with Montaigne: *Moral Philosophy from Montaigne to Kant: An Anthology*, vol. I (Cambridge etc.: Cambridge University Press, 1990). It opens with the claim to which my volume is eminently hospitable, that 'the problems that engaged moral philosophers during the seventeenth and eighteenth centuries . . . are at least as significant as those of epistemology and metaphysics' (1). In the course of adumbrating his non-religious interpretation of Christianity, Dietrich Bonhoeffer identified Montaigne, along with Jean Bodin, as the literary origin of belief in the autonomy of ethics, *Letters and Papers from Prison* (London: SCM 1967) 359.

life and this, for the most part, is not my concern. [52] Nothing in my discussion actually hangs on the question of whether I have done justice to Descartes in the desultory and rather offhand observations offered so far. Most importantly, even if justice has been done, I have no interest in burying any more than in praising Descartes in the presence of Pascal. The immediate purpose of contrasting the two men is to highlight the significance of different ways of engaging with Montaigne in light of the social and cultural accompaniments of the scepticism that he (Montaigne) epistemologically adopted. What has sparked the whole exercise is Polanyi's acknowledgement of Descartes as Locke's predecessor. It is to Descartes himself that we now turn.

It profits to draw attention to an interpretation by Peter Schouls of *Descartes and the Enlightenment,* which is germane, important and generally persuasive.[53] Tracing the connections between Descartes and the French Enlightenment, he demonstrates to just what a considerable extent the central Enlightenment themes of freedom, mastery and progress are sheer Descartes. 'One might say that the spreading of the Enlightenment amounted to the growing acceptance of an integral part of Descartes' position, the Cartesian concepts of freedom, mastery and progress' (12). In dealing with these themes, Schouls finds himself 'examining the very foundations of Descartes' total position' (6). In the course of doing so, he makes illuminating reference to Descartes' work, *The Passions of the Soul.*

> It is the only work in which he [Descartes] deals with an area of life in which he believes each individual can walk the road of progress to the end. Once that journey has been completed, the highest level of autonomy which is possible in that area of life has been reached: man then has exempted himself from being subject to God and has achieved complete mastery in that area of life. In this declaration of independence, *The Passions of the Soul* present what is perhaps Descartes' clearest articulation of the spirit which pervades the Enlightenment (172).

---

52. Although Desmond Clarke's volume, *Descartes,* is the go-to biography in English, Vrooman's earlier and readable *Descartes: A Biography* (New York: Putnam, 1970) also gives a good idea of the atmosphere surrounding Descartes' life. See too Stephen Gaukroger's intellectual biography, *Descartes.*

53. Peter A. Schouls, *Descartes and the Enlightenment* (Edinburgh: Edinburgh University Press, 1989). Page references to this work are usually given in the text from now on.

The 'spirit which pervades the Enlightenment' is the spirit of moral autonomy. Schouls integrated his verdict into the not unfamiliar thesis that the will has a foundational role in Descartes' work such that 'it was Descartes' unrelenting exercise of free will which for him established the autonomy of reason' (60).[54] The fall has not affected the freedom of the human will.[55] Ensuing 'self-mastery' makes the Cartesian project 'messianic'.[56] Reason is liberated by a combination of method and free will (31). Freedom is 'even more basic than . . . the *cogito*, for we cannot reach the *cogito*, nor attain the liberation and validation of reason, apart from acts of free will' (40).[57]

While Schouls argues his case effectively, a conscientious caveat is in place. The main Enlightenment text that he treated was Condorcet's *Sketch for a Historical Picture of the Progress of the Human Mind*, but he omits to say that Condorcet finds fault with Descartes where he finds none with Locke.[58] However, our concern is with Schouls' exposition of Descartes and not with the connection he makes between Descartes and

---

54. This claim is widely accepted, including by Charles Taylor in *Sources of the Self*, chapter 8, whose contribution I detail below, and by the challenging and provocative study by Lawrence Lampert, *Nietzsche and Modern Times: A Study of Bacon, Descartes and Nietzsche* (New Haven, CT/London: Yale University Press, 1993) 242. Because Schouls orients the discussion as he does, I am focussing on his formulations.

55. Clarke, *Descartes*, 292; also his reference to Descartes' Fourth 'Meditation', 346.

56. So Denis Diderot judged: Schouls, *Descartes*, 180. For self-mastery as a provisional moral code in *Discourse*, see *Philosophical Writings*, I, 123-24. At one stage, what eventually became the celebrated *Discourse on the Method of rightly conducting one's reason and seeking the truth in the sciences* was comprehended under a title that began: *The Plan of a universal Science which is capable of raising our nature to its highest degree of perfection*, I, 109.

57. See also 45. This is not to overlook the fact that, formally, from early on, Descartes argued that the intellect should be directing the will; see *Rules for the Direction of the Mind* in *Philosophical Writings*, I, 10. However, the question of priority – whether intellect drives the will or the will the intellect – cannot be reduced in the way in which I have just framed it because neither intellect nor will are undifferentiated concepts. For Descartes' exposition of the freedom of the will in the *Principles of Philosophy*, see *Philosophical Writings*, I, 205-7. In more than one set of replies to his *Meditations*, Descartes had to elaborate on the nature and freedom of the will: *Philosophical Writings*, II, 117; 133-34; 291.

58. Nicolas de Condorcet, *Sketch for a Historical Picture of the Progress of the Human Mind*, tr., J. Barraclough (London: Weidenfeld & Nicolson, 1955) 122; 132-33. In light of Mark Mitchell's reference to Voegelin in comparison with Polanyi, see Schouls' reference to Voegelin in connection with Condorcet, *Descartes*, 6, n. 5. For Schouls' disagreement with Voegelin on Condorcet, see *Descartes*, 138, n. 11.

the Enlightenment. The case Schouls makes with regard to the freedom of the will and the significance of *The Passions* in Descartes' authorship seems compelling. *The Passions* is, indeed, a high celebration of the free human will, which 'renders us in a certain way like God by making us masters of ourselves, provided we do not lose the rights it gives us through timidity'.[59]

Schouls is no maverick interpreter of Descartes. Sartre, who certainly found cause to disagree with Descartes, lauded the way in which the latter rested his intellectual enterprise on a magnificent humanistic affirmation of the freedom of the will.[60] Before that, Kierkegaard had insisted that Descartes had entered into doubt in freedom, thus inverting any claim about the relationship between thought and will that stipulated the primacy of the former.[61] Nietzsche called 'the rule of reason' in Descartes a 'testimony of the sovereignty of the will' (*WP* 95). Hegel is also illuminating here.[62] The strength of the Cartesian will is exposed in the conviction that we can '*acquire an absolute power*' over the passions of the soul, mastery over good and evil, joy and pain.[63] When Michael Polanyi described Nietzsche's conviction that we choose our own values as a 'modern radical form' of 'demanding absolute autonomy for our thoughts', and this as a demand that 'goes back at least to Descartes', there is at least a hint that moral demand lies behind Descartes' epistemological programme.[64]

---

59. Descartes, *Philosophical Writings*, I, 384 and see the discussion that proceeds until the end of the work. Cf. Descartes' remarks on the human will and the image and likeness of God in his *Fourth Meditation* in *Philosophical Writings*, II, 40.
60. J.-P. Sartre, *Descartes* (Paris: Trois Collines, 1949) 24.
61. See Reidar Thomte's introduction to Kierkegaard, *The Concept of Anxiety* (Princeton: Princeton University Press, 1980) viii-ix. See also Kierkegaard's remarks, quoted here, on Descartes' substitution of the epistemological for the existential against the background of his (Kierkegaard's) rumination on scepticism and the ethical. Kierkegaard is the psychological and, we may opine, theological opposite of Descartes when he writes that 'man is a helpless creature, because all other understanding that makes him understand that he can help himself is but a misunderstanding, even though in the eyes of the world he is regarded as courageous – by having the courage to remain in a misunderstanding, that is, by not having the courage to understand the truth, 'To Need God is a Human Being's Highest Perfection' in *Upbuilding Discourses*, eds. Howard and Edna Hong (Princeton: Princeton University Press, 1990) 297-326, quotation from 310-11.
62. See Robert B. Pippin, *Modernism as a Philosophical Problem: On the Dissatisfactions of European High Culture*, 2nd edition (Oxford: Blackwell, 1999) 69.
63. *Philosophical Writings*, I, 348. The italics are Descartes' own, in the section title.
64. *Meaning*, 108.

As for Nietzsche himself, it is not surprising that he found Descartes congenial in this respect. He certainly had his criticisms of Descartes. Against Descartes and his philosophical predecessors, he agreed with Leibniz 'that consciousness is merely an *accidens* of experience and not its necessary and essential attribute' and against Descartes he agreed with Hegel on the wrong-headedness of positing 'being' without 'becoming'.[65] Descartes was 'superficial' (*BGE* 191). Yet what Nietzsche liked about Descartes was that he had the strength of soul to think hard and the courage to strike out (*EH*, 'The Wagner Case: A Musicians' Problem', 3). Descartes may be faulted philosophically but, spiritually, he redeems himself in a modest measure. In that respect, the spirit and mood of the Cartesian enterprise appealed to the thinker – that is, Nietzsche himself – who would one day propose that we not only rise above but also banish into an ugly past the whole business of externally given good and evil.

Nietzsche also exalted a form of individualism and it is easy to miss what is apparently a rather similar individualism in Descartes if we concentrate on Descartes' search for and presumed discovery of a universal method. A stark individualism attends that search, though its interpretation should probably be rather subtle and nuanced.[66] Descartes constantly trumpets his discoveries as his very own, not just *by* himself but *for* himself. Granted the need to be vigilant in reading Descartes – he has been described as 'full of pranks' – we should note that he alleged of the *Discourse* that his 'present aim . . . is not to teach the method which everyone must follow in order to direct his reason correctly, but only to reveal how I have tried to direct my own'.[67] Descartes kept up his insistence on this point. Eudoxus, representing Descartes in *The Search for Truth*, declares:

> It was never my intention to prescribe to anyone the method which he should follow in his search for truth, but simply to describe the method which I used myself: if it should be thought to be defective, it would be rejected; if good and useful, others would use it too, I left it up to each individual to use it or reject it entirely as he saw fit.[68]

---

65. Nietzsche, *The Gay Science* [*GS*], trans. Josefine Nauckhoff (Cambridge: Cambridge University Press, 2001) paragraph 357.

66. Clarke's biography, *Descartes*, guides us into the biographical nooks and crannies that we should need to explore in order to construct an interpretation.

67. *Philosophical Writings*, I, 112. Cf. 118: 'My plan has never gone beyond trying to reform my own thoughts and construct them upon a foundation which is all my own'. It is Hiram Caton who calls Descartes a prankster: Lampert, *Nietzsche*, 159.

68. *Philosophical Writings*, II, 419.

We may be wary of taking Descartes at his word here and judge that he *de facto* recommends universality just as firmly as *de jure* he insists on individuality.[69] It is an interesting enough question, which will not be settled simply by consulting his published philosophical literature. Whatever we conclude, we cannot neglect the self-image that Descartes promotes when he flaunts his method as his own creation even where it is tacitly, we may judge, or even palpably universal. It is not surprising that Schouls ascribes to him a kind of creator-consciousness. At all events, the note of breakthrough, the tint of presumed originality in Descartes' literature from his *Rules for the Direction of the Mind* through to the famous *Discourse* and *Meditations*, is not easy to miss.

Where Descartes announces his novelty in the last-named work, it is in the context of a defensive role he aspires to play, the defence of theism against a recrudescence of atheism in modern form. Because of the critical role he plays in the story of those who lament his epistemological errors and their religious consequences, we owe it to him to keep this in mind. In this role, Descartes will offer proofs that, he reckons, 'leave no room for the possibility that the human mind will ever discover better ones'.[70] This is a great claim, but one called forth by great stakes. In the preface to his *Meditations*, Descartes several times parades his project as the championship of truth against atheism, atheism being that system of thought or way of thinking which embraces the beliefs that God does not exist and that the human soul is not distinct from the body. The arguments designed to vanquish atheism are the fruit of method rightly applied.[71] It is the self-proclaimed distinction of Descartes' method that truth has been established on its rational foundations. The truth in question is theistic truth. Obviously, that is religious truth of the highest order.

CARTESIAN ALIENATION

Schouls' analysis forces us, if not to modify, at least to supplement the important thesis that Charles Taylor argued vis-à-vis Montaigne and

---

69. '[O]ne of Descartes' fundamental assumptions . . . is that each person's reason is like every other person's reason, and that therefore a correct description of the workings of one person's reason holds for all', Schouls, *Descartes*, 23.
70. *Philosophical Writings*, II, 7.
71. In his preface to the *Meditations*, Descartes observes that the atheists are 'generally posers rather than people of real intelligence or learning', II, 6.

Descartes as sources of the modern self.[72] In his account of the historical *Sources of the Self,* Taylor highlighted the importance of tracing the sense of self that underlies moral ontologies. His essay constituted a sustained investigation of how moral ontologies reflect concepts or suppositions about selfhood and the 'spiritual intuitions' that undergird them (8). A 'background picture . . . underlies our moral intuitions' (41) and there is a 'spiritual outlook' behind and associated with our epistemologies (10). Taylor's claim that moral reasons motivate the generation of intellectual frameworks is one important way in which he corrects, challenges or significantly modifies what lies on the surface of Polanyi's approach to intellectual history as exemplified by Polanyi's remarks on Locke and epistemology in *Personal Knowledge.*[73] Taylor distinguished at the origins of modernity between a strand of thought about the self that is disengaged and one that is thoroughly first-personal. These are rival strands, contrasting entrées into modernity. Descartes inaugurates the former stance and Locke proceeds to intensify it. The latter stance can claim Augustinian pedigree but on its way to Goethe and Wordsworth via Rousseau there was a turning-point whose representative figure was Montaigne.

> Montaigne is at the point of origin of another kind of modern individualism, that of self-discovery, which differs from the Cartesian in both its aim and method. Its aim is to identify the individual in his or her unrepeatable difference, where Cartesianism gives us a science of the subject in its general essence; and it proceeds by a critique of first-person self-interpretation rather than by proofs of impersonal reasoning (181-82).

Montaigne needs no help from science, a fact that indicates that he is on to something different from Descartes in relation to self-understanding. Montaigne is in pursuit of the individual, not the essence. Descartes may indeed couch his enterprise in terms of the individual, but it is the individualism of intellectual method, not of its human object. 'At bottom, the stance toward the self is flatly opposed in these two enterprises' (182).

---

72. Taylor, *Sources.* Page references in this volume are given in the text below.
73. See, e.g., *Sources,* 23. In light of Taylor's discussion of the relation of Montaigne to Descartes, note that, in the course of discussing Montaigne and Descartes, Toulmin remarks that '[e]pistemology involves not just intellectual, but also moral issues', *Cosmopolis,* 41.

The modification of or supplement to Taylor's analysis that Schouls encourages is with respect to the similarities, as opposed to the contrast, between Montaigne and Descartes. Their philosophical stances toward the self may, indeed, be flatly opposed but is that true of their religious stances? If we look at matters from Pascal's point of view – whether or not that point of view is correct – the attitudinal stances of the two men are not so flatly opposed, even if they are not flatly identical. Viewed in light of the humble self who needs a re-directed will *coram deo*, Montaigne and Descartes do not offer flatly opposed attitudes. Both stances are broadly self-defining on the criterion Taylor deploys in his study of Hegel: 'The modern subject is self-defining, where on previous views the subject is defined in relation to a cosmic order.'[74] In any case, Schouls' and Taylor's analyses are basically complementary. Schouls offers a plausible and apparently persuasive characterization of what underlies Descartes' whole epistemological programme. Descartes' creation of method is a kind of self-definition and self-definition is a product of self-image (18). For his part, Taylor emphasizes the place or presence of self-mastery and strength of will in the Cartesian enterprise in a way that dovetails with Schouls' analysis.[75]

Taylor also formulates the contrast between Montaigne and Descartes in terms of the former exemplifying the 'engaged' as opposed to the latter's 'disengaged' self.[76] Leaving Montaigne to one side, the adjective is rather dramatically apt in relation to Descartes. To all appearances, Descartes' philosophical disengagement is symptomatic of wider personal disengagement. Discussing Polanyi's legacy, Mark Mitchell remarked that '[m]odern rootlessness is, at least in part, a

---

74. Charles Taylor, *Hegel* (Cambridge: Cambridge University Press, 1975) 6.

75. Chapter 8 of Taylor's *Sources* is devoted to Descartes but the force of its argument depends on its place in the volume as a whole. We could modify, perhaps significantly, Taylor's contrast between Montaigne and Descartes in another direction, too. Toulmin rightly both draws attention to Descartes' individualism and observes an affinity between Montaigne and Descartes that Taylor does not mention, because while 'Montaigne also wrote *as an individual*' he 'always assumed that his own experience was typical of human experience generally', 41. In the course of his investigation into early modern philosophy, Toulmin also 'put Montaigne and Descartes face to face', 36. 'Modernity has two distinct starting points, a humanistic one grounded in classical literature, and a scientific one rooted in 17ᵗʰ century natural philosophy' (43). For important questions put to Toulmin on the origins of modernity, see Pippin, *Modernism*, 184, n. 7.

76. See Taylor, *Sources,* chapter 8; also, 178. Taylor regards the 'ideal of the disengaged self' as a modern variant of the Platonic idea of mastery, a variant promoted by 'the modern scientific world-view' (21).

function of scepticism concerning the sacred nature of one's family or home, which are reduced to mere accretions we must, often with considerable pain, scrape away as we pursue that for which our hearts truly long.'[77] Polanyi apparently held that '[p]hilosophical rootlessness has produced geographic rootlessness, and to reverse the habit of geographic rootlessness, we must go to the source of the problem and retool our philosophical assumptions'.[78]

These words could be seized on by anyone sniffing around for an excuse for another spat with Polanyi or a sympathetic commentator on his legacy. This time the argument would be about the way geographic and philosophical rootlessnesses should be related. It is an argument that would take me a step too far afield and generate a suspicion that the early pages of this volume are dedicated to a running battle with Polanyi. It behoves us to let sleeping dogs lie pacifically here, especially since tracking forms of rootlessness would take us on a most tortuous path where the dangers of getting lost would be at least as great as the perils of rootlessness itself.[79] Polanyi does not mention Descartes in this connection, but Descartes did exemplify geographical rootlessness. In early seventeenth-century France, whence Descartes hailed, 'the wanderers, the irregulars, the independents, resentful of authority, unsubmissive in spirit' were abroad, although it is not implied that each of these descriptors applies to Descartes.[80]

We must certainly not lump together every philosophical, moral and social misfit, to couch matters in the politically incorrect terms in which people could regard a type of wanderer from a traditionalist point of view, and Popkin's study is again commendable for its admirably scrupulous insistence on attending to the relevant distinctions here and discouraging us from branding all non-conformity with the same label. Even so, we must place Descartes against this variegated background. Just as the religious patriarch, Abraham, was one social nomad among

---

77. Mitchell, *Michael Polanyi*, 163.
78. Mitchell, *Michael Polanyi*, 168.
79. Nietzsche is amongst those who connect intellectual and geographical solitude, if not rootlessness (*HH* 2.1.237). Ruminating on Heraclitus, Nietzsche said: 'To walk alone along a lonely street is part of the philosopher's nature', *Philosophy in the Tragic Age of the Greeks*, trans. Marianne Cowan (South Bend, IN: Gateway, 1962) 66.
80. J.S. Spink, *French Free-Thought from Gassendi to Voltaire* (London: Athlone, 1960) 12 and see Gaukroger, *Descartes*, 135-39, on the distinction between *libertinage flamboyant* and *libertinage érudit*. See too Robert Mandrou's remarks on nomadism, *From Humanism to Science: 1480-1700* (Harmondsworth: Penguin, 1978) 219.

many, his story unintelligible apart from his social background (whatever his religious distinction), so it is with philosophical patriarch, Descartes. The tramping nomadism of Descartes' day was not an entire social novelty in Europe, but the geographical landscape of his day was spattered with post-Reformation blood, spilled over the years of religious strife. Descartes trod this European earth for nine years in search of truth and method in the early seventeenth century. He did not create the climate in which he lived and laboured any more than he created the nomads so if, indeed, philosophical rootlessness grounds geographical rootlessness, then Descartes does not lie at the bottom of it all.

Whether or not Polanyi and a host of others are right in judging that Descartes got his epistemology badly and fatefully wrong and so made a grave and momentous philosophical blunder, a discomfiting personal attitude to humankind or its representatives in his day comes to light in Descartes' philosophical disengagement. There is a famous passage in his *Meditations* where Descartes remarks:

> We say that we see the wax itself, if it is there before us, not that we judge it to be there from its colour and shape; and this might lead me to conclude without more ado that knowledge of the wax comes from what the eye sees, and not from the scrutiny of the mind alone. But then if I look out of the window and see men crossing the square, as I just happen to have done, I normally say that I see the men themselves, just as I say that I see the wax. Yet do I see any more than hats and coats which conceal automatons? I *judge* that they are men. [81]

Taken in the overall context of his life and thought, this looks as though it is not only from a philosophical point of view that Descartes viewed others from the standpoint of a spectator. [82] It was also from a personal, existential point of view. This fact has engendered commentators' language that either enshrines a moral judgement or lends itself to the possibility of such judgement. Descartes, said David Levin, '*prefers* the

---

81. *Philosophical Writings*, II, 21.
82. In the *Discourse*, Descartes writes that for nine years 'he did nothing but roam about in the world, trying to be a spectator rather than an actor in all the comedies that are played out there', *Philosophical Writings*, I, 125. 'In doing this', he adds, 'I was not copying the sceptics, who doubt only for the sake of doubting and pretend to be always undecided; on the contrary, my whole aim was to reach certainty – to cast aside the loose earth and sand so as to come upon rock or clay.' See also I, 115.

distance of vision ... even when it means dehumanisation'.[83] Of course, if Descartes did have such a preference, we should not necessarily essay a moral judgement on him, because such things as trauma, unshakeable anxiety or lack of a sense of safety could, in principle, have decisively formed his psyche. Iain McGilchrist quotes Levin in the course of his discussion on 'Descartes and Madness' and then does so again: 'What could be a greater symptom of madness than to look out of one's window and see (what might, for all one knows, be) machines, instead of real people?'[84] McGilchrist himself probes the question of schizophrenia in this connection. [85] Was Descartes in a bleak 'nomadic prison'?[86]

If readers have already generously given the author the benefit of the doubt when he protests impartiality as between Descartes and Pascal, they may react to this brief excursus on Descartes with the judgement that it is in pretty awful taste, an unedifyingly irritating portent of things to come in subsequent chapters, despite the fact intellectual history rather than personal psychology has been solemnly touted as the authorial sphere of interest. I am not unsympathetic to that reaction, but McGilchrist's thesis on intellectual and cultural history and his positioning of Descartes within it illuminates the question of epistemology. In a remarkably impressive essay, McGilchrist approaches Western culture from the perspective of brain science. His thesis is that the calculative left hemisphere is physiologically meant to function as the emissary of the integrative right but that it has usurped the position of the latter and that the narrow forms of rationality that have come to dominate in the Western world are physiologically and, thus, psychologically aberrant. Taylor's Cartesian 'disengagement' and Levin's 'dehumanisation' are expounded neuroscientifially.[87] McGilchrist regards Descartes' celebrated principle – 'that I could take it as a general rule that the things we

---

83. Quoted in McGilchrist, *The Master and his Emissary*, 168.
84. McGilchrist, *The Master and his Emissary*, 333. The question of moral judgement on a given individual is obviously affected where the notion of madness is seriously countenanced.
85. *The Master and his Emissary*, 439.
86. This is Ben Mijuskovic's phrase used in relation not to Descartes but to Thomas Wolfe, quoted in Hywel D. Lewis, *Freedom and Alienation* (Edinburgh: Scottish Academic Press, 1985) 117.
87. Although McGilchrist does not discuss Taylor himself, he makes an illuminating connection between Descartes and Robert Musil's towering and haunting novel, *The Man Without Qualities* (to use the common, if not felicitous, translation of the German title).

conceive very clearly and very distinctly are all true' – as 'the fallacy that was to derail the next three centuries of Western thought', and posits that this is the product of the imbalance of the respective hemispheric functions.[88]

It is in this context that McGilchrist discusses 'Descartes and Madness'.[89] His purpose is 'to illuminate the links between his [Descartes'] philosophical enterprise and the experience of schizophrenia, and when his account on Descartes and madness is read in the context of his very detailed investigation hitherto of the brain and Western culture, it is sobering. Citing Descartes' own observation that it is 'a mental disorder which prizes the darkness higher than the light', McGilchrist comments:

> Descartes was rather keen on branding those who saw things differently from himself as mad. Dominated by the left hemisphere, his world is one of comedy and light – he was, after all, the spectator in all the comedies the world displays. But there is madness here, too, which, as I have suggested, approximates the madness of schizophrenia.[90]

As far as the main line of my argument in this volume goes, McGilchrist could be dead wrong on Descartes, just as Pascal could be dead wrong in his difference from him. My purpose is deliberately to introduce questions and considerations around and about Descartes that are designed to queer an epistemological pitch. From a theological point of view, the latest set of questions or considerations are no distraction from the task of locating the significance of epistemological questions in Western intellectual history. The third chapter of Genesis provides a compressed but seminal account of the connection between morality, knowledge and illusion. We read there that Eve perceived the fruit of the tree of knowledge of good and evil under three aspects (3:6). Firstly, it was good for food. Secondly, it was pleasing to the eye. Thirdly, it was desirable for gaining wisdom.

---

88. *The Master and his Emissary*, 328.
89. *The Master and his Emissary*, 332-5.
90. *The Master and his Emissary*, 349-50. Approximation is important: McGilchrist does not actually call Descartes schizophrenic, judging it likely 'that schizophrenia is a relatively modern disease, quite possibly existent only since the eighteenth century', 261. It is a kind of 'misplaced hyper-rationalism'. McGilchrist also discusses Montaigne and Toulmin's work in this connection, 323-25.

Eve's perception was illusory. There was no illusion in relation to the first two aspects; according to Genesis 2:9, 'Out of the ground the Lord God made to spring up every tree that is pleasant to the sight and good for food' (NIV) and this description surely comprehends the tree of the knowledge of good and evil, along with the tree of life. It is different with the third perception. The tree was not desirable for gaining wisdom. Eve just thought she saw that it was, but God had not made it so. The account is far from hinting that God deliberately tried to trip up Eve and Adam with a gratuitous prohibition. Creation entails the existence of something other than God and the possibility thereby exists of entering into a relationship with creation that by-passes God. Divine prohibition informs humankind in imperative form about the destructive consequences of entering into immediate relationship with the created order. What Eve thought was a sense perception was, in reality, intellectual judgement and it constituted illusion – *maya*, to deploy the terminology of Hindu thought – or 'the opposite of holy fact', as Charles Williams put it.[91] In ordinary life, sustained illusion, the taking of things to be what they are not – in fact, the taking of things as the very opposite of what they are – constitutes a form of madness when it is sustained in a clinical context and becomes constitutive of perception. We must reckon with the possibility of a condition of spiritual madness. If Jesus was not, as his family believed him to be, clinically insane, were his opponents clear of the charge of spiritual insanity?[92]

The question of spiritual illusion has been introduced to underline the point that Eve did not make an innocent epistemic mistake or epistemological error. The compressed account in Genesis does not include an explanation of why Eve trusted the word of the serpent instead of the word of God. However, the disordered desire on which she acted has an implicit, but unmistakeable, moral basis. Only so is the divine punitive reaction explicable. If Eve saw things as she did, we may go as far as to say that there went into her perception a desire to see things as she did, but even if we have reason to suspend judgement or improve on that formulation, she was certainly responsible for the settled perception that segued into action. No New Testament author more than John insists on the moral basis for the rejection of light. 'This is the

---

91. See Williams' powerful treatment of illusion in his chapter on 'The Opening of Graves' in his novel, *Descent Into Hell* in *Charles Williams Omnibus* (Oxford: Oxford City Press, 2012) 865-78.

92. See, e.g., Mark 5:21-31, for the verdicts of family and of Pharisees. For the insanity of idolatry, see, e.g., Isaiah 44:12-20 and Daniel 4:28-33 for the juxtaposition of spiritual and physical insanity.

verdict: Light has come into the world, but men loved darkness instead of light because their deeds were evil' (John 3:19). To the Pharisees, Jesus says: 'If you were blind, you would not be guilty of sin; but now that you claim you can see, your guilt remains' (9:41). There are differences between pre-lapsarian humankind and post-lapsarian religion. There are similarities too.[93] The epistemological error that is the mark of spiritual derangement has a moral root.

At risk of protesting too much, I underline that Descartes is the occasion to talk about these things. To stand in partial, let alone comprehensive, judgement on him even at the end, let alone at the beginning of this volume, would be professionally as well as morally sickening. In any case, to return to the more sober language of epistemology and moral sensibility, to claim as McGilchrist does that there is a physiological basis for epistemological moves (in the case of Descartes, putatively faulty moves) is not to unearth a moral basis.[94] As for morality, just as Nietzsche was interested in the physiological basis of moral development, so there is theological reason for enquiring about the moral basis of physiological development.[95] In theological perspective, the cultural evolution of *homo sapiens*, and so the physiological evolution with which it interlocks, has taken its course under the sign of the fall as well as creation. In this perspective, epistemic and epistemological error are fruit rather than root. The significance of Pascal in our account has been that he introduces theological considerations that impinge on the question of the connection between epistemology and moral sense. Considering Descartes in his own right generates that question as well. He has led us to a point where we are summoned to be theologically alert, whatever we make of the man himself.

Polanyi's account of Locke is also such a summons and theologians have heard and heeded it. They have done well to hear, but have they done so well to heed? When we come to an alternative account of Locke in our

---

93. There is a good case for taking James 1:14-15 to be an echo of Genesis 3:6: see Dale L. Allison Jr, *James: A Critical and Exegetical Commentary* (London/ New York: Bloomsbury T & T Clark, 2013) 253, n. 249.

94. Of course, neuroscientists have long talked in these physiological terms. For just one example, see, in the context of his overall discussion of the brain, J.Z. Young's observation that '[e]very philosopher's theory of knowledge . . . is influenced by the whole life system of the individual who propounds it', to which he adds 'and the culture of which he is part', *Philosophy and the Brain* (Oxford: Oxford University Press, 1988) 172.

95. See, e.g., the 'Note' that concludes the first book of Nietzsche's *OGM* (p. 245).

next chapter, we shall brook no theological intervention or interference. In the present chapter, there has been theological intervention, whether or not theological interference, but a comparable intervention in the discussion of Locke would amount to an interference. In his case, we shall be concerned simply with what he said and with its implications for Polanyi's thesis whereas, in discoursing around and about Descartes, we have been concerned not just with what he said and but with surrounding interpretive possibilities. It is principally for the sake of flagging up those possibilities that we have engaged with him.

He must now be allowed one more word.

DESCARTES AT THE END

His own rootlessness and somebody else's moral crisis combined to kill Descartes. Obviously, the socio-cultural backcloth of Descartes' intellectual endeavours cannot be depicted in monochrome. Turbulence in moral philosophy and crisis in moral conviction were abroad in his time and place as much as were epistemological questions. Descartes' preoccupation with questions of mathematics, science and epistemology did not prevent him from taking cognizance of the moral turbulence of his day. The women in his life testify to this. They sought intellectual illumination in relation to conspicuously moral issues. Queen Christina squeezed the life out of Descartes in the bleak Scandinavian mid-winter when, at break of day, she forced him to help her discover an ethical code and impart to her the nature of the greatest good. Throughout those moral dawns, Christina kept in mind 'our own personal reality as the goal to be studied, explained and hopefully mastered', maintaining that 'the greatest of all sciences is that of knowing how to live and to die well.'[96] In requesting and receiving instruction on these matters, she was certainly partly taking him at his word. 'We should endeavour above all else to live well', Descartes had written. [97] Whether Christina subsequently lived well or not, it is a moot point whether Descartes died well, instructing her in moral matters when and where he did. Princess Elizabeth of Bohemia was content to be complicit merely in squeezing the literature out of him, for it was partly at her behest that he produced *The Passions of the Soul.*

---

96. Quoted in Vrooman, *Descartes*, 242.
97. See Descartes' preface to the French edition of *Principles of Philosophy* in *Philosophical Writings*, I, 186. References incorporated into my text below are to the part and section numbers of the translation of the Latin edition as found in *Philosophical Writings*, I, 193-291.

In light of Polanyi's ruminations on faith and rational demonstration, we owe it to Descartes to report that he professed the supreme certitude of faith in the life and soul of humans who function as God intended, although he lodges this claim in a literature that will produce in the informed reader at least the shadow of a suspicion that the profession is contrived. In his *Principles of Philosophy*, Descartes assures us 'that whatever God has revealed to us must be accepted as more certain than anything else' (I, 76); that 'the natural light is to be trusted only to the extent that it is compatible with divine revelation' (I, 28); that 'although the light of reason may, with the utmost clarity and evidence, appear to suggest something different, we must still put our entire faith in divine authority rather in our own judgement' (I, 76). Elsewhere, Descartes observes that although 'what has been revealed by God is more certain than any knowledge . . . faith in these matters, as in anything obscure, is an act of will rather than an act of understanding'.[98] These words show that Descartes does not zealously advocate a faith whose material content is obscure, and this means that the Bible gets us off to a pretty hopeless start because Genesis does not furnish us with clear and distinct matter when it gets us out of the blocks.[99] In the second set of his replies to objections to the *Meditations*, Descartes remarked that '[t]he sin that Turks and other infidels commit by refusing to embrace the Christian religion does not arise from their unwillingness to assent to obscure matters (for obscure they indeed are), but from their resistance to the impulses of divine grace within them, or from the fact that they make themselves unworthy of grace by their other sins.'[100] Nonetheless, and attending assiduously to both the social and literary context of these remarks, we are bound to ask whether all this consistently torpedoes what Descartes has claimed on behalf of reason and to wonder whether we should instead read with scepticism what Descartes claims for faith.[101]

Still and all, whatever Descartes has surrendered to reason, whether to his own as an example for others or to universal reason and concomitant universal assent, he purports to offer to us what is, substantively considered, a religiously conservative accomplishment. Descartes

---

98. *Rules* in *Philosophical Writings*, I, 15.
99. Clarke, *Descartes*, 253.
100. *Philosophical Writings*, II, 106. However, the nuances of this point can only be grasped if we follow his accompanying exposition of it.
101. There is surely a good case for adopting Caton's hermeneutical rule in reading Descartes, which is that he views faith in subordination to reason: see Lampert, *Nietzsche*, 162.

surveyed a scene that was not of his own making, featuring a revival of Classical and pagan scepticism. His resolute and creative opposition to this enabled Descartes to present himself religiously as one who resists novel tendencies, a *defensor fidei*, albeit in the form of a rational explorer.

If, in our assessment of Descartes' epistemology, we are inclined to emphasise less his expressions of pious faith than his rational performance, we should with equal conviction emphasise that, for Descartes, the rational is powered by the moral in the sense that he views the studied exercise of doubt as a sign of the moral strength of a soul that will not submit to fear.[102] To discover things for yourself is a mark of self-mastery. Schouls puts it boldly but not hyperbolically: 'At least in practice, Descartes' revolution in the sciences was accompanied by a revolt against the traditional Christian view of the place of man. For Descartes, man has the first word and the last in the matter of determining what is and what is not to be accepted as truth' (37-38). If this is so, while we may honour Descartes' motives in seeking a health of mind that humankind was lacking, it is clear that Abraham's quest for the heavenly city (Hebrews 10:11,16) and Descartes' quest for an earthly order are not manifestly variants on one and the same pursuit.[103]

Montaigne, Descartes and Pascal oblige us to pause at the portals of engagement with John Locke on Michael Polanyi's terms. Polanyi may be right to swell the company of the many who think that Descartes got his epistemology wrong. He may further be right on the connection between an objectivist view of knowledge and the drive for human perfection. [104] The role of Descartes' epistemological error in the formation of modernity is another matter. Two germane questions arise in connection with Polanyi's diagnoses. The first is whether, on the one hand, Descartes' epistemological error, if such we judge it to be, underlies the disasters of Western intellectual history, if such we

---

102. Schouls, *Descartes*, 35. He quotes Koyré: 'Whereas Montaigne "*submits* to doubt as its slave, through weakness . . . Descartes employs doubt as his tool, or, if one prefers, as his weapon"' (36).

103. See a very early writing of Descartes, *Philosophical Writings*, I, 3. Of course, if Abraham pursued a heavenly goal, it was via an earthly one – he unwittingly sought new heavens and a new earth; and Descartes believed in immortality. Yet, to adapt slightly a phrase of Washington Irving's, we should in the last resort be readier to say of Descartes than of Abraham 'that earth divides with Heaven the empire of his thoughts', *Tales of the Alhambra* (Granada: Miguel Sánchez, n. d.) 96.

104. Mitchell, *Michael Polanyi*, 54. Mention was earlier made of Descartes' allusion to 'raising our nature to the highest degree of perfection' in the original title of *Discourse on Method*; see *Philosophical Writings*, I, 109.

judge them to be, along the lines Polanyi set out or, on the other hand, Descartes' putatively mistaken epistemological moves are undergirded by a deeper anthropological stance of which they are a symptom. The second is whether Polanyi's reading of intellectual history in relation to early modern epistemology, as expressed in his observations on Locke, collides with a perspective such as that of Pascal, as expressed in his observations in the *Pensées*.

Both these questions are about the significance of epistemology. A correct interpretation of Locke will give us another angle on the question. To this we now turn. [105]

---

105. Though I do not explore it, the manifestly plausible claim that Descartes wrongly understands emotion and embodiment ultimately, if somewhat indirectly, makes an important potential contribution to my aim to re-locate the significance of epistemology by modifying it. Antonio R. Damasio's influential *Descartes' Error: Emotion, Reason, and the Human Brain* (New York: Avon, 1994) presents a powerful case. Damasio by no means disagrees with Descartes on everything (see his reference to Descartes' *Passions of the Soul*, 124). However, in developing his argument on the bodily basis of mind and that 'feelings have a say on how the rest of the brain and cognition go about their business', even providing a kind of 'frame of reference' for cognition (160), Damasio shows how Descartes' error consists not only in 'the separation of the most refined operations of mind from the structure and operation of a biological organism' (250) but also in the belief that 'thinking and awareness of thinking, are the real substrates of being (248). (For the distinction between emotions and feelings, see 270, n. 1). For McGilchrist's criticism of Damasio, see *The Master and his Emissary*, 185.

Chapter 2

Restoring a Measure of Faith in Locke

Approaching Locke

Cool, clear-headed, far from the ignoble strife or restless spirits of men such as those whom we met in the previous chapter, Locke plods dispassionately along his tranquil philosophical way. So it may seem to those who turn the pages of his principal philosophical text, and the one that principally occupies us, *An Essay Concerning Human Understanding*. Appearances are deceptive. Locke was deeply immersed in the political struggles of his day. In exile, he lived in the Netherlands for over five years. In England, before that, more than one biographer reproduces a report from the early 1680s that, in Oxford, 'John Locke lives a very cunning unintelligible life. . . . No one knows where he goes.'[1] Still, we shall not get drawn into the intrigues of Locke the man and duly adhere to Michael Polanyi's concerns. Although Polanyi's influence on theologians is not confined to it, his *Personal Knowledge* has apparently and understandably made the most impact on them. This is the volume containing the passages quoted at the beginning of the previous chapter.

---

1. So Maurice Cranston, *John Locke: A Biography* (Oxford: Oxford University Press, 1985) 221 and Roger Woolhouse, *Locke: a biography* (Cambridge: Cambridge University Press, 2007) 177. For relevant detailed coverage, see too the magnificently thorough work by Richard Ashcraft, *Revolutionary Politics and Locke's Two Treatises of Government* (Princeton: Princeton University Press, 1986).

In challenging Polanyi's reading of Locke, my ultimate aim is to put pressure on the position that highlights epistemological factors at the origins of modernity. In order to shake off Polanyi's legacy, we have to get straight on Locke's religious epistemology and do so against the background of his general epistemology.

Locke does not normally emerge from expository and philosophical commentary on his work as either wholly clear or wholly consistent in some key areas of his work and there is no need to quarrel with a judgement to the effect that he was willing at important junctures to sacrifice logical consistency to perceived common sense. Locke's religious epistemology, no more than his general epistemology, has relaxed the furrowed brow of every philosophical commentator who has sought to grasp its logic.[2] The account that follows will feature on this score neither charges of inconsistency against Locke nor pressure for acquittal on such charges. Definitive or comprehensive interpretation is not my ambition. It is possible to offer a defence of Locke as arraigned on the charges made by Polanyi and company without either a dogmatic interpretation of or a comprehensive verdict on his religious epistemology.

From the outset, we must set our faces firmly against any attempt to draw conclusions about Locke's religious epistemology from just one of his works, and most certainly not the one from which Polanyi quoted – Locke's *Third Letter on Toleration*. It looks as though Polanyi took Locke's words here to be representative of Locke's epistemological convictions, but it will not affect my argument if it turns out that Polanyi was not strictly committed to that supposition. As he neither disclaims nor defends this supposition in so many words, he could, in principle, claim that the problem of modernity that exercises him comes to light in words such as those cited from the *Third Letter*, which at least manifest an important strand in Locke's thinking, even if they are not entirely representative. Nonetheless, it is regrettable that Polanyi gives the impression that the words he cites well represent Locke's epistemology. Throughout his literary corpus, Locke sets up the relation of faith to knowledge in a variety of ways and the *Third Letter* cannot be singled out as characteristic. On the contrary, whatever we make of Locke's variations when it comes to interpreting him, Maurice Cranston long ago and quite rightly remarked in relation to the *Third Letter* that in it

---

2.   Paul Helm's statement of the problem in 'Locke on Faith and Knowledge', *Philosophical Quarterly* (January, 1973) 52-66, remains useful. On the wider front, Nicholas Wolterstorff alludes to internal difficulties in Locke's work in terms of: 'Locke is to be counted among Locke's most acute critics', *John Locke and the Ethics of Belief* (Cambridge: Cambridge University Press, 1996) xv.

'Locke was forced . . . to acknowledge a more sceptical attitude towards religion as such than he had previously admitted'.[3] We might add that it was more sceptical than anything he published later, too, unless we partially except the fragmentary *Fourth Letter on Toleration*.[4]

Even when we consider them on their own terms, in isolation from what Locke wrote elsewhere, Polanyi overestimated the scope of Locke's remarks on faith in the *Third Letter*. If Polanyi was equating what he took to be Locke's understanding of the 'mere personal acceptability' of faith with 'subjectivity', we must respond that 'subjectivity' in a political context and 'subjectivity' in a general epistemological context do not necessarily amount to the same thing. This must be kept firmly in mind if what is described in terms of Lockean 'subjectivity' is explicitly or implicitly equated with 'mere personal acceptability'. When Locke distinguished faith from knowledge in the *Third Letter*, he was aiming to limit the scope of legitimate magisterial authority in matters where intellectual conviction does not amount to demonstrative knowledge. The authorities should not be allowed to legislate or adjudicate on matters about which we cannot actually *know* the truth. That is the context in which Locke distinguishes as he does between faith and knowledge in the *Third Letter*. What Locke was explicitly disowning when contrasting faith with knowledge here was not the potential for any sort of objectivity attaching to faith, but, rather, an objective demonstrability that would function as a legitimating ground for magisterial coercion.[5] Correspondingly, if Torrance, when charging Locke with misguided epistemological privacy, was equating that privacy with what Locke claimed for faith in the *Third Letter*, he misunderstood. What counts politically as a private opinion need not lack legitimate pretension to publicly demonstrable *rational objectivity*, even when it is not demonstrable *knowledge*, when what is at stake are the rational grounds of religious belief and not the grounds on which magistrates can compel religious conformity.

Locke's critical interlocutors can sometimes display extraordinary carelessness in reading his work, presumably because they concentrate their reading on his *Letters on Toleration* and, even here, they fail to take into account the context of Locke's epistemological remarks. Thus Mark Mitchell thinks that Locke is allied with William of Ockham in holding that religious belief is immune from fact and in separating science from

3. Cranston, *John Locke*, 367.
4. *Works*, vol. v, 549–74.
5. Peter L.P. Simpson makes the same mistake in relation to Locke's denial of objectivity in his *Political Liberalism: A Defence of Freedom* (New Brunswick, NJ/London: Transaction Publishers, 2015) 111, fn. 11.

religion accordingly.[6] The preliminary point to be made here is that the context as well as the content of Locke's epistemological observations in his writings on toleration has to be factored into any wider judgement on Locke. His claim to fame may have been to find a 'new way of ideas'; what he opposed in this Third Letter was a 'new way of persecution'.[7] Locke says that once we get clear on what the issue really is – and he avers that his interlocutor has lurched about at this point – we should also get clear that nothing short of 'certainly knowing' the truth of one's religion can justify magisterial coercion (143).[8] The question is not whether the Christian religion is 'true': it indubitably is.[9] The question is not whether the earliest Christians were asked to believe it: they were. The question is not whether Christians ought to doubt the basic historical facts constituting or undergirding Christianity: they should not. 'Any who call themselves Christians' are in possession of a 'sure' and 'full' revelation' (157). The question hinges on whether we are dealing here with matters *demonstrably* known, yielding a strictly corresponding certainty.[10] Believe, be assured, be confidently persuaded by all means; but realise that all this is 'short of true knowledge' (179).

These averments may or may not entail the kind of threat to faith that troubles Polanyi, but, at all events, Locke's studied and influential presentation of the relation of faith to knowledge came in the celebrated *Essay on Human Understanding*, where he set forth programmatically the philosophical principles of his religious epistemology. For that reason, I shall give an account of it. When Locke came to defend the *Essay* against the criticisms of Edward Stillingfleet, bishop of Worcester, it looked as though he had rather changed his epistemological tune from the *Essay* itself.[11] However, it was not changed to the tune he sang in the

---

6.   *Michael Polanyi*, 178, n. 21.

7.   *Works*, v, 142. From now on, where possible, page references to Locke's work are placed in the body of the text.

8.   The argument about what the argument was about is still going on in the *Fourth Letter, Works* v, 554.

9.   Very near the beginning of his *Second Letter Concerning Toleration*, Locke had told his interlocutor that: '[t]rue religion and christian religion are, I suppose, to you and me, the same thing' (*Works* v, 67) and at the very end, he made clear that he had not demurred from his interlocutor's conviction that '"bringing souls to salvation"' was, in Locke's words, 'the best design any one can employ his pen in' (137). Both suppositions are re-stated in the Third Letter, *Works* v, 144; 335.

10. Locke is capable of using the word 'certainly' in what looks like a loose sense in relation to knowledge of Christian basics such as the birth of Christ in Bethlehem and his suffering under Pilate, 153.

11. See Helm, 'Locke'.

Third Letter. In his correspondence with Stillingfleet, Locke included a rough attempt to separate the spheres of faith and knowledge, assigning them to epistemically independent spheres, but not along the lines of the subordination that appears in the third and fourth letters on toleration. The *Essay* itself also differs from the toleration writings in a way we should not suspect from Polanyi's account. Locke varies his tune, whether or not this produces grating dissonance. It would be most unfortunate if all this conveyed the notion that Locke was so different in different places as to be all over the place overall. Still, it would be unjust to foreclose that possibility definitively. What I shall seek to show is that, even when not read *in meliorem partem*, Locke does not emerge at the place where Polanyi or his followers locate him.

Nothing in my argument particularly hangs on an interpretation, still less on the plausibility, of Locke's argument in the *Third Letter*, nor am I concerned with the philosophical plausibility of Locke's argument in the *Essay*. However, I am concerned with the correct interpretation of the *Essay*. While my argument is not optimally advanced by taking aim and firing away at all Locke's casual interpreters, it is in order to give preliminary notice that he has been very carelessly interpreted by an interpreter of interest to us, Thomas Torrance. In contrast to Colin Gunton in *Enlightenment and Alienation*, Torrance cited Locke directly as well as citing Polanyi's quotation from Locke. In 'The Framework of Belief', Torrance wanted to draw attention to the crisis in Western epistemology wherein Locke played a leading, perhaps *the* leading, part. He offered textual evidence from the *Essay on Human Understanding* to claim that, in Locke, rational, demonstrative knowledge is 'sharply contrasted with belief which is no more than an "ungrounded persuasion" of the mind, for it is only extraneously and not evidently related to the thing believed'.[12] In support of this claim, Torrance cited chapters xv. 1-3 and xix. 11ff. from book IV of the *Essay*.[13] He straightforwardly misread the text. In chapter xix, it was not 'belief' but *'enthusiasm'* that Locke dubbed 'an ungrounded persuasion'. Directing his energies towards dismantling 'enthusiastic' epistemological principles, Locke studiously, pointedly, deliberately and programmatically distinguished enthusiasm from faith as well as from reason. 'Enthusiasm' constitutes a third ground of assent to a given proposition alongside grounds in faith and in reason and it is a ground that, unlike those two grounds, is categorically rejected.

---

12. *Belief in Science*, 7.
13. Locke, *An Essay Concerning Human Understanding*, ed. Peter Nidditch (Oxford: Clarendon, 1975). Whenever possible, section references to this *Essay* are incorporated into the main text.

Further, Torrance unquestioningly identified the 'faith' of chapter xv with the 'faith' of chapter xix. From a commentator's point of view, the terrain here gets a little bumpy, but what is clear is that 'faith' is not used uniformly in these two chapters, as I shall document below. Although, for myself, I believe that problems of interpretation have been exaggerated here, that does not matter; it may be granted that the way in which Locke's usages of faith are to be related is open to debate.[14] What is both necessary and sufficient to say at this stage is that, in chapter xv, Locke uses 'faith' as a term in general epistemology. It is what is maximally attainable when we fail to demonstrate a proposition delivered by reason. What Locke is describing is the exercise of deducing the rational probability of a proposition and the appropriate form of assent to it. Here, Locke is discussing what we might term 'rational faith'. However, in chapters xviii and xix, we have moved onto religious epistemology and are now talking about '*religious* faith', which is a different animal. In this latter context, 'faith' is the mode in which we grasp a proposition not deduced or delivered by reason at all, but proposed in the name of revelation. Religious and rational faith are not the same thing. When Locke is discussing *general* epistemology, faith is *not* contrasted with reason; it is contrasted with knowledge, faith and knowledge being alternative *products* of the operations of reason. On the other hand, when Locke is discussing *religious* epistemology, faith *is* contrasted with reason, for it furnishes here an alternative *method* to the general rational method of attaining cognitive grip on a proposition.

At risk of giving worthy and good-natured readers sleepless nights wondering whether they have wandered into Act 2, Scene 2, I have briefly indicated flaws in the interpretation of Locke so as to get polemics out of the way. Those flaws and polemics do matter. Turning, now, to Locke's text in its own right, the stretch of land before us will appear a little colourless to some readers but it should not prove to be barren and should be traversed in the assurance, if not of Canaan beyond, at least of wider and perhaps more enticing pastures that will eventually come into view. The *Essay* contains the systematic summary attempt that Locke made to state the principles of religious epistemology and stands at the heart both of his philosophy and his contribution to the history of philosophy. The engine of his religious epistemology pounds away within it.

---

14. I make a limited attempt at interpretation in Stephen N. Williams, 'Restoring "Faith" in Locke', *Enlightenment and Dissent* No. 6 (1987) 95-113. I remain committed to this, as I do to my harmlessly general 'John Locke and the Status of Faith', *Scottish Journal of Theology* (40.4) 1987.

Essay on Human Understanding

Locke treated the principles of religious epistemology in his *Essay* only as his opus drew faithfully to its close in Book IV. He specifically tackled the question of faith in relation to reason in chapters xviii and xix of that Book, the latter chapter having joined the work only at its fourth edition. We need to understand them against their wider background.

Generally speaking, Locke's examination of the way, nature and scope of knowledge in the *Essay* produced a coalition of what we may loosely term empiricist, idealist and sceptical elements in the outcome of his analysis. This outcome is a relatively attenuated sphere of knowledge. Such knowledge as we possess is rational and yields 'certainty'. In chapters xiv and xv of Book IV, Locke presents a heralded and superficially rigid distinction between what we know, admitting of certainty, and what we may judge to be the case, admitting of no more than probability. There are degrees both of knowledge and of probability (IV.ii). Probability is in principle capable of reaching such a high degree that it raises our assent to a given proposition practically to knowledge and we are in the vicinity of certainty. Yet, even at such high altitude the distinction between knowledge and judgement, between certainty and probability, is not supposed to lapse. In this context, what I have called rational faith – we have not yet got to religious faith – is aligned with judgement and probability. It belongs to the sphere of opinion and not of knowledge. If a proposition is judged, but not known, to be true, it is rightly entertained as a matter of opinion for it is at best highly probable. Assent to it is a matter of faith. Religious categories and concepts are not on the table at the moment.

When Locke introduces faith into his general epistemology, its alignment with opinion has no necessary connection at all with the *private* opinion we have heard about from his critical commentators. Nor is the faith in question a matter of ungrounded persuasion. Life, says Locke, is lived mostly 'in the twilight of probability' (IV.iv.2). Probabilities can be either objective or subjective. An objective probability obtains when it is impossible even in principle to attain anything higher. A subjective probability obtains when an individual has not in practice gone beyond probability. When it comes to deciding what is objectively probable, public grounds and accepted criteria for holding beliefs and adjudicating their tenability should be invoked. There may be cases when a person is justified in maintaining the truth of a proposition that formally can be no more than probable with all the confidence rightly placed in the truth of a proposition demonstratively established and, as such, known. These are cases are of what Leibniz, for example, termed 'moral certainty'.[15] In the case of such high probability, assent is effectively *necessary* (xv.2; xvi.6). Yet, so long as we are talking about probabilities, we remain formally within the sphere of faith and opinion.

That is how Locke understands the relationship between faith and *knowledge*. Faith and *reason*, as we shall shortly see, is a different kettle of fish. Before he gets onto that discussion and after examining the degrees of assent that are involved when we gauge the probable truth of a proposition, Locke offers an extended treatment of reason, including an attack on the use of the Aristotelian syllogism in epistemology. He notes different significations of the word 'reason'. In general epistemology, it refers to a faculty in humankind that elevates us above the beasts, enlarging our knowledge and regulating our assent as we try to interpret the data provided by our senses. In this context, Locke is willing to contrast 'rational' with 'intuitive' knowledge. That is not because he regards intuition as irrational, but because 'rational knowledge' is a phrase that can be used in the more restricted sense of 'demonstrative knowledge'. There is thus a sense of 'rational' where we do, indeed, use it to mean 'demonstrable' and in such a case we contrast rational knowledge with judgement, judgement being an intellectual operation that pertains to the probable and not to the demonstrable. What Locke is most certainly not doing is overthrowing the more general rationality of non-demonstrative judgement. 'Judgement' kicks in when we cannot actually demonstrate the connections of ideas that are not intuitively known, but it can and certainly ought to be rational. We withhold the word 'rational' from such judgement only when we are quite deliberately using the word 'rational' in the sense of 'demonstrable'. This is an equation we make only in specific contexts. Normally, in general epistemology, the rational is not confined to the demonstrable, as the most casual perusal of Locke's talk of intuition and judgement will reveal. 'To place the emphasis on demonstration as the source of rationality, or to identify it with criteria, misses some of the most fundamental aspects of Locke's concept of reason.'[16] For Locke, '[t]o be rational means a number of things'.[17]

The concept of rationality in Locke's thought cannot be comfortably netted in the course of a brief expedition such as that on which we have embarked. We can just allow salient features of Locke's general

---

15.   G.W. Leibniz, *New Essays on Human Understanding*, eds. J. Bennett and P. Remnant (Cambridge: Cambridge University Press, 1981) 68.

16.   See the whole piece from which this sentence is taken, John Yolton's extended review of J. Dunn's *Locke* in *The Locke Newsletter* (1985) 88-95, quotation from 86.

17.   Yolton, *The Locke Newsletter*, 89.

epistemology to surface. So what happens when Locke moves onto religious epistemology? Now that he has contrasted faith with *knowledge*, both of these being the potential product of rational operations, he asks what we are to make of a contrast we familiarly encounter, namely, the contrast between faith and *reason*. Locke thinks that it is extremely important to understand that distinction correctly. If we are to uphold it in a way that is valid and useful, we must get rid of its usual invalid and dangerous deployment in much contemporary discourse. We may validly speak of faith as opposed to speaking of reason. We may not validly speak of faith as being opposed to reason. The proper distinction between faith and reason is not an antithesis. 'However faith be opposed to reason, faith is nothing but a firm assent of the mind; which if it be regulated, as is our duty, cannot be afforded to anything but upon good authority, and so cannot be opposite to it' (xvii.24).

In matters religious, we must have reason for believing. That is where the 'enthusiasts' go astray. They reject that principle. When reason cannot be made to serve their purposes, their cry ascends: 'It is a matter of faith and above reason' (xviii.2).[18] For all they care, the enthusiasts' 'above reason' can be contrary to everybody else's reason. That, Locke says, will not do. If we have rightly concluded that some propositions are truly contrary to reason, we should have achieved that conclusion on good, objective grounds. Such propositions are 'inconsistent with or irreconcilable to our clear and distinct ideas' (xvii.23). Enthusiasts do not think that there is any objective test to be passed. As far as Locke is concerned, there is no valid sense of rationality whereby it would be rational to maintain a position such as that maintained by the enthusiasts.

However, as long as we do not understand it in the enthusiastic sense, there is a valid, legitimate religious appeal to propositions 'above reason'. Some propositions are not rationally *deduced*; that is, they are not established by the procedures deployed in general epistemology. A credible proposition that emerges absent that procedure may rightly be described as being 'above reason'. It is distinguished from propositions established 'according to reason', but it is also distinguished from propositions 'contrary to reason' (xvii.23). Even though such propositions are not rationally deduced in the standard procedural way of general epistemology, they may validly procure our assent on condition that they are not opposed to what is rationally known to be true. Take characteristic religious assent to propositions above reason. Here,

---

18. It has been wryly and justly observed that the only point at which Locke gets enthusiastic in his *Essay* is when he gets on to 'Enthusiasm', Richard Aaron, *John Locke* (Oxford: Oxford University Press, 1970) 1.

assent is not the outcome of the kind of rational procedure applicable in general epistemology. In general epistemology, reason may pursue knowledge, fail to attain it and attain faith instead. Whether knowledge or faith is the product, rational deduction is the procedure. Not so when distinctively religious epistemology is in question. In this context, the faith/reason contrast properly applies where we are attending to the *method* of deducing the truth or probable truth of a proposition. That is, religious faith refers to the mode of accepting a proposition not made out by reason at all. It is thus trading in commodities 'above reason'.

Locke aims to make the rationality of religious belief in particular consistent with the rationality of belief in general, but the rationalities are not isomorphic. This is a key move in the fourth book of the *Essay*, but it is understandable if complaint is made that it results in a fairly complex picture, which threatens to play merry havoc with the good-willed interpreter innocently in conscientious search of an above or across the board consistency.[19] It would take us too far afield here to chase up the scattered but sometimes significant remarks pertaining to religious epistemology that powder discussions in the *Essay* prior to the focussed treatment in Book IV. However, we should review at least one area covered in the chapter on 'Degrees of Assent' in which Locke is still orbiting around general epistemological matters (IV.xvi). Locke tells us here that probability obtains in the case of two sorts of propositions: (a) those relating to what is observable (to which there may be empirical human testimony) and (b) those relating to what is not observable (to which there is empirically none). Not only are there two *sorts* of propositions, there are also two *grounds* for taking propositions to be (probably) true. The first ground is 'the conformity of anything with our own knowledge, observation and experience'; the second is 'the testimony of others, vouching their observation and experience' (xv.4).

Now something interesting turns up in the discussion. Locke allows that there are cases where we may be rationally justified in suspending our usual grounds for judging a proposition to be true. There are cases where something *contrary* to common human experience and to the

---

19. In light of our subsequent discussion, what are we to make of Locke's claim that revelation advances us in our knowledge (IV.vii.11)? Nonetheless, we might smugly suggest that if we could integrate the germane claims made on behalf of general and religious epistemology in the *Essay*, it would probably take us even further away from Polanyi and those who follow his lead than we shall already be travelling; see Richard Ashcraft, 'Faith and Knowledge in Locke's Philosophy' in John Yolton, ed., *John Locke: Problems and Perspectives* (Cambridge: Cambridge University Press, 1969) 194-223.

ordinary course of things may vouch for a proposition, making assent to it reasonable. Locke does not tell us explicitly which type of proposition is in question here but he does tell us what the exceptional ground of assent is. It is miracle. A well-attested miracle gives us grounds for assenting to the proposition to which it putatively bears witness. God may use the very unusual nature of such an event to testify to a proposition that he wants us to receive as true (xvi.13). General epistemology includes space for religious appeal.

The plot thickens further. Now that he has specified an exceptional ground of assent, Locke proceeds to introduce what he describes as one more 'sort' of proposition. He does not spare his readers some hard work. Already, we may have wondered whether the sort of proposition to which miracles can in principle bear witness is one of the two sorts he has mentioned before getting onto miracles, or whether it is a new sort of proposition. Now a new sort of proposition is explicitly mentioned and we are not explicitly told how it should be related to those sorts of propositions that have gone before. Whatever we conclude from an investigation into this and however obvious such a conclusion may be after we have sifted the possibilities, Locke informs us that the salient feature of this new sort of proposition is that it is a proposition to which we may give wholehearted assent even if what is proposed does not agree with 'common experience or the ordinary course of things' (xvi. 13). Assent in this case is unimpeachably warranted on the ground that it is a proposition to which God testifies. As such, it 'carries with it an assurance beyond doubt, evidence beyond exception' (xvi.14). It is a *revealed* proposition. Assent to it is called *faith*. If God has revealed something, we must assent to the content of his revelation with complete confidence and as necessarily as we ever assent when we *know* something to be the case.

Faith and revelation are worlds away from enthusiasm and although they do not take the epistemic form of rational knowledge, they do not lack its epistemic confidence. Well-informed and intellectually scrupulous religious believers have no less confidence in God than does the enthusiast. What the former have and what the enthusiast lacks is ground for confidence. We need to be properly intellectually satisfied – a need not felt by the enthusiast – that we are in actuality dealing with a revealed proposition before it procures our assent. Furthermore, we need to understand the said proposition aright before we assent to it. This is a point at which the reason that conducts us in life and in our general epistemology is brought to bear on putative revelation. Reason does three things in this respect. First, it can ascertain the intelligibility of the proposition in question. Second, it can reject any claim to revelation that stands in contradiction to what is known. Third, it should produce evidence that the proposition in question is actually revealed. In all this, Locke is crystal clear about the fact that, in the cases now under discussion, reason is not the *source* of a revealed proposition. That is why we talk of a proposition being above reason and with impeccable propriety describe our assent to it in terms of faith and not of reason. Not only is the description proper, the assent may also be. For this to be the case, reason must be summoned to validate and legitimize the operation of a faith that assents to things above reason.

Balancing acts are involved here for which few commentators on Locke have been tempted to award maximum points. It is not difficult to see the general problem. Locke proposes utterly confident assent to *what* God has revealed while apparently remaining logically committed to the belief that we cannot rationally possess a kindred degree of confidence *that* God has revealed something. Whether or not some modification can get Locke over this hurdle without much philosophical injury is a question difficult to answer with any degree of satisfaction on the evidence of the *Essay* alone. At all events, Locke's programmatic statement is:

> Reason I take to be the discovery of the certainty or probability of such propositions or truths, which the mind arrives at by the deduction made from such ideas which it has got by the use of its natural faculties, viz., by sensation or reflection. Faith, on the other side, is the assent to any proposition, not thus made out by the deductions of reason, but upon the credit of the proposer as coming from God, in some extraordinary way of communication. This way of discovering truths to men we call *revelation* (xviii.2).

In sum, Locke maintains that, while reason is not the source of all valid beliefs, it must be involved in the validation of all beliefs. We should note that, with respect to revelation, Locke holds that while the scope of what God may in truth reveal is unrestricted, what we may intelligibly communicate to others is restricted. Nothing believed on the basis of revelation can command assent of firmer confidence than something known by reason. As we have noted, Locke insists that nothing can be rightly received as revelation if it contradicts rational knowledge, but unimpeachable epistemological principle must allow that rational assessment of the truth of propositions that relate to things outside the compass of ordinary human experience proceeds differently from the way that it proceeds in the case of ordinary experience.

Where does all this leave us with respect to the interpretations of Locke I am challenging? At the very least, the absolute bare minimum, the picture is far more complicated than we should suspect on the basis of those interpretations. Locke sustains a deliberate and steady intention to align revelation, reason and faith so as to outlaw false antitheses and to establish proper distinctions. In the name of the alliance between revelation, reason and faith, he allows us to call reason 'natural revelation' and revelation 'natural reason enlarged' (xix.4). Enthusiastic appeal to knowledge is put to the sword. Should we be minded to do what Locke thinks that we should not, that is, to pit reason and revelation in competition, even if not in contradiction, then reason appears to take the lion's share of the credit. It 'must be our last judge and guide in everything' either by establishing the truth of a proposition or by validating the claim that it is actually revealed, in which (latter) case, the revealed proposition become 'one of her [reason's] own dictates' (xix.14). Of course, this reason is the gift of God to humankind. Moreover, God can reveal things above reason in the appropriate sense. Further, it is the wisdom of reason to learn just how little it knows substantively from its own resources.

From one point of view, rational assent to the claim that a proposition is revealed may be viewed as an expression of rational power in the form of a rational confession of its own limitation. From another point of view, the same thing can be viewed in the opposite way, i.e., as an admission of rational limitation in the form of a rational expression of power. Locke claims that revelation trumps rational improbability; while it cannot trump rational *knowledge*, it can triumph over the rationally *improbable* (xviii.9). It will be recalled that we live life in the twilight of probability.[20] We can certainly look at Locke's achievement in more than one light, but it is undeniably wrong to describe faith or belief as at best subjective opinion in contrast to objective knowledge. Faith may not be knowledge, but it is fully objective. Its epistemic confidence is potentially very high and full indeed. Reason may regulate religious faith but not banish it to the sphere of private opinion when it is well founded. In Locke's thought, neither rational nor religious faith are reduced to the effete subjectivity or the muted privacy of mere personal opinion.

Of course, we may still discern in all this the seeds of a destructive epistemology along lines at least akin to those that trouble our theologians or Michael Polanyi. It may be urged that Locke has still given the advantage to reason over faith, reason's judgement being not

---

20. '[P]robability', said Bishop Butler in his introduction to *The Analogy of Religion Natural and Revealed* (London: Bell, 1886), 'is the very guide of life'.

just rationally indispensable but logically final. Even when it adjudicates in favour of the revealed claim, it will never allow faith to scale the pinnacle of rational knowledge, however high it goes up the epistemic ladder and however firm its asseverations about the absolute reliability of divine testimony. Some will conclude that all this is a bad thing, both religiously and more widely damaging.

How should we respond to this judgement? One way to do so is by extending our investigation of Locke. The *Essay* sets out its position abstractly in the sense that particular religious claims are not put to the test. It offers only an intellectual structure, intellectual principles. Investigation into the rational proof of Locke's religious pudding best proceeds by turning to the work in which his claims for Christianity are put to the test: *The Reasonableness of Christianity*. Here, Locke seeks to apply the epistemological proposals of the *Essay*. The *Essay* had offered a demonstration of the existence of God in the form of a cosmological argument (IV.x). Further, it had ascribed a theoretical place to miracles without scorn and with patent encouragement to readers disposed to persist in upholding the authority of Scripture.[21] As we now move beyond the principles of religious epistemology to the grounds of Christian belief, we shall find confirmation of the claim that Locke needs to be cast in an alternative light to that in which he appears in Polanyi's work. More than that, we shall be in a position to understand the significance of that discovery for the thesis being developed in this book.

The Reasonableness of Christianity

It has been observed that the title of Locke's work 'epitomized the substance of English theology for a hundred years'.[22] While Locke's *Reasonableness* applies epistemological principles, it is not a treatise on epistemology. Its avowed aim was to deal principally with justification, faith and salvation and not with reason, faith and revelation. [23] It was published in 1695 after Locke had been led to examine the question of justifying faith. He was clear that faith justified. But in what does such faith consist? *Reasonableness* is Locke's answer to that question. His

---

21. See IV.xix.16 for reference to 'Scripture'.
22. Alan Richardson, recording Mark Pattison's observation in *History Sacred and Profane* (London: SCM, 1964) 21.
23. *The Reasonableness of Christianity as delivered in the Scriptures*, ed. John C. Higgins-Biddle (Oxford: Clarendon, 1999). Chapter and section (not page) numbers are usually given in the main body of the text from now on. I have reduced capital letters that begin words in Locke's original text to the lower case.

investigation had a wider scope and his motives were broader than we can explore here. Our interest is in the surface of the text where Locke applies his epistemological scheme to soteriological questions.

His answer to the question: 'In what does faith consist?' is apparently simple. It is this: 'Believe in the Lord Jesus Christ and you will be saved'. This belief can be expressed as belief that Jesus is the Messiah, although more or less kindred or close Christological titles (as Locke regarded them) can alternatively be used.[24] Of course, we have slid here from talk of 'belief in' to 'belief that', but Locke has no problem with that. He glosses 'believing on him' as signifying 'no more than believing him to be the Messiah' (9.82). He is little troubled by the objection that this means that he is concerned with propositions and not with trust, with *fides historica* and not *fides salvifica*. If folk 'please to call the believing that which our Saviour and his apostles preached and proposed alone to be believed, an historical faith, they have their liberty' (11.191). What they are not entitled to do is to deny that it is simultaneously a saving and justifying faith. Objection: 'the devils believe and tremble' (11.193). Indeed, they do, but their fault is not that they get tangled up in a false estimation or overestimation of the importance of assent to propositions. Their problem is that their belief is not accompanied by repentance. To say that belief in Jesus as Messiah suffices for salvation is to say that it suffices *as belief*. It is not to say that belief suffices for salvation. Repentance is a necessary condition for salvation.

Before remarking on the question of whether belief for Locke is in fact a necessary, if certainly not a sufficient, condition for salvation, it should be noted that Locke ran into heavy controversy over the content of what he thought it sufficient to believe. Do we not, so went the rejoinder to him, need to believe what the apostles proposed for our belief in the rest of the canonical Scriptures? Locke was accused of stark reductionism. Debate over this point encompassed the question of fundamental articles of faith and led Locke to *Vindications* of his *Reasonableness*, the second of which was longer than the *Reasonableness* itself.[25] We shall not pursue him over these hills and dales. What

24. Philip Doddridge pithily observed that 'a question arises' here 'concerning the extent of these words' ('belief that Jesus is the Messiah') as quoted in the lively and well-researched study by Alan P. F. Sell, *John Locke and the Eighteenth Century Divines* (Cardiff: University of Wales Press, 1997) 200.

25. A prominent allegation Locke had to face in connection with *Reasonableness* was that of Socinianism: see Victor Nuovo's 'Introduction' to Locke's *Vindications of the Reasonableness of Christianity* (Oxford: Clarendon, 2012) xix-lxxvii. To confute it, Locke vigorously protested his allegiance to the theology of the New Testament.

detains us from pursuit is interest in the way that Locke advertises in
Reasonableness the utter confidence of the assent of faith, doing so without
any overt hesitation, misgiving or embarrassment. 'The faith which God
counted to Abraham for righteousness, was nothing but a firm belief
of what God declared to him, and a steadfast relying on him for the
accomplishment of what he had promised' (3.24). Abraham's 'relying
firmly on the promise of God, without any doubt of its performance,
gave him the name of the father of the faithful' (13.245). The confidence
of faith has a companion confidence because those who possess only
the 'light of nature' can themselves have confidence, confidence in the
divine bounty and goodness. So it is confidence all round and all the
way down. As recipients of promise, such as Abraham, had confidence,
so we, beneficiaries of fulfilment, may have it. We ought to have it in
full measure: belief that Jesus was the Messiah deserves entertainment
'past doubt' (4.26). Locke likes to quote the Johannine text that reports
the disciples' confession that they believed *and were sure* (my italics) that
Jesus was the Messiah (6:69).[26]

How do we become assured? Above all, because his miracles attest
Jesus' claim.[27] Locke does not isolate miracle; we also encounter in
his work its familiar twin in the tradition of Christian apologetics,
prophecy. However, the reference to the epistemic force and place of
miracles found in the *Essay* engenders the supposition that miracles are
likely to be religiously important for its author. It is a supposition amply
confirmed on reading *Reasonableness*, which also embodied the *Essay*'s
criteria of intelligibility and conformity to precedent knowledge (moral
knowledge being particularly relevant in *Reasonableness*) for affirming
revelation. In *Reasonableness*, we learn that miracles are designed to
convince us of messianic claims (4.27-29); the Jews were justified in
accepting them on that basis (7.55-57) and they were necessary for the
receipt of Jesus' mission (8.73-76). The epistemological pattern set out
in the *Essay* is in evidence in the *Reasonableness*. It was reported earlier
that, in the *Essay*, miracles can in principle so accredit a proposition
that we are entitled not only to believe it but also to believe it with
assurance. Principle becomes practice in *Reasonableness*. If *Reasonableness*
differs at all with regard to religious epistemology from what we might
expect from a reading of the *Essay*, it is not because Christian faith turns
out to lack epistemic muscle. Just the opposite. It is because Locke uses
in *Reasonableness* language that is rather excessive even for that highest

26.   'Being sure' is not the best translation of the Greek.
27.   Locke essayed a short 'Discourse on miracles', which was published posthumously,
      Works, vol. viii.

probability which, according to the *Essay*, necessarily procures assent. Locke's assured faith in *Reasonableness* is, if anything, stronger than what the *Essay* may be supposed to permit. If, in the *Essay*, space is created for the maximal epistemic status for the claims of faith and revelation that Locke's philosophy of knowledge will allow, *Reasonableness* fills the space to the point of overflow. Jesus is the Messiah. God has revealed it. That is sure. And it is certainly not a dictate of reason.

The exact nuances of the soteriological accompaniment of this staunch defence of the impeccable epistemic credentials of Christian faith in *Reasonableness* are not easy to determine dogmatically. Locke needed to specify how we should describe the exact and important religious distinction of Christianity in relation to the wider religious experience of humankind (14.257-60). Are faith and receipt of revelation necessary for salvation? Locke does not waver on the question of the necessity of faith for salvation in the case of those who hear the Word. To be saved, we must believe in the Word of revelation. Yet Locke effortlessly, it seems, conjoins this with what he judges to be the case for those who have not heard the gospel, where it is clear that '[n]o body was, or can be required to believe, what was never proposed to him to believe' (13.243). God, says Locke, quoting Scripture, requires of each '[a]*ccording to what a man hath, and not according to what he hath no*t' (14.252).

So what exactly hath a man without knowledge of Christ? Soteriologically speaking, a lot, it would seem.

> The same spark of the divine nature and knowledge in man which, making him a man, showed him the law he was under, as a man, showed him also the way of atoning the merciful, kind, compassionate Author and Father. . . . He that made use of this candle of the Lord, so far as find out what was his duty, could not miss to find also the way to reconciliation and forgiveness, when he had failed of his duty (14.252-53).

What is that 'way'? 'Repentance, asking pardon, and amendment' (14.253). Nature has revealed this as a way of reconciliation, giving hope of atonement. The gospel, 'having said nothing to the contrary, leaves them to stand or fall to their own Father and Master, whose goodness and mercy is over all his works' (14.254).

While the formulations seem to betray no hesitation, Locke does not conceal the fact that they are fetched out of rather deep theological waters when he concedes that someone may possibly press the question: 'What need was there of a Saviour?' (14.254). Locke's first answer is that if divine wisdom deemed it fit to send a Saviour, that is good enough for us. His constructive elaboration is more detailed. Whatever human reason may know in principle and whatever was discovered by human reason in practice, reason was never able to establish the knowledge either of God or of our duties comprehensively and persuasively enough to ground a universal religion adequately. Priests and philosophers in different ways failed people. Priests corrupted religious knowledge. Philosophers kept it to themselves. By way of contrast, Jesus, his mission established by indubitable miracles, established a religion that could and did become universal, not local; public, not private (14.274-89).

It is in relation to the question of knowledge of our duties that Locke displays the most deliberate and systematic epistemological interest in his *Reasonableness*. Priestly corruption prevents worthy religious practice by detaching it from virtue. As for philosophers, their limitations are various. These include the sheer difficulty of establishing a full system of morality with confidence (the common crowd would never follow the reasoning anyway) and the sheer difficulty of collating its diverse elements even if someone somehow managed to gather into one the scattered fragments. Confident subscription to a universal *vera religio* is simply unavailable until the appearance of Jesus. Locke crafts his epistemological scheme here with some care. Morality, religion and the responsible conduct of life must be founded on either reason or revelation (14.268-74). In principle, an assured and true religion could be rationally discovered. In practice, it never was. Further, it was always going to be all but impossibly difficult. 'A clear and convincing light', something for us to depend on 'with certainty', an 'unerring rule', a 'sure guide', authentic religious authority – all this was unavailable save through Jesus Christ. Reason vouches in the appropriate way for the fact that what Jesus teaches is substantively true. What moral knowledge reason independently possesses is not contradicted but edifyingly amplified in Christianity. As for 'the truths revelation has discovered', Locke says that it 'is our mistake to think, that because reason confirms them to us, we had the first certain knowledge of them from thence' (14.278). On the contrary, '[t]he truth and obligation' of the teaching of Jesus 'have their force, and are put past doubt to us, by the evidence of his mission. He was sent by God; his miracles show it; and the authority of God in his precepts cannot be questioned' (14.273).

Locke offers a number of reasons why Jesus appeared. Outward reformation of worship, encouragement in piety and the promise of spiritual assistance were all needed (14.244-46). However, Locke gives less time to these considerations than to those previously mentioned. Indeed, even after he has given full weight to all the items in his cornucopia, it may be judged that he has not satisfactorily answered the question: what need is there for a Saviour?[28] Most certainly, we have a revealed religion that is a way of salvation. At the same time, forgiveness is available through penitence without knowing Christ. Although, when it comes to the treatment of the Saviour, he inserts the vocabulary of 'hope of atonement' into his discussion, Locke includes no treatment of atonement. Is salvation, then, minus atonement? Locke has his defenders who read him on this point 'conservatively' in relation to traditional insistence on atonement.[29] Whether or not we find them persuasive, what Locke thinks is at stake in the discussion of the reasonableness of Christianity is ultimately the possibility of *vera religio*. That is through and through a soteriological matter. Locke is dealing with something he regards as religiously important over and above the epistemological dimensions of assurance and faith that feature in the *Essay*. If Locke invests any religious significance in his invocation of revelation, it is because what Christians believe to be revealed is the way of salvation. It would be tendentious and unwarranted to propose here that Locke was eager to get his epistemology right for the sake of soteriology. What can safely be said is that everyone in Locke's day knew that if reason could banish revelation, it would have struck at the soteriological point of Christianity. Its soteriological point is announced in the first sentence of *Reasonableness*. And '[i]n *The Reasonableness of Christianity* Locke laid the cornerstone of his life's principal effort.'[30] There is more than the struggle for epistemology at stake – significantly more. Before elaborating on this, we return to the concerns of Polanyi and company.

---

28. Locke does not formulate an argument to the effect that the ontological necessity for a Saviour does not entail universal cognitive necessity that we should know the Saviour in this mortal life if we are to be saved. Nor does he argue that the lack of universal cognitive necessity in this mortal life does not entail a lack of ontological necessity.

29. E.g., W.M. Spellman, *John Locke and the Problem of Depravity* (Oxford: Clarendon, 1988) chapter 5. For a rather surprising reference to Locke in the history of the doctrine of atonement, see Horace Bushnell, *The Vicarious Sacrifice, Grounded in Principles of Universal Obligation* (New York, NY: Scribner, 1866) 29.

30. Higgins-Biddle, 'Introduction' to *Reasonableness*, cxiv. This substantial essay is an excellent introduction to Locke's volume. 'To fully illuminate the nature of the Fall' was one of Locke's great authorial aims, W. M. Spellman, *John Locke and the Problem of Depravity* (Oxford: Clarendon, 1988) 103.

FROM REVELATION TO RECONCILIATION

After commenting on his *Third Letter*, I have in the foregoing exposition drawn on two major works by Locke. I have referred to the fact that Locke followed up both of these with defences or elaborations. I have also noted that Locke has more variations on the theme of reason and revelation than are found in these two major works or in the letters on toleration. Casting our net over the whole of his authorship, we might, on the one hand, find evidence that relatively weakens the hand of revelation in Locke's thought. In *Two Treatises of Government*, the natural light of reason seems to shine brighter than it does in *Reasonableness*, making revelation the less distinctive.[31] On the other hand, we might witness the position of revelation strengthened. If we peruse Locke's posthumously published *Paraphrases* of Paul's epistles, we discover that he has no evident difficulty in reproducing and vouching for the strong claims for revelation made by the apostle. In fact, this volume not only brings to light Locke's commitment to the truth of revelation more than does any other, it '[m]ore than any of Locke's other writings . . . stresses the superiority of revelation to reason'.[32] Note also that, in commenting on Paul in these paraphrases, Locke moves away from the purely intellectualist view of faith itself (as distinct from repentance) that we find in the *Essay* and in *Reasonableness*.

If we must conclude anything in the round, it is that Locke sought to give religious belief a status that permits it (a) to apprehend cognitively what reason cannot apprehend and (b) to do so on impeccably rational grounds, and that (c) he applies this permission to the most important conceivable issue, that of soteriology. His texts embody an intention to show that religious belief is armed with full rational warrant and is entitled to apprehend what demonstrative knowledge does not. Locke needs to make no apology at all for making an alleged exception in the case of religion. If religious belief is epistemically inferior to demonstrative knowledge, it is rationally no less assured. Granted, we must allow an interpretation of Locke that emphasises that, as a matter of manifest logic, demonstration gains the upper epistemic hand over faith

---

31.   See Peter Laslett's introduction to Locke's *Two Treatises of Government*, 2ⁿᵈ ed. (Cambridge: Cambridge University Press, 1967) 87-90. For a different point of view, see Peter Schouls, *The Imposition of Method: A Study of Descartes and Locke* (Oxford: Clarendon, 1980) 220-21.

32.   A.W. Wainwright in his substantial and helpful introduction to *A Paraphrase and Notes On The Epistles of Saint Paul To The Galatians, 1 and 2 Corinthians, Romans, Ephesians*, volume 1 (Oxford: Clarendon, 1987) 31.

if we are comparing relative strengths. But if faith must concede that, it concedes as little as possible within the terms of what the distinction requires. Locke makes faith as distant as it can possibly be from inability to apprehend confidently what reason cannot. In epistemic practice, it concedes barely an inch and epistemological principle is designed to show how that can be the case.

Of course, those who are partial to Polanyi's reading of intellectual history at this point, even if they are open to the interpretive corrections I suggested at the beginning of this chapter, may seize avidly on these last formulations. As Troeltsch said somewhere of historical criticism: give it an inch and you give it an ell. Is the crack not there in Locke and is that not the trouble? The answer is: 'no' – even if the crack is there, it is not the trouble as Polanyi perceives it. Suppose that we make an ungrudging concession to Polanyi and company with regard to the epistemic supremacy of demonstrative knowledge over faith in Locke's philosophy. Given the way Locke argues this, how significantly is the epistemic status of faith imperilled? If any contemporaries or successive generations tried to push Locke's logic in the direction of weakening the claims of revelation, others could with equal, if not greater force and justice, push back to strengthen the claims. Locke's thought overall as easily encourages those so inclined to find a way of philosophically strengthening his overt ambitions in religious epistemology and their theological application as it does those inclined to reduce the strength of faith and revelation. That is to say the least and why not, at least, say what Wesley said in recommending that readers of Locke's *Essay* make 'full use of all the just remarks made by this excellent writer' while castigating his errors?[33] When we discern in Locke's major philosophical treatise (the *Essay*) and primary theological essay (the *Reasonableness*) such possibilities for revelation as we have discovered, we can but wonder at the ready adoption of the suggestion that Locke dispelled what mattered epistemologically as far as belief and revelation are concerned and that this is the breach that opened out into modernity. Locke essayed strong claims for revelation in a climate where Herbert of Cherbury, assorted free-thinkers and perhaps Thomas Hobbes had flaunted or were flaunting, with more or less aplomb, radical alternatives.[34]

---

33. John Wesley, 'Remarks Upon Mr. Locke's "Essay On Human Understanding"' in *The Works of John Wesley*, volumes 13-14 (Grand Rapids: Baker, 1996) volume 13, 455-64, quotation from 464. The introduction and conclusion to Wesley's essay do not give us a flavor of the sandwich in between.

34. The possibility that Locke drew on Hobbes in his interpretation of the reasonableness of Christianity has long intrigued. There are other possible

To pursue an enquiry into how the historical demise of revelation in intellectual circles was specifically related to Locke's thought and writings would evidence an excessive preoccupation with Locke in particular. In relation to him, it could be argued that the most that I have gained by examining his thought is to suggest the possibility that the blame for the critical shift that troubled Polanyi may not be squarely and with confidence placed on the shoulders of Locke himself. But perhaps this just means that we have to name other names instead of Locke's. Is it not the epistemological trouble, rather than the epistemological troubler, that matters in an analysis of the crisis in Western thought of the kind that preoccupies the likes of Polanyi, Gunton and Torrance?

Well, in that case, Locke has given us big shoes to fill in his vacancy.[35] Far more important, my discussion of *Reasonableness* against the background of the *Essay* has aimed to do more than alert us to the strength of Locke's personal intention of maintaining the status of revelation in his defence of Christianity and of maintaining it with a robust epistemological conscience. It has alerted us to the soteriological interest in the defence of revelation. Pascal returns to mind. Pascal's implicit answer to the 'why' of the demise of revelation is to direct us to look for reasons of the heart. We do not have to be Pascal or even religious to suspect that when we are in the thick of Western Christian religious concerns, with talk of penitence and salvation dominating the foreground, reasons of the heart will make their presence felt. Two logically distinct but closely related possibilities thus emerge. The first is that the battle over revelation is also and perhaps fundamentally a battle over soteriology. The second is that with the shift to that perspective, we shift also from speaking of reasons of the head to speaking of reasons of the heart.

As for the legacy of Locke himself, of all who immediately tried to enlist him in their cause, the cause of a radical critique of Christianity, the deists were singularly important historically. They are extremely suggestive on the question of epistemology and soteriology. They pulled Locke as far as they could into their quest for a rational religion encumbered as little as possible by revelation. Although popular definition of deism

---

Lockean sources: see Ashcraft, *Revolutionary Politics*, for an interesting account of Robert Ferguson's work on this score, 55-64.

35. As for big shoes, note Gilbert Ryle's comment that '[i]t is not much of an exaggeration to say that one cannot pick up a sermon, novel, a pamphlet or a treatise and be in any doubt, after reading a few lines, whether it was published before or after the publication of Locke's *Essay on Human Understanding*. . . . The intellectual atmosphere since Locke has had quite a different smell from what it had before Locke', quoted in Schouls, *Imposition*, 3.

specifies an absentee creator God, deism has long proved difficult to define accurately when its texts are scrutinized properly. Herbert of Cherbury, whose general epistemology Locke criticized, was once called the father of deism, but the distance between Herbert and the deists has often been emphasized.[36] Bolingbroke, Middleton and Wollaston have all in their turn been accorded and denied the appellation 'deist'. Samuel Clarke, deeply exercised by the whole phenomenon of deism, distinguished four kinds in his day.[37] The first kind professed belief in the existence of an eternal, infinite, independent and intelligent Being, but denied Providence. A second accepted the doctrine of Providence as part of a proper doctrine of God but submitted that God did not concern himself with the question of whether actions are morally good or bad. A third gloried in the denial of the immortality of the soul. A last breed could be unearthed that was actually hospitable to orthodox beliefs but established them all by the light of nature.

'Deism' thus names an immensely complex and multi-faceted phenomenon.[38] A figure like Charles Blount fits somewhere into almost any analysis of deism, but he was writing before Locke produced his major works. Still, it is instructive to record John Oman's comment on Blount's translation of the *Life of Apollonius of Tyana*: 'This was the first definite attack on revelation, and it derived its force, not from itself, but from being an indication of the far more dangerous attack which was expressed in life, not in writing.'[39] The work of Anthony Collins and that of John Toland are historically particularly close to Locke, but the book that became known as the 'Bible of deism' was the later work by Matthew Tindal, *Christianity as Old as Creation*.[40] Although the claim has been made that Tindal has been over-exposed at the expense of Toland, he rightly remains in the limelight in analyses of deism, even if he ought

---

36. On Herbert, see R. Bedford, *The Defence of Truth: Herbert of Cherbury and the Seventeenth Century* (Manchester: Manchester University Press, 1979).

37. Samuel Clarke, *A Demonstration of the Being and Attributes of God* (London, 1728) 158-90.

38. See Wayne Hudson, *The English Deists: Studies in Early Enlightenment* (London: Pickering & Chatto, 2009). In Hudson's volume, it comes to light that Clarke's was not the only four-fold classification: see that of a different four early on by Jacques Abbadie (36).

39. John Oman, *The Problem of Faith and Freedom* (London: Hodder & Stoughton, 1906) 91.

40. The page references in the text below are to the first edition (London, 1730). I use the third edition in Stephen N. Williams, 'Matthew Tindal on Perfection, Positivity and the Life Divine', *Enlightenment and Dissent*, no. 5 (1986) 51-69.

to share it.[41] It is in connection with Tindal that a remark particularly salient for our purposes was made by Hans Frei in the seminal historical-theological study that influenced early 'narrative theology'. Frei put it like this:

> There was only one seemingly watertight device for protecting the theological indispensability of historical revelation against deistic insinuations of a natural nonpositive saving knowledge of God. This was a root-and-branch affirmation of the specific historical event of original, inherited and natural inexpungeable guilt, the fatal moral, metaphysical and noetic flaw which could be wiped out only by a similarly factual saving occurrence.[42]

At first glance, this formulation may give the impression that fall and redemption were wheeled in to protect revelation and that this constitutes a logical alternative to the position that revelation was retained in order to protect fall and redemption. In fact, this is certainly not what Frei intended to convey.[43] His emphasis was on the theologically substantive *affirmation* not on the *genesis* of doctrinal reasoning: the events of fall and redemption were *affirmed* in order to protect the notion of revelation because the events were precisely what constituted the material content of doctrine and substance of revelation.[44] Frei was alerting us to the connections between the defence of revelation and the defence of historical redemption or reconciliation. It was in this connection that reference to Tindal was included in his discussion of the neologians. Frei did not examine Tindal's work, but it behoves us to do so briefly.

---

41. For a proposal that we demote Tindal in order to accord to Toland a higher place, see Peter Harrison, *'Religion' and the Religions in the English Enlightenment* (Cambridge: Cambridge University Press, 1990) 167. Peter Byrne was at the same time continuing the tradition of giving Tindal pride of place in *Natural Religion and the Nature of Religion: the Legacy of Deism* (London: Routledge, 1989).
42. *The Eclipse of the Biblical Narrative* (New Haven: Yale University Press, 1974) 61.
43. While he did not, as far as I know, declare himself in print on precisely this matter, my conversations of many years ago with Hans Frei, who was my *Doktorvater*, convinced me that he endorsed the thesis I argue in this volume about the primacy of the soteriological.
44. I do not for a moment deny that the concepts in my investigation can be matched up differently in modernity; Harrison's *The Fall of Man* is amongst the volumes that document how Francis Bacon and the Baconian tradition sought to use reason to remedy the fall.

Accounts of Tindal's 'Bible' often miss its characteristic feature, which is the logical deduction of practically every significant theological claim from the idea of God.[45] An early statement in his work seems too innocuous to announce much in the way of rigorous method, yet it does indicate the direction of intellectual travel. 'If . . . you allow that we are to measure what is pleasing or displeasing to God (which takes in the whole of religion) from what our reason teaches us concerning his nature, you allow all I contend for' (30). Indeed, if we are to ascribe the word 'rigour' at all to Tindal's lengthy piece, it is not to its logical presentation, which is a literary tumble-dryer of an affair, the same items constantly reappearing in different order. Rather, it is to the relentless adherence to the principle of logical deduction from the divine attributes. This could profoundly irritate Bishop Joseph Butler, who retorted that '[n]othing . . . but omniscience could justify Tindal in maintaining that God must reveal Himself perfectly to every one in every place at all times'.[46] Such alleged hubris surfaced precisely in the confidence of a rational deduction from the very idea of God. The conclusion from which Butler demurred was reached *a priori* by Tindal because he found it entailed in divine justice and immutability. Tindal did not deny that historical revelation occurred in some form. What he denied was that God could reveal anything in history of religious importance, unless it were a republication of what reason could and should independently know. It could not be important if what is revealed is both theoretically and practically accessible to our cognition in other ways.

In so far as Tindal deployed principles of religious epistemology, he had recourse to Locke. He explicitly did so quite summarily, although the summary nature of his appeal managed to reflect a pervasive assumption and grounded a religious epistemology that Tindal paraded ubiquitously.[47] His discussion certainly helps to bear out the claim that when the deists made epistemological use of Locke, they were 'flashy and superficial'.[48] Tindal tried to market his reason in the form of canned

---

45. However, in *Natural Religion*, Peter Byrne indicated the priority of the idea of God Tindal's argument, as did H.E. Allison, briefly and neatly in *Lessing and the Enlightenment* (Ann Arbor, MI: University of Michigan, 1966) 14, though I think that the universal identity of human nature, which Allison takes to be presupposed in Tindal's argument, could be deduced *a priori* from Tindal's concept of God.

46. See Oman, *The Problem of Faith*, 127.

47. Tindal's discussion should be picked up from the end of the twelfth chapter of his work.

48. John Yolton, *John Locke and the Way of Ideas* (Oxford: Oxford University Press, 1956) 204.

empiricism, and logical deduction from the idea of God turns out to be the ingredient that flavours everything eventually served up. Knowledge-claims in religion must be validated according to the security of their rootage in 'self-evident notions'. It is clear that the claims of general epistemology Tindal makes are motored by religious concerns. He never tires of repeating that the only scheme of knowledge compatible with deity is a scheme that bestows universal, knowable religious truth. The substance of that truth is essentially moral and the moral is the religious. 'Was there any thing but morality necessary to constitute true religion; we might be so certain that the goodness of God would give us a demonstration for it, equal to that he has given us for morality' (131). The 'plainness of God's precepts' is 'agreeable to infinite wisdom directed by infinite goodness, which certainly will give us equal degrees of evidence for religious truths, which so much concern us as it has done for truths of less importance' (130-31).

Not only is morality the essence of religion, Tindal also insists on a rational-moral criterion for knowing the ways of God. He keeps up his discussion on this point for a long time but I leap here to what he does at the end of it.[49] Having established his positions with unmistakeable clarity, he trains his fire to marked purpose on one thinker: Samuel Clarke. According to Tindal, Clarke is fatally inconsistent. Clarke reasons away well enough for the most part, admirably deducing his conclusions from the being and attributes of God. Then he proceeds to ruin the performance by introducing historical revelation. This is manifestly inconsistent. Why should anyone of otherwise sound reasoning so lapse? The answer is not hard to find. Samuel Clarke believes that God effected reconciliation in history. Reconciliation requires revelation, for neither the principle of mediation nor the person of the Mediator is known to the natural religion of reason. Tindal attacks the doctrine protected by revelation, as well as the protective casing of revelation itself. The idea of a Mediator is heathen. It is a slight upon God and the humanity he created in his image.

> I may venture to say that the Dr's [Clarke's] description of human nature in all but one pair (and that too perhaps but for a day) is a libel on the dignity of human nature; and an high reflection on the wisdom and goodness of its author; in placing them, without any fault of theirs, in an unavoidable state of degeneration and corruption for 4,000 years together, and continuing the greatest part still in the same state (390).

---

49.   His final chapter is the only one devoted to rebuttal of an opponent.

Tindal identified the cause of epistemological confusion amongst the orthodox. It stems from soteriological conviction, soteriological confusion, soteriological illusion. Because of the problems that surround the definition of deism and identification of who belongs there, it would be wrong to dogmatise on just how representative Tindal is of deism as a whole. He has been classified with the 'constructive' as opposed to the 'critical' deists, but that very classification is variously presented, sometimes being understood in thematic, sometimes in chronological terms.[50] What we can confidently say is that in his denial of the fall and of historical redemption and in his concomitant assertion of human moral or religious self-sufficiency, Tindal definitely identifies the grain of a foundational plank in the deistic criticism of traditional Christianity.

Ernst Cassirer long ago detected in Tindal's work evidence of a shift from more broadly intellectual concerns to interest in "'practical reason'".[51] Whether or not there is a shift at quite this juncture, Cassirer makes a significant comparison. He compares Tindal to Kant on account of their shared moral interest. Cassirer's comparison does not negate the truth that the bold 'onto-theologizing' of which Tindal is representative was a target for Kant's *Critique of Pure Reason*.[52] Nor would anyone reading Tindal be likely to confuse him with the sage of Königsberg. Yet, if anything would have impelled Kant to keep the hand of friendship extended to the author of *Christianity as Old as Creation*, even after he (Kant) had awakened from his dogmatic slumbers, it is surely what Tindal had to say about moral error. Tindal castigated human proneness to seek distraction from true moral religion at all costs, especially by rites and belief in miracles. He maintained that the 'positivity' we assign to revelation, and which grounds such errors, tends inexorably to corrupt the moral incentive. Either you have morality or you have a God acting in history. Once connection with Kant is established in this area, there is no reason for abstaining from doing what Garrett Green did, which

---

50. For a 'constructive' Tindal, see Leslie Stephen, *History of English Thought in the Eighteenth Century*, vol. 1 (New York, NY: Harcourt, Brace and World, 1962) 113-37; for a 'critical' one, see E.C. Mossner, *Bishop Butler and the Age of Reason* (New York, NY: Macmillan, 1936) 74-78.

51. Ernst Cassirer, *The Philosophy of the Enlightenment* (Princeton: Princeton University Press, 1951) 174.

52. Immanuel Kant, *Critique of Pure Reason*, trans. Norman Kemp Smith (London: Macmillan, 1933) 525. However, perhaps Tindal's way of arguing cannot be mapped clearly onto Kant's distinctions between theists and deists and various types of deism.

was to compare Tindal to Fichte.[53] In Fichte's *Attempt at a Critique of all Revelation*, we witness the dire struggle to slot revelation somehow into moral requirements, the moral being the criterion of the religious.

We are back, then, with morality. In *The Authority of the Bible and the Rise of the Modern World*, Reventlow located Locke's thought in the context of his discussion of Christianity as a scheme of moral action, a scheme that Reventlow found played a formative role in the development of biblical criticism. We noted that, according to Locke, on the one hand, God has moral requirements that are not adequately known without Christ and if we are serious about the will of God, we should search out these things. On the other hand, ignorance of what is revealed cannot possibly disqualify us from salvation. There is a natural religious knowledge of the propriety of penance for the attainment of reconciliation. In breaking with a special and religiously significant revelation in history, the deists made a crucial soteriological as well as epistemological move. In Tindal, its nature becomes plain, whether we deem the move logically compelling, permissible or faulty. He knew that talk of revelation would continue just as long as did talk of reconciliation. Samuel Clarke illustrated the plain and classical connection. Denying the need for reconciliation was, in this historical context, a vitally necessary and promisingly sufficient condition for the denial of revelation.

John Dryden observed that deists were 'rationalists with a heart-hunger for religion'.[54] It is quite a poignant description, especially when we recall a chapter-title, many years on, in the volume by William Temple from whose indictment of Descartes I quoted earlier: 'The Hunger of Natural Religion'.[55] Pierre Bayle characterized the conflict of his day as one between the champions of reason and the champions of religion for the souls of men. [56] Perhaps Lord Halifax got close to explaining the religious sensibilities underlying deism, or at least its Tindalian Bible, when he observed that 'there should not always be storms or thunder, a clear sky would sometimes make the Church look more like heaven'.[57] For decades after the Reformation, the battlefields of Europe lay under the dark, shadowy residue of storms and thunder. We must not

---

53. See Green's introduction to Fichte's work, *Attempt at a Critique of all Revelation* (Cambridge: Cambridge University Press, 1978).

54. Quoted in Paul Hazard, *The European Mind, 1680-1715* (New Haven: Yale University Press, 1953) 256.

55. *Nature, Man and God*, lecture xx.

56. See Hazard on Bayle, *The European Mind*, part 1, chapter 5.

57. In *The Character of a Trimmer* (1684), quoted in Basil Willey, *The Eighteenth Century Mind* (New York, NY: Columbia University Press, 1940) 10.

underestimate the importance of this dismal social scene in impelling 'the flight from authority'.[58] If deism was party to a cultural revulsion from a theological dogmatism that masqueraded as religious virtue, proving its style in bloody feud, we can easily agree that the impetus behind deism had a moral component. To that extent – however we wish to connect the 'religious' and the 'moral' conceptually or historically – it commands our sincere sympathy. 'Give us a moral God and a moral soul', said the radicals of the day or, better: 'Reason informs us that we have a moral God; give us a moral soul to go with what we have'. 'Revelation' seemed to block the gift. It secured the intrusion of fall and reconciliation in history.

In a detailed study of John Toland, R.E. Sullivan concluded in relation to the deists that '[t]heir sense of the demands of a personal God was usually less urgent than their sense of the obligations which were theirs as reasonable beings.'[59] At this point, Sullivan was contrasting the deists with Pascal. Pascal and the deists are occupied with different phenomena, detained by different features of religious reality. As far as Pascal is concerned, what we attend to in the things of the spirit is a matter of will directing mind to concentrate on some intellectual object. From his point of view, when we are in thrall to a different spiritual sense of things than is required by the knowledge of a personal God, we are dealing spiritually less in different aspects of the one putative truth than in different attitudes to the one commanding truth.

When deists attended to 'obligations', they were attending to what they took God to require morally of us. Reasonable beings are morally obligated to live as such. Revelation as traditionally understood in Christianity contradicts moral order for it introduces a non-rational and non-moral criterion into religious obligation. A question arises, then, about the relations of revelation and reconciliation, of reason and moral sense. The traditional Christian claim that God has reconciled us to himself in Jesus Christ contradicts the claim that we can be saved by living morally. It collides with a properly formed moral sense and imposes a sense of our inadequacy and the inadequacy of the works of our hands. When reason ousted or usurped revelation to the extent and in the way that it did in the eighteenth century, was this the product of a deeper conflict than a conflict between reason and revelation so as to be, rather, a conflict between a moral sense that powered reason and a belief in reconciliation protected by revelation?

---

58. Jeffrey Stout, *The Flight from Authority: Religion, Morality and the Quest for Autonomy* (Notre Dame, Indiana: University of Notre Dame Press, 1987).

59. R.E. Sullivan, *John Toland and the Deist Controversy: A Study in Adaptations* (Cambridge, MA: Harvard University Press, 1982) 276.

From preliminary ruminations on Descartes and his day, we have been led through an enquiry into Locke's thought to ask this question. Pascal has made his presence known in the course of the enquiry. The contours of an alternative picture to that set out in the work of our epistemologically interested interlocutors are palpably, if not yet boldly, appearing. These contours can be depicted more boldly. In attempting to do so, I shall claim as an ally one whose massive thought stands unmistakeably behind that of Thomas Torrance and Colin Gunton though, in saying this, we are not inducting them into a community of his like-minded disciples. Enter Karl Barth. Turning to his *Protestant Theology in the Nineteenth Century*, we find that the logic of Barth's investigation into the Enlightenment supports the line of thought pursued in this volume. Polanyi was concerned about how Locke paved the way for a momentous development that came on with the Enlightenment. Having just looked at Locke without the eyes of Polanyi, we now turn to look at the Enlightenment through the eyes of Barth.

Chapter 3

Troubled Giant[1]

In an essay on 'Barth on the Western Intellectual Tradition', Colin Gunton sketched Barth's theological response to the Enlightenment as it was set out in his *Protestant Theology*.[2] He reported that Augustinian and Enlightenment thought have points of historical and theological connection and that Barth was committed to overthrowing both types of thought. Gunton covered three areas: the ontological, cultural and epistemological, but the greatest of these is the epistemological.[3] The epistemological legacy bequeathed by Augustine to Christendom, one that dogged the Enlightenment, was the separation of reason and faith. As Gunton draws out the themes of *Protestant Theology*, he concentrates on the epistemological question.

Prima facie, Gunton's account is justified to a degree with respect to Barth's analysis of the breakdown of revelation and the advent of Schleiermacher on the tide of reason's fatal incursion. Yet, a closer scrutiny of Barth's argument leads us to underline in bold the '*prima facie*' and 'to a degree'. There are points where Barth could consistently have

---

1. The title of this chapter has been lifted from F. S. Northedge, *The Troubled Giant: Britain Among the Great Powers, 1916-39* (London: Harper Collins, 1966).

2. 'Barth on the Western Intellectual Tradition' in John Thompson, ed., *Theology Beyond Christendom: Essays on the Centenary of the Birth of Karl Barth* (Allison Park, PA: Pickwick, 1986) 285-301.

3. We glean this from the essay as a whole, but note the reference to the 'particular importance' of epistemology on p. 289.

slanted and slightly modified formulations in his account so that I should
be freed up to say instead more firmly what I want here to intimate only
mildly: 'Gunton's account is not *really* justified.' A slight but significant
internal adjustment in the formulation of Barth's argument or flow of his
account here and there would have shown that Gunton's concentration
on epistemology missed the mark. Rather than pussyfooting around, let
me put it like this: careful reading of Barth shows that Gunton's reading
of Barth is lopsided. Granted, Barth argued that the introduction into
Protestant dogmatics of reason as judge of religious truth opened the
door and eventually led to the elimination of revelation. He also argued
that the natural knowledge of God as a regulative principle in dogmatics,
which enabled reason to adopt this role, was theologically disastrous.
This seems to be all about epistemology. But is faulty theological
epistemology really the root of all evils as far as Barth is concerned in
this volume? In attempting to answer that question, I eschew substantive
theological evaluation of Barth as much as I have eschewed philosophical
evaluation of Locke or any evaluation of the figures under discussion in
the first chapter of this work.

Thomas Torrance observed that

> the danger of natural theology lies in the fact that once its ground
> has been conceded it becomes the ground on which everything else
> is absorbed and naturalized, so that even the knowledge of God
> mediated through his self-revelation in Christ is domesticated
> and adapted to it until it all becomes a form of natural theology.
> Barth reached this judgement through extensive examination of
> the history of German Protestant theology which it is extremely
> difficult, if not impossible, to refute.[4]

In what follows, I do not address the subject of natural theology
directly nor is there any attempt to expound Barth on the natural
knowledge of God across the corpus of his theological work. My interest
in Barth is restricted to his reading of the history of thought with special,
though not sole, reference to *Protestant Theology*.[5] In this context, I shall
not be suggesting any radical adjustment of Torrance's verdict so far as it
goes, but what underlies Barth's judgement on theological epistemology
should not go unnoticed if that judgement is placed in a wider context.

---

4.   *Transformation and Convergence*, 290.
5.   Karl Barth, *Protestant Theology in the Nineteenth Century: Its Background and
     History* (London: SCM, 1972). Page references to this work will usually be
     supplied in the main body of the text.

This is the more germane to my argument especially if Barth's influence has directly or indirectly aided or lain behind the epistemological sightings of Gunton and Torrance discussed earlier. A consideration of Barth's historical analysis in its own right potentially yields good fruit in terms of my discussion. When Colin Gunton takes up Barth's analysis, he mildly spices our investigation by connecting Barth and Polanyi.[6] This is a dish I must reluctantly pass up. Barth alone is fare enough.

KARL BARTH'S TROUBLES

Colin Gunton observed that gone were the days when Barth was simply pitted against Schleiermacher.[7] True; but it remains that Barth's dissent from Schleiermacher motors his historical investigation in *Protestant Theology* even if it is not the only factor that does so. In pursuing Schleiermacher, Barth is scrupulously critical of those who would take such dissent as a licence for operating in the fashion of Brunner, for instance, who refused to hearken seriously to Schleiermacher and condemned him before the trial began (21). Barth's volume was the product of a series of lectures on Schleiermacher and on theology from Schleiermacher onwards (26). The first part of *Protestant Theology* is called 'Background' and the second 'History'; the second part commences with Schleiermacher. In the published event, Barth spent more time on the eighteenth-century background than on the nineteenth-century history. In fact, he has largely shot his historical and theological bolt not just before arriving at Schleiermacher but also before arriving at those thinkers whom Gunton identified as being crucial alongside Schleiermacher, namely, Kant and Hegel. Gunton rightly noted the controlling function of the concept of 'absolutism' in Barth's analysis.[8] It is a term borrowed from the sphere of politics because Barth believed that it was from the political angle that the eighteenth century is best viewed as a whole (54).[9] 'Absolutism' conveys how Barth wanted to think about the whole.[10]

6.   See the fleeting reference to Polanyi in 'Barth on the Western Theological Tradition', 291.
7.   'Barth on the Western Theological Tradition', 292.
8.   Gunton connects Barth on absolutism with Polanyi on rationalism in 'The Truth of Christology' in Torrance, *Belief in Science*, 91.
9.   But note Max Beloff's observation that '[t]he history of art is as essential to a full understanding of eighteenth-century absolutism as the history of political theory', *The Age of Absolutism, 1660-1815* (London: Hutchinson, 1954) 47. Barth distinguished between 'political' and 'enlightened' absolutism.
10. Barth also refers to eighteenth-century absolutism in a portion of *Church*

'Absolutism' in general can obviously mean a system of life based upon the belief in the omnipotence of human powers. Man, who discovers his own power and ability, the potentiality dormant in his humanity, that is, his human being as such, and looks at it as the final, the real and absolute, I mean as something 'detached', self-justifying, with its own authority and power, which he can therefore set in motion in all directions without any restraint – this man is absolute man (60).

This man imparts to life both an outer and an inner form.

If there is such an external cast for the eighteenth century, and one that we can identify, it is perhaps most allowable to comprehend it in terms of a striving to reduce everything to an absolute form . . . [the will for form being] a will to which all things we find existing about us are mere material to be moulded by man (55; 63).

Barth proceeded to examine the outer form in a variety of fields, including nature, architecture, fashion, education, literature and music. However, it is in Barth's treatment of the inner form that we hear the tones and encounter the presuppositions of his treatment of eighteenth-century theology. He searched for some psychological common denominator that would furnish us with the clue to the inner life of eighteenth-century 'man'.[11] He found it by focussing on Renaissance humanist man, celebrant of complete rational autarchy in a rational world governed by God. This man migrated from antiquity into northern Europe and thence to eighteenth-century Europe. This is the man of late pre-Christian and extra-Christian antiquity – the Stoic with a dash of the Epicurean in him. 'The inner attitude to life of the eighteenth century consisted of the fact that Cicero and Plutarch were now taken seriously' (77). Philosophy is 'a practical teaching of life' deriving from an attitude towards life based on the 'complete authority of the rational man in a rational world with a religious background' (77). Leibniz is

---

Dogmatics I/2 (Edinburgh: T & T Clark, 1956), see 293, to which I shall later advert. Colin Gunton remarks that 'Barth's analysis of the Enlightenment as a whole as the "Age of Absolutism" is one of the possible theological analyses of the monistic tendencies of modernity', *The One, the Three*, 30, n. 37.

11. I retain the standard translation 'man' when referring to Barth's account, however inclusive his German usage was designed to be. It is another matter when he is talking about Mary, *Church Dogmatics*, I/2, 140 (cf. 193)!

the prime exemplar.[12] He is the true father of the Enlightenment (35). In his life, Leibniz embodied this transfigured humanism and in his thought, he gave it classic expression. What is eighteenth-century man but Leibniz's monad?

> This simple and utterly individual, indeed unique spiritual substance is the fountain-head of all reality. The utterly self-sufficient monad is an emanation, an image, a mirror of God Himself and is therefore nowhere limited by things outside it, but only in its own being; which has no windows, and changes only in its inner principle, its own most peculiar striving; which is always the best it is possible for it to be, and which can therefore transform itself by the tendency of its own most peculiar nature; but it cannot be destroyed, cannot perish, and is immortal like God himself who created it (78).

In this account, Barth is identifying a form of rationalism. However, the importance accorded to reason is the expression of will – the will for form (75). Rationalism may be the substance of humanism, but the substance is itself the expression of an underlying spirit. We can trace Barth's account through his discussion of 'The Problem of Theology in the 18th Century' (80-135). Prior to that chapter, he has prepared us for his accusation that theology capitulated to the *Zeitgeist*. Sadly, this means that the theologian is at heart a Stoic humanist who will approach theology as one resolved to master it in absolutist fashion. Barth expounds this under the rubric of 'humanization'. Humanization is

> if not the abolition, at least the incorporation of God into the sphere of sovereign human self-awareness, the transformation of the reality that came and was perceived from outside into a reality that is experienced and understood inwardly . . . incorporated into human capabilities, comprehended as such a reality as can be begotten of man's capability and must be so begotten to count as reality (84).

The 'problem' – that is, the subject-matter – of theology is humanized in four ways: by the incorporation of Christianity into (a) the State (b) morality and the bourgeoisie (c) science and philosophy (d) inwardness

---

12. Leibniz emerges in an interestingly different light from Barth's standpoint in Timothy J. Gorringe, *Karl Barth: Against Hegemony* (Oxford: Oxford University Press, 1999) chapter 5.

and the individual. It is in this last case that we discern the pure form
of the general tendency of the time. Like the Renaissance and Leibniz,
and before the Romantics and Goethe, eighteenth-century man found
in himself 'something eternal, almighty, wise, good, glorious' (113). At
this point, Barth lets loose with a hostility unequalled in his attitude
towards any other group or individual in any other group. Pietism is the
trouble. It is the religion of grasping, not of being grasped. It is the twin
of rationalism and no true heir to the Reformation. In this context, Barth
dilates on the notion of reason (*ratio*). 'Reason' is the normative concept
characteristic of the time, not in the narrower sense of an entity that
eliminates mystery but in a broader sense every bit as deleterious for it
embraces the ability to see the limitations of human understanding and,
consequently, to know something of what lies beyond that boundary.
Reason is in command of mystery not by directly cognizing but by
directly locating and therefore demarcating its content.

Barth certainly regards reason as the normative concept characteristic
of the time; equally certainly, he judges it to be such only because it is
the expression of something other than its conceptual self. It expresses
an underlying spirit and so a proper grasp of its conceptual dimensions
requires that we penetrate deeper than it if we want to understand human
depths. Barth's discussion of Pietism reaches its term in his criticism of
its doctrines of grace and justification; in other words, in its soteriology.
Pietists had an unhealthy concern for what takes place within us rather
than an adequate orientation to what is in Christ for us. They head
back to Pelagianism. Moralism is the enemy at the gate. At the root of
the will for form, expressed by reason, is the will for morality, which is
moralism (109). Philosophical moves and the pursuit of science furnish
theoretical foundations and justification for a prevenient Christian
moralism (101). It is the moralistic principle that drove people to seek
a new-formed Christianity (104). What this new-formed Christianity
took to be natural and rational basically embodies the will for form,
the will for self-disposal, a 'moralism that was desiderated' (106). As
Barth is clear on the moral root, so he is clear on its relation to matters
epistemological.

> The new picture of the world, mathematically scientific thought,
> anthropocentric, autonomous philosophy, the virtue of 'historical
> truthfulness', and with this the distaste for miracle . . . is not a
> foundation and a cause, but an instrument, indeed one might
> go so far as to say a garb, for the criticism . . . Man makes the
> opposition to older Christianity which had come about through

his new moralism into a contrast between the modern and the obsolete presuppositions for cosmology and epistemology – in order to justify himself (108).

It follows that when we interpret Enlightenment thought and the Enlightenment era, we must safeguard the distinction between 'the real, primary and pioneering reasons for the criticism' of the Bible and 'very plausible, secondary, useful aids to that criticism' (109). Yet again, I invoke Reventlow's account of *The Authority of the Bible and the Rise of the Modern World*. The line Barth takes in *Protestant Theology* is both consistent and overlaps with Reventlow's detailed and persuasive account, one that shows how the historical-critical movement in biblical studies has deeper roots than in scientific thought and goes back to Renaissance humanism.

However, when Barth comes to the story of theology, it does, indeed, unfold *on its surface* as the story of the tragic fate of theological epistemology. For Barth, this comprises the essential tragedy of Protestant theology. We learn this when he gets into his account of it in the chapter on 'Protestant Theology in the Eighteenth Century'. In this chapter, Barth names the names and reports the moves that brought Protestantism into an aporia in which it remained, structured or shaped by Schleiermacher into a more permanent form of habitat. Schleiermacher does not get it anything like as hard from Barth as do his Protestant predecessors, who made sure that the seed of his thought fell on soil that would bear bad fruit in abundance. Several of these predecessors are named. One figure, in particular, emerges out of the shades of what for most of us is relative historical obscurity not into the light of the gospel but into the light of the eighteenth century, a light world away from the gospel. Barth's comments on this figure are of critical significance and sum up the lesson not only of the eighteenth but also of the nineteenth century. *Primus inter pares* he may be, but once Barth gets onto him, he loads a goodly proportion of the blame for theological catastrophe onto him. He is referring to one Johann Franz Buddeus (1660-1727).[13]

BARTH AND BUDDEUS

Barth does not spend long on Buddeus in *Protestant Theology* but what he says there is devastating. There are at least two other places in Barth's

---

13. The significance of Barth's treatment of Buddeus on the question of revelation and reconciliation is highlighted by Frans H. Breukelman, *The Structure of Sacred Doctrine in Calvin's Theology*, ed., Rinse H. Reeling Brouwer (Grand Rapids, MI/Cambridge, UK: Eerdmans, 2010) 234-41.

corpus where Buddeus features in the context of concerns broadly identical with or cognate to those in *Protestant Theology* and I shall review these first. The first reference is easily overlooked, for Buddeus' name is rather inconspicuously mentioned. It crops up in Barth's celebrated exchange with Brunner over nature and grace.[14] In this exchange, Barth clearly showed that he viewed any epistemological issues that arose between him and Brunner as fundamentally soteriological in nature. He accused Brunner of failing to understand what he (Barth) really maintained on the question of natural theology. Behind Brunner's talk of human capacity for 'word' or for 'revelation', and behind his distinction between a formal and a material *imago Dei* constitutive of humanity, there is a fateful creeping Pelagianism. Should we not say of Brunner's drowning man, the sinner who needs rescue, that he really wants to swim just a little (82)? Barth fears that for all Brunner's vaunted celebration of grace, there is a 'new' doctrine of the Holy Spirit about to break forth in Brunner's work, one that lamentably requires that the Holy Spirit have a point of contact in humans for his divine activity.

As far as Barth is concerned, what Brunner is doing here is nothing theologically novel. In propounding his theological anthropology along with a proposal that the task of natural theology is a task for his theological generation, Brunner is actually recommending 'that we should walk in the way upon which Protestant theology entered in the age of "rational orthodoxy"' (94). There is reason to fear that Brunner is possessed of the spirit of the late seventeenth and early eighteenth centuries. Heading the cast of spirits now grimly summoned from the shades of those times is our man, Buddeus. He is no more prominent than the others whom Barth mentions – Christian Matthias Pfaff, Jean Alphonse Turretini, Jean Frédéric Osterwald and Samuel Werenfels. All four of these appear in *Protestant Theology*, but in *Protestant Theology* Buddeus is accorded much greater significance than they are or at least given a much higher profile. Meanwhile, in *Natural Theology*, Barth fears Brunner, the Thomist and Brunner, the Neo-Protestant less than he worries about Brunner, the theologian, who unfortunately sports the garb of rational orthodoxy. If Brunner is seeking to institute 'a *theologia naturalis* consisting of propositions and instruction directly obtained from natural evidence of the kind that was introduced into Protestant theology two hundred years ago', will we now witness a resurrected Wolff, Semler, Lessing and Schleiermacher following in his train (112)? In alluding here to the fact that rational orthodoxy paves the way for

---

14. John Baillie, ed., *Natural Theology* (London: Bles, 1934). Page references appear in the body of the text from now on.

Schleiermacher, Barth sums up precisely the contention of *Protestant Theology* and Barth's strictures against Brunner are noticeably darkened by the shadow of Buddeus and his kin.

Buddeus also appears in a second work, where he occupies a far more prominent position than he does in the debate with Brunner. This is at the juncture of the discussion of religion and revelation in *Church Dogmatics*.[15] Here, Barth narrates a tale of misspent Protestant attempts to relate religion to theology. The polemical but constructive expositions of the Trinity, Word of God and Incarnation that launch his *Church Dogmatics* are designed to 'fix the reality of revelation in God' and this is, *ipso facto*, to deny our ability to find in humans the possibility for it. At some stage after the Reformation, Protestant theology took a fatal step in the way in which it related religion and revelation. Where Buddeus has an innovative role in *Protestant Theology*, in *Church Dogmatics*, Barth traces the dangers he wishes to identify to a time before Buddeus. Even so, the emphasis falls on the fatal birth of Neo-Protestantism whose generation is witnessed in the movement of rational orthodoxy at the beginning of the eighteenth century. In this connection, the guilty parties are two: Salomon van Til (Reformed) and Buddeus (Lutheran). They effectively torpedo dogmatics. 'Dogmatics now begin quite openly and unilaterally . . . with the presupposition of the concept and description of a general and natural and neutral religion, which as *religio in se spectata* [religion regarded in its own right], is the presupposition of all religions.'

Both van Til and Buddeus specify the content of our natural knowledge of God, including the affirmation that it cannot lead to salvation. Like van Til, Buddeus is clear that *religio naturalis*, stemming from the natural knowledge of God, must indispensably be supplemented by revelation. Nonetheless, *religio naturalis* contains the *notiones* that constitute the *bases et fundamenta omnis religionis* [the bases and foundations of all religion] by means of which we can identify the supplementary revelation. Natural religion thus functions in two ways. Firstly, by virtue of its insufficiency for salvation, it enables us to discern the need for revelation. Secondly, by the religious direction it is able to provide on the basis of its knowledge, it enables us to identify that revelation when it appears.

Barth holds that it is impossible to exaggerate either the material significance or the historical consequences of this approach. In the work

---

15. *Church Dogmatics* I/2, 280–297. Quotations in the text below are from these pages. In the company of Pfaff, Werenfels, Osterwald and Turretini, Buddeus has already put an early appearance in I/2 (see p. 4). Indeed, Buddeus makes an early appearance in *Church Dogmatics* I/1 and is thereafter an occasional visitor to its pages; see *Church Dogmatics* I/1 (Edinburgh: T & T Clark, 1975) 7.

of van Til and Buddeus 'there emerged clearly and logically what was perhaps the secret *telos* and pathos of the whole preceding development'. Humans naturally, independently of revelation, possess knowledge of the form and the content of the relation in which we stand to God. That is, humans have religion. Revelation becomes 'a historical confirmation of what man can know about himself and therefore about God even apart from revelation'. This is classic Renaissance stuff. Despite any substantial material orthodoxy they or their contemporaries retain, Buddeus and van Til put Protestant theology on the slippery slope by exposing Christian faith to rational adjudication. Wolff proceeded to harmonize the claims of reason and revelation; neology proceeded beyond that to submit Christian dogma and Scripture to the test of critical reason and of criticism founded on *religio naturalis*; Kantian rationalism proceeded further still to change *religio naturalis* into *ethica naturalis*, leaving revelation on the scene only in drastically attenuated form. Then Schleiermacher, Strauss, Feuerbach, Ritschl and Troeltsch all piled in with their peculiar reductions. This is all a sad commentary on the work of Buddeus and van Til. Both opted to understand revelation in the light of religion instead of *vice versa*. There you have it: modern theology. 'Neo-Protestantism means "religionism". . . . At the end of the period which started with Buddeus, theology had lost any serious intention of taking itself seriously as theology.'

If all this sounds severe and perhaps constitutes as painful a part of *Church Dogmatics* as any, the denunciation of Buddeus gets stronger still when we return to the pages of *Protestant Theology*. Here, Buddeus distinctly holds the key to the development Barth traces. We hear nothing of van Til, nor is Buddeus related to seventeenth-century theology along the lines of the discussion in *Church Dogmatics*. In *Protestant Theology*, it is reason and revelation, not religion and revelation, that are under scrutiny although, of course, the themes overlap considerably. Here, Buddeus is the manifestation of eighteenth-century man in Christian dogmatics. It is he who takes the decisive step into a new theological age when, following the inclinations of his Pietist friends, he gives theology its new theme. 'The reality of the salvation that has been received, the reality of the man who is to be renewed through faith . . . also, in his view, forms the criterion for the greater or lesser worth of revealed truth' (142).

Barth is persuaded that if you gaze at the reality of man, you are led to seek out the 'possibilities of man in general' and this means that human reason apart from justifying grace, though endowed with prevenient grace, is in line for positive reassessment. This all yields bitter fruit in Buddeus' conviction that human reason, on the basis of a natural knowledge of God, is able to distinguish between true and false claims to revelation. Reason thereby has some control over revelation by its grasp of general, universally perceptible, religious truth. Reason is a rival to revelation as a source of religious knowledge. Bitter fruit and fearful prospect: 'Can the possibility be avoided that others will come who will make more energetic use than Buddeus feels to be right of this discriminatory capacity assigned to reason and of the exalted position consequently ascribed to men?' (142)

As reason and revelation are in effect already juxtaposed on the same level, reason in truth gains a concealed advantage over revelation. Buddeus' combat with Wolff, who took the next decisive step, was needless. Wolff stabilized the balance between reason and revelation, making them spheres of equal import. Externally, this was a turning-point.

> Two spheres of equal size . . . means that the two require and supplement each other so that fundamentally the one knowledge is completely and totally also that of the other: reason is also revealed in its own way and revelation is rational in its own way, the only difference being that each has its own character (156).

While Locke does not enter the picture, Barth would have said this of Locke too. The Wolffian turning-point is in reality a sharpish curve along the Buddean road. Consider neology. The neologians, who dispassionately dismantled a key Christian doctrine or two like the Trinity and original sin, are neither particularly new nor particularly interesting. Buddeus and his Pietist collaborators had already bartered their authentic Protestant birthright for the celebrated mess of pottage (158). True, Buddeus did not basically invent the new intellectual method. What he did was simply to do things in the humanistic way dictated by his century. He invented it *for theology*.

> Did not Buddeus do more for the innovation with which we are concerned than the men who are now to be described in the usual way as neologists, whose merit (if it can be called that) ultimately was that they went a few more steps – though not very long steps – along the road opened up by Buddeus' dogmatics, which ascribed to reason the significance of a material criterion for revelation? (163)

This is Barth's angle of approach to the thinkers whom he discusses both before and after Schleiermacher. Buddeus constructed the perfect runway for Neo-Protestantism.

Channel-Hopping

Barth's discussion of Buddeus in *Protestant Theology* obviously went way beyond a description of historical theology at the time of the Enlightenment. It publicised the gravamen of his theological opposition to modern theological method. It is the responsibility of theology to begin and stay with revelation in Christ. Revelation in Christ is intellectually unprotected once the natural knowledge of God equips reason with adjudicatory powers. The abolition of revelation awaits only the historical realization of a logical process. So Barth believes and believes firmly. Perhaps talk of 'historical realization of a logical process' is a slightly tendentious way of putting it, implicitly tying him down to a Hegelian way of approaching history and intellectual history to which he is not committed. Be that as it may, as far as Barth was concerned, this particular historical process, however conceptualised, should never have been initiated. At several junctures in his account in *Protestant Theology*, Barth expressed dismay that Protestant theologians ignored warning signals that were flashing clear and strong. Even after Kant, repentance was possible. Indeed, precisely because Kant's work brought to such a conclusion the project unwittingly fathered by Buddeus, there was a golden opportunity for recovering the Reformation heritage, now that bad trees had manifested themselves in the production of bad fruit. When Kant announced that *'[t]he biblical theologian proves that God exists by means of the fact that he has spoken in the Bible'*, he held out, despite himself, the possibility of a healthy retrieval of theological method (312). Unfortunately, Schleiermacher and his successors continued in the way of their forefathers, Buddeus and his seed, who caused the theological people of God to sin. While historical contingencies and personal reprehensibilities clutter the scene Barth depicts, blame must also be securely attached to him, i.e. Buddeus, who introduced into theology the conceptual opportunity and logical tool to dismantle revelation.

In his discussion of eighteenth-century Protestant thought, Barth did not stray over the channel. Yet, when he embarked on his discussion of religion and revelation in *Church Dogmatics*, he took, as he put it, a text that applied to both sides of the channel. Its author was Paul de Lagarde who proposed that the word 'religion' is used in opposition to the word 'faith' in the era Barth is examining. This language is a sign of subversion and 'presupposes the deistic criticism of the universally Christian concept of revelation'.[16] The spectre of deism lurks behind – better, the

---

16.   *Church Dogmatics* I/2, 284.

spirit of deism courses within – the theological enterprise that so bothers Barth. Barth well knew that the faith/religion contrast was not simply of epistemological significance, and that vital soteriological investments were at stake. The 'universally Christian concept of revelation' being controverted on the scene graced by the deists was, as we have observed, a concept of revelation of the way of reconciliation.

On one reading of deism and at the least in one prominent strand of it, we may think that we encounter the classic demonstration of Barth's thesis about the implications of allowing reason to judge revelation, for one proposed defining characteristic of deism is a move towards collapsing reason as judge of revelation into reason enthroned as the source of religious knowledge. When Crous proposed this a long time ago, he cited the examples of Charles Blount and Anthony Collins.[17] One of Reventlow's accomplishments was to give due place to English deism in its historically formative impact on wider European notions of biblical authority and, hence, of revelation. In light of the references by de Lagarde, Barth, Crous and Reventlow to deism, we should miss at our peril the chance to hop briefly back over the channel to see whether we can offer supplementary remarks on Barth's thesis.

Locke was convinced that where reason rightly judges revelation, no threat to revelation is involved. The 'reason' that Locke hauls on stage, and to which he assigns responsibility for judging whether a proposition really is revealed, is a reason that has firmly secured some material knowledge of God apart from special revelation, available, for example, in a cosmological argument. As is the case with Buddeus and in accordance with his own philosophical approach, Locke's natural knowledge of God functions as a criterion of what may validly be claimed in the way of theological knowledge. For him, this is theologically unimpeachable because, from a theological point of view, it does not falsely arrogate anything to reason theologically *a priori*. The reason why claims to revelation ought to be tested against our material religious knowledge is simply because such knowledge is *de facto* in our possession. What is religiously known apart from revelation – and, for that matter, anything known *simpliciter* – possesses *ipso facto* the logical potential to play a role in adjudicating the credibility of a claim that something has been revealed. As far as Locke is concerned, we cannot set *a priori* theoretical limits to what reason can know naturally and thus cannot deny it the possibility of independent theological significance. *De facto*, reason does not have sufficient knowledge to eliminate the need for revelation.

---

17. See S.G. Hefelbower, *The Relation of John Locke to English Deism* (Chicago, ILL: University of Chicago Press, 1918) 26. Hefelbower is critical of Crous.

Furthermore, the empirical evidence for revelation is compelling without reserve. So from Locke's point of view, Barth's worries are groundless and his methodological strictures misplaced.

On this view, Barth is guilty of an error that has more than one dimension. It could be said that he illicitly draws conclusions about the potential of reason abstracted from any consideration of the performance of reason, instead of limiting reason, as he should, in accordance with its actual performance, religiously successful or otherwise. What he says theologically about revelation should be affected by the religious performance of reason. On top of this, it will then be contended that Barth ignores the fact that the overwhelming *de facto* empirical evidence for revelation subverts any human attempt to eliminate revelation in the name of reason. In practice, where reason rightly judges revelation, it cannot rightly eliminate it and must even endorse it. So things appear to the Lockean eye.

How, then, did deism, especially when professing its philosophical allegiance to Locke, justify its move to eliminate revelation in the name of reason? The obvious place to go in order to search out the deist move from Locke is to one of the deist heavy-hitters, John Toland, and his *Christianity Not Mysterious*.[18] Issued just after Locke's *Reasonableness* and apparently taking its argument just one step – but a drastic step – further, this work seems, at first glance, to illustrate nicely and exemplify well the mechanics of a characteristic deistic move away from Locke. Locke's reason did not arrogate to itself a claim to be the source of all significant religious truths because it had no grounds for denying the categorical possibility of truths above reason and empirical evidence compelled it to assent to the actuality of their existence. Toland got rid of the category of 'truths above reason', leaving no logical space within the framework derived from Locke for truths that are not directly authorized by reason.

What is going on formally looks fairly clear at first blush until we notice that Toland is, in point of fact, not at all precisely attacking what Locke is protecting although, of course, he dissents from Locke's conclusions. Toland's categorical 'truths above reason' are truths that defy rational criteria of intelligibility. Locke, however, does not subscribe to such truths. To the extent that Toland's argument is effective, it is so against certain views of the *nature* of religious propositions, i.e., their intelligibility or lack thereof, and not of their *source*. There is mischief in the pot when 'above reason' becomes systematically ambiguous between 'above rational intelligibility' and 'beyond reason as source'. Toland muddies the waters. When Locke sanctions adherence to propositions about reason, it is in

18. John Toland, *Christianity Not Mysterious* (London, 1696).

the latter sense of the phrase. Toland does not demonstrate that Locke's 'above reason' is precarious in the sense that Locke understood that phrase, even if he thinks that he has demonstrated it.

Tindal must be allowed to enter the fray again in this connection. Much as he does not want to be against Locke, he concedes that he cannot be with Locke on the 'above reason' business, as far as he can tell.[19] Quite apart from the question of intelligibility, which he thinks the category of 'above reason' is bound to raise, Tindal's philosophy of religion compels him to demur from the allocation of conceptual space to truths above reason in Locke's sense, i.e., to truths with a non-rational source. The doctrine of the Trinity (a crucial casualty in the transition from Wolff to neology) comes up for special scrutiny here. Locke had notoriously got himself into hot Trinitarian water in the exchange with Stillingfleet, bishop of Worcester. Tindal's way of expressing his troubles over the Trinity somewhat collapses the objection to the 'above reason' epistemic status of revealed truth in the form advanced by Locke and a Toland-type worry over intelligibility. While Tindal attends better than does Toland to 'above reason' in the sense of source of truth, in the end, with Toland and Tindal alike, we are frustrated by conceptual unclarities in the deist move away from Locke on premises that deism shared, as far as possible, with Locke.

Tindal's position on reason as judge of revelation is best assessed not narrowly, by microscopic examination of his treatment of this particular question, but in light of his overall project, and perhaps we should say this more widely of deism. Its overall project can be described as a lay liberation theology that deists believed was in the best tradition of the Reformers and were sure was in the best interests of everybody else. For Tindal, the Reformers are praiseworthy on account of the admirable nature both of their goal, the freeing of the laity from the suppression of papacy, and their grasp of the principle needed to achieve their goal.[20] The principle in question is 'the Protestant principle, of every man's being obligated to judge for himself in all religious matters, without prejudices or partiality'. So where, if at all, did the Reformers go wrong? In their failure to realize that their programme could never be effective unless it be the case that 'there are no doctrines of divine original contained in the Gospel dispensation, but what by their innate excellency are knowable to be such; as being writ in our minds and put into our hearts (Jeremiah) by God Himself'.

By the criterion of the law of nature – necessarily a perfect law (because, necessarily, God would not give any other) and necessarily an immutable law (entailed by divine immutability, which is analytic in

---

19. Williams, 'Matthew Tindal'.
20. For what follows, see *Christianity as Old as Creation*, 299-315.

divine perfection) – we can 'judge antecedently to any traditional religion what is, or what is not, a law absolutely perfect, and worthy of such a being for its legislator' (59). This, of course, is precisely the reduction Barth feared, couched, in Tindal's case, in terms of ontological deduction. That is Barth's point: once reason discovers any natural knowledge of God, it is plain that it must logically function to judge claims to revelation. It is equally plain that the right to judge cannot be arbitrarily curtailed just in order to protect ourselves against rational disposal of revelation altogether. The theological scandal is that reason has been arrogated both a *de jure* and *de facto* power over our response to the revelation of the triune God. Nothing in principle now prevents natural knowledge from being judged to be materially other or more imperially extensive than it was *contingently* judged to be by its orthodox defenders. So Barth judged and he tells us that is what actually happened. Orthodoxy could not control what natural knowledge got up to. Natural knowledge could and did become greater than its avowedly orthodox defenders allowed, to the point of containing all that we need religiously. It becomes reflexive knowledge of its own religious sufficiency. No revelation is needed; religiously significant truth is obtainable elsewhere. However weak deist logic may have been in its exercise of seeking to erase Locke's religious conclusions, Locke had shifted theological conflict onto the terrain ruled by reason and where there is no principled protection for revelation. So Barth would have told us to read the Locke-deist connection.

The deists were glad to enter into Locke's inheritance, but Buddeus consciously countered them. It throws important light on our enquiry to note briefly where Buddeus differed from the deists of his day because it introduces an important new factor into the question of his difference from Barth in a later day. If, for Tindal, reason dispensed with revelation, for Buddeus, on the other hand, reason positively required it. For Buddeus, the capacity or power by which reason is able to adjudicate is also that whereby it recognizes or establishes its own limits. How did Buddeus justify or, at least, explicate this?

BUDDEUS IN SELF-DEFENCE

Introducing Buddeus in his volume on *Protestant Theology*, Barth alluded to an essential theoretical background to his theological work. This background comprehended his prior philosophical contributions. Although he does not specify which he had in mind, Barth must have meant Buddeus' *Elementa philosophiae practicae* (1697) and the *Institutiones philosophiae eclecticae* (1703). In his *Institutiones*, Buddeus expounded his conviction that, since life is a *praxis pietatis*, so philosophy is a practical science that directs us to happiness.[21] The will, not just the intellect, is thus lively and directive in the philosophical quest. This is a point Buddeus takes up in his *Institutiones theologiae dogmaticae* (1723-24; hereafter *Dogmatics*), the only work of his on which Barth directly comments.[22] Happiness and sorrow stem from an inclination of the will. Because the will underlies the intellect, it must be healed if the understanding is to be sound. Healing grace is needed right at the inception of philosophical or theological work. Indeed, Buddeus will argue, the natural knowledge of God includes perspicuous intimations of this.

Buddeus believed that there was not only a natural knowledge of God but also a natural moral sense of obligation. One thing that characterizes religious and moral knowledge is the facility with which they are acquired. Both the existence of God and our need to worship him are known if we just apply our minds to the matter. If we do, these truths will be perceptible with little difficulty (1.I.12). Truly, this whole important religious business does not require too much attention in that undemanding, conscientious investigation will lead us to an unproblematic apprehension of the truth concerning the supreme end of humankind (1.I.5). This kind of attitude pervades Buddeus' introduction – the introduction that landed him in Barth's bad books. For example, the deduction of the soul's immortality is 'clear from afar to sound reason' and our duties towards ourselves and others should be known with minimal difficulty (1.I.13).

In these matters, 'reason instructs all people quite clearly' (1.1.14). A persuasive argument to God's existence need *never* be difficult. In treating arguments for the existence of God, Buddeus adduces three kinds of proof (2.1.6). First, there are metaphysical arguments, which are forms of cosmological argument, based on phenomena that *clearly* point to the living God. Second, there are physico-theological (*physica*) arguments, which are forms of teleological argument yielding a conclusion about God *evidentissime* (most evidently) from the world's harmony. Third, there are empirico-historical evidences, which comprise the historical testimony of Gentile cultures.

---

21. For the philosophical context of Buddeus' operations, see the brief account in Lewis White Beck, *Early German Philosophy* (Cambridge, MA: Belknap, 1969) 255-58.

22. Buddeus' fateful argument unfolds in part 1 of *Dogmatics*, which I shall now follow. Wherever possible, section references are given in the body of the text below.

This last set of arguments is particularly telling for our purposes. According to Buddeus, primal religion is revealed and characterized by the promise of redemption that came to Adam and to the patriarchs. *Vera religio* is that religion where the promise is grasped. When God himself is the direct author of the sacrificial system, as is the case in the Old Testament, sacrifices have a particularly prominent function as indicators of the need for redemption. However, this state of affairs does not detract from the universal nature of revelation and rob it of a religiously significant role. If Old Testament sacrifices show forth a mode of redemption guaranteed by known promise, pagan sacrificial systems signal the need for redemption felt by the conscience. Gentile, pagan religion is the corruption and degeneration of primal sacrificial religion and its ignorance is shown in the institution of a set of sacrifices that do not materially point to Jesus Christ. Yet, their institution is evidence of the preoccupation with the question of redemption that pagan and patriarchal religion share. Pagan rites demonstrate the vestiges of their origin in the form of manifested awareness of the question of redemption rather than in the material substance of the rite.

Since the question is known but the answer not, the marks (*notae*) or characteristics constitutive of any genuinely revealed religion that might come along are also known. One crucial criterion on which we judge whether or not a religion is revealed is whether or not it shows humans the way of redemption. The person so placed as to judge revelation according to that criterion is *ipso facto* so placed as to need redemption. Rational power is predicated on religious need in the sense that reason is rooted in a knowledge that the basic human condition is one of soteriological need and so the people who are wielding any rational, adjudicatory instruments placed in their hands by the Saviour and Creator God are people who know that they need to be redeemed. Rationally, we judge on the basis of what we know and we know that we do not know the way of redemption that we know we need.

The contrast with Tindal, our prime deist example, is stark and strong. Buddeus maintained that a vital and central component of our empirical, natural knowledge of God is a knowledge of the need for redemption. Tindal denied it. For Tindal, the essential nature of the human condition is effectively deduced from the idea of God. From his point of view, the data to which Buddeus refers in his account of the empirical history of religion and his account of the human condition must be assessed against the test of deductive reason. On this assessment, it is plain that sacrifices that allegedly demonstrate the need of redemption cannot have been instituted by God. They were instituted by priests. On that point, of course, Tindal had plenty of company.

How can Buddeus logically meet Tindal's *a priori*? Answer: by appealing to conscience. It is conscience that accounts for the fact that the intellectual path to affirming the knowledge of God is quite easy and for the almost imperceptibly greater ease in grasping the basics of active religious requirements that are inalienably associated with such knowledge. Buddeus rebuked the deceased Herbert of Cherbury (1.1.17-18). Among Herbert's common religious notions is the notion that penitence is adequate for the restitution of a broken relationship with God. God, says Herbert, forgives and no reconciliation in history is required. Wrong, says Buddeus. Herbert's denial is the outcome of refusing to heed the deliverances of conscience on the matter of divine majesty. A conscience informed by the knowledge of God's majesty judges penitence alone to be quite inadequate. Conscience most certainly possesses such knowledge. What else does the empirical history of religion, with its proliferation of propitiatory rites, amply demonstrate?

According to Buddeus, then, revelation is a revelation of the way of salvation. Conscience knows that reconciliation with God is needed and Christianity, as a religion of reconciliation, qualifies as a candidate for the status of *vera religio* and, on material examination, passes the test. Christianity testifies to an historical mediation and Mediator. That is its essence. Consequently, it is the essence of theology. With such talk, we are returned to Barth.

The Trouble with the Troubled Giant

Barth's report on Buddeus' position is brief and accurate, but accurate only as far as it goes. There is a sin of omission. Barth omits reference to *conscientia* in Buddeus. This is regrettable, whatever his distaste for the pietistic conscience. As Buddeus sees it, any move on the part of reason to dismantle revelation is thwarted by conscience. A deist who sought to deduce from the powers of reason or from the being of God that rational adjudication of the claims of revelation either permitted or compelled the rational disposal of revelation would quite simply be refusing to pay heed to an unmistakeable voice, the voice of conscience. Although, writing before Tindal, Buddeus does not address the Tindalian *a priori*, he would have seen it as a case of technical reason operating illicitly outside its ontological basis where conscience is domiciled.[23] Of course, Barth

---

23. The distinction between ontological and technical reason is borrowed from Paul Tillich, *Systematic Theology*, volume I (London: Nisbet, 1953) 80. Although Tindal's peculiar a prioristic mode of argument was his own and not universally characteristic of deist writings as such, the point about conscience

dismisses *theologically* the position adopted by Buddeus here; for him, a conscience formed without knowledge of God's revelation in Christ is no surer a guide in matters of religious truth than is a reason so formed. It is no part of my task to adjudicate the theological issue between them. However, had Barth attended specifically to the connection in Buddeus' thought between conscience and the requirement for the aforementioned revelation of the way of reconciliation, he might have smoothed those bumps in the path of his historical exposition that lured Gunton into overemphasising the place of epistemology in Barth's historical account.

The conjunction of two things in my account at this point hints at the possibility of a degree not quite of internal dissonance, but at least of internal untidiness, in Barth's account. One is the concession that it is not altogether surprising if Gunton or any others should read Barth's story as primarily a tale of theological epistemology, as Barth's strictures on Buddeus might indicate *prima facie*, although this is presumably the result of not attending carefully enough to what Barth is saying in *Protestant Theology* before he gets onto the theology itself. The other is connected to Barth's explicit warning that epistemology is not the bottom line. If the spirit of eighteenth-century 'man' is that of arrogant self-sufficiency and that spirit has penetrated theology in the form of faulty method, then the question arises of whether couching the problem of Protestant theology in epistemological terms is (literally) too superficial. The introduction of the question of conscience, absolutely key as far as Buddeus' defence of revelation is concerned, surely helps us to adjust and strengthen Barth's account of eighteenth-century villainy towards revelation. [24]

The element of slight but significant tension in Barth's account can be given a concrete demonstration in connection with conscience by drawing attention to the first full-length discussion of any thinker in *Protestant Theology*, namely, Jean-Jacques Rousseau.[25] This chapter occupies a prominent place in Barth's account not just by virtue of its being the first such discussion but also because Barth treats Rousseau at greater length than he does any other thinker in either the eighteenth or the nineteenth centuries. He dwells on the detail of Rousseau's life and

---

applies universally to deism.

24. Of course, Barth is well aware of the role of the concept of conscience with respect to the issue in question: *Church Dogmatics* I/2, 285-86 on Walaeus and Wendelin. It is just that he does not advert in *Protestant Theology* to its role in Buddeus' theological reasoning.

25. The earlier, abbreviated, English translation of Barth's volume was titled *From Rousseau to Ritschl* (London: SCM, 1959).

pays systematic attention to Rousseau's writings with a kind of attentive orderliness that is quite distinctive when we closely compare it with his accounts of other thinkers in this volume. Barth's study of the eighteenth-century background to nineteenth-century Protestant theology takes us up to Hegel, and Barth's story can be read up to that point roughly as: 'From Leibniz to Hegel'. However, when we place his discussion of Rousseau alongside his discussion of Hegel, Barth at least gives the documentary impression of having mastered the corpus of Rousseau's work far more thoroughly than that of Hegel. At risk of exaggeration, it seems that his discussion of Rousseau is an essay (necessarily brief, of course) in disciplined interpretation while the chapter on Hegel is rather impressionistic. Indeed, despite the interest and importance of Barth's contributions on Lessing, Herder, Kant and Novalis, which come after Rousseau and before Hegel, the discussion of Rousseau emphasises a point that, once made, incomparably throws into sharpest relief Barth's major claims about Protestant theology in these centuries. What is that point?

Barth wanted to connect two ages: the age of rationalism and that of the Romantic reaction to the Enlightenment. Time spent on the eighteenth-century background is designed to establish the way in which rationalism, at one with Pietism, landed Schleiermacher on a track that, for all his Romantic originality, he did not lay down. Barth welded together the age of Enlightenment and the age of Goethe. They meet in Rousseau. Barth is sensitive to Rousseau's reputation for having overtly broken with rationalism in the direction that became Romanticism. He does not demur from emphasis on what is new in Rousseau, but he is clear that the new is dialectically the self-realisation at the same time as it is the abolition of the old. Barth contends that the absolute will for form needs to break its own exterior mould in order to realise its inner instinct. It does so in Rousseau's thought. Eighteenth-century man is actually fulfilled in Rousseau, whether he knows it or not (and he typically does not). Leibniz and Rousseau are two sides of the same coin. Rousseau discovers, quite simply, himself – him himself, just as he is *in* his own being and *as* his own being. Philosophies that advanced rationalism promote particular forms of self-formation and Rousseau brings this fact to light.

In his discussion of Rousseau, Barth proceeded in the direction that we should anticipate on the basis of his earlier descriptions of eighteenth-century man before he arrived at Buddeus and his confederates. Barth's discussion hinges on the Pelagian rejection of original sin and, with respect to Rousseau, Barth declares that 'the church doctrine of original

sin has seldom, I believe, been denied with such disconcerting candour
and force and in so directly personal a way' (224). What is striking
about Rousseau is that here the secret that man is good 'is blurted out
so expansively and with such assurance' (224). If anyone took offence at
this, including the Pietists, they simply did not know themselves. 'The
eighteenth century did not understand itself for as long as it failed to
understand what a splendid, radiant and at the same time profound
Pelagianism Rousseau was offering it' (231).

In the same breath as he said this, Barth proclaimed with unbending
finality that those who typically resisted Rousseau's epistemological
moves towards the sufficiency of natural religion had no cause to do so
and had only themselves to blame for what Rousseau got up to. While
Barth does not mention Buddeus by name, it is either because he is too
spiritually weary to do so or because he assumes that it is evident at
whom he is pointing the finger. If he assumes the latter, he is entirely
warranted in doing so. The charge Barth brings against the thinkers who
exhibited righteous indignation towards Rousseau is identical to that
which he brings against those who trumpeted their negative reactions
to Wolff and neology. To put it crudely, Barth's point boils down to:
'After Buddeus, what do you expect?' When Barth arrives specifically
at Rousseau's denial of revelation in the epistemological names of
reason and conscience grounded in natural religion, he expounds that
religiously most famous portion of Rousseau's writing, the 'Confessions
of a Savoyard Vicar' in *Emile*. Then, finally, the reason-revelation theme
brings Barth's discussion towards its conclusion.

> That was what was theologically new about Rousseau: the
> fact that he broke completely with the doctrine of original sin,
> which had long been under fire from all sides, and with the
> conception of revelation also generally threatened for a long
> time. . . . Rousseau's new gift to theology ultimately consists
> in this very widening of the concept of reason by means of the
> discovery of man's spirit nature. . . . It is from Rousseau onwards
> and originating from Rousseau that the thing called theological
> rationalism, in the full sense of the term, exists (233-34).

These are excerpts between whose lines Barth fills out the claim
that the kind of reason he has in mind and is pledged to expose is that
expansionist reason that comprehends the whole nature of humankind.
This comprehensive operation is the authentic telos of the notion of
reason that has been insinuating itself into the Protestant theological

heartlands long before it breaks the cover of flimsy orthodoxy. The ultimate intrinsic secret of reason is its imperial demand. Rousseau brings this to light.

Let us, for the sake of argument, suppose that Barth has soundly characterized what happened in Protestantism between rational orthodoxy and Schleiermacher. Then one thing emerges very clearly in the account of Rousseau. It is this: the guiding religious development in the Enlightenment depths and in early Romantic theology is not felicitously described in terms of epistemology. It is a matter of fundamental anthropology, surfacing in epistemology. That is why I have judged that Barth could have finessed his story here and there so that this truth about epistemology was consistently foregrounded. If 'reason' was fundamental for Karl Barth, it was in a sense expanded beyond its use in an epistemological tussle over the rival claims of 'reason' and revelation. On his own explicit terms, the collision between Rousseauite and Barthian understandings of Christianity is the collision over the doctrines of humanity and of grace, a collision in the root perception or conviction about humanity before God and under the gospel. Rousseau needs no redeemer in historical space nor reconciliation in historical time. He needs no grace. Therefore, he needs no revelation. Conscience commands nothing in that respect. Barth knows and draws attention to the importance of conscience in Rousseau's religious philosophy. He quotes from *Emile*:

> Conscience! Conscience! Divine instinct; immortal and celestial voice; assured guide of a being who is ignorant and pressed hard, but intelligent and free; infallible judge of good and evil, it is you who make man resemble God; it is you who are responsible for the excellence of his nature and the morality of his actions; without you I sense nothing within me which raises me above brute creation, except the unhappy privilege of straying from error to error. . . . Heaven be praised. . . . We can be men without being scholars (199-200).

Though Barth does not say so, conscience connects Rousseau and Buddeus. From Buddeus' point of view, that which testifies to the need for revelation, that is, conscience, does so because it testifies primarily to the need for grace. If reason proceeds to dispose of revelation, conscience must somehow have been disposed of first. In his bittersweet search for self-definition, Rousseau has searched for freedom and for whatever independence of God is available to him. Buddeus will say that liberation from the need for revelation is achieved only if you first banish that which should conduct us to revelation and allow conscience, which is a divinely appointed guardian of revelation on the territory of the spirit as well as of the mind, to roam illicitly and unconstrainedly free away from its uncontestably proper human domain. It takes an act of will for that to happen. It is not intellectual slippage.

Barth has also confessed the fundamental nature of the will in the project of self-definition. He has shown clearly that Rousseau's struggles with Christianity are only secondarily epistemological. Further, he has earlier affirmed that Buddeus' own epistemological error arose out of an erroneous understanding of justification: 'with the Pietists, Buddeus allows justification to issue in a work that takes place within man and thinks that in conversion he can establish certain *actus paedagogici* ['pedagogical acts'] independent of the work of the Holy Spirit. Against the background of such a doctrine of grace, his epistemology must become what it did become' (142). Theologically, Barth affirmed revelation as an act of grace. It is not just gracious as an act of revelation but it is a revelation of grace in its content. Grace comes through Jesus Christ and in the reconciliation of humankind in and through Christ. Barth could, then, have written the story of Protestant theology in the eighteenth century as the story of conflict between what powered reason and what is illuminated in revelation, i.e., between the impulse for human self-definition and the gospel of Christ, crucified and risen. He does so materially but not, I think, as consistently explicitly and clearly as he might have done. Hence Gunton could seize on epistemology in his name.

However, I do not want to make a small mountain out of a relative mole-hill. My interest is in enlisting Barth in the cause of modifying an explanation of the decline and eventual demise of Christianity couched in terms of epistemology. If I have wrongly judged either Gunton's appropriation of Barth or the internal texture of Barth's account, my main point remains. It ought to be said that nothing along the remaining stretch of Barth's lengthy journey through Protestant thought modifies either his account or my account of his account. Hegel is a hinge figure in one respect for, if the eighteenth and nineteenth centuries formed a unity such that the latter fulfilled the former, Hegel was the prime representative of that unity. In him the hopes of all the years were fulfilled: 'Was it worth waiting for another after he had come?' (385). Yet Hegel, however bloated his reason, received in Barth's account a much more relaxed ride that did rational orthodoxy. True enough, only someone unfamiliar with the literary ways of Barth would automatically expect him to flail the stick around blatantly at the point at which the opposition might be thought keenest. However, the comparative restraint in the treatment of Hegel is not a literary device. With all the delectable, rich, rational Hegelian intricacies, we should have thought that, with him, we should have reached, if not the apogee of rationalism, at least a point where we shall hear from Barth the severest strictures. There is a good reason why we do not (and I do not have in mind the possibility of a Barthian predilection for Hegel). The severest has already been said, and said in relation to Buddeus. The rotten pith has been laid bare, especially with Rousseau. The one to blame when a gale devastates a house is the one who opened the door. Enlightenment man entered the household of faith by courteous permission of Buddeus.

Perhaps it is because Barth is so carried away by the epistemological sins of Rousseau and others that, by force of exposition, he ends his account of Rousseau on an epistemological note. Yet one cannot help feeling, if slight exaggeration be pardoned, that this note is a relative whimper after the strident attention drawn to Rousseau's sins, which were not foundationally epistemological. This judgement on Rousseau is, of course, consistent with the fact that Barth understood Enlightenment reason as the instrument of deep humanist sensibility. Humanist sensibility, of which reason is the instrument, is in collision with grace, God's way, salvation, reconciliation in and through Jesus Christ. To say that revelation communicates the grace is inadequate: revelation is an act of grace. But it obviously is that only because grace is God's Word to humankind. Just as the methodological account of the Word of God in *Church Dogmatics* is undergirded by the triune nature of God, so is Barth's interest in epistemology in *Protestant Theology* undergirded by the question of grace. It follows that if those who are broadly or in greater detail persuaded of or very sympathetic to Barth's position place the spotlight on epistemology, then the modern critical mind is not being understood according to the depth that characterises Barth's point of view. If so, we are not likely to get the remedy quite right for the troubling modern condition. It is more the symptom than the underlying disease that has been diagnosed.

I have argued that, although Barth can look as though he is couching the problem of modernity in *Protestant Theology* in terms of epistemology, of reason and of revelation, he is not fundamentally doing so. One must certainly beware of getting into the habit of working with a false distinction between revelation and reconciliation in reading Barth. What is revealed is our reconciliation. [26] Moreover, we might be

---

26.   For the constant and consistent verbal and conceptual association of revelation

encouraged to appreciate the force of Barth's concentration on the sins of reason in developing his opposition to eighteenth-century theological anthropology if we reckon with César Chesneau Dumarsais' observation that 'reason is to the philosopher what grace is to the Christian'.[27] Yet, there is nothing deeper for the Christian than grace. A question that has arisen in the course of my account so far is whether there is something deeper for the philosopher than reason. One philosopher certainly thought so and to him we now turn.

INTRODUCING NIETZSCHE

Before he gets to the multi-part volume of *Church Dogmatics* in which he sets out his understanding of reconciliation, Barth provides a discussion of theological anthropology that includes treatment of the man who represented 'with less restraint and we might almost say with greater honesty . . . the spirit of all European humanity as fashioned and developed since the 16th century.'[28] This man is Friedrich Nietzsche.[29] He was one of a number of significant contemporaries who drew inspiration from the Renaissance, especially in its Italian form. Barth agrees with the judgement that the Italian Renaissance was the 'mother and model' of all European humanity in the modern age.[30] He names the mighty implicated in the mighty movement he tracks: Leibniz and Goethe, Kant and Hegel. Not surprisingly, we are reminded of the flow of discussion in *Protestant Theology*. Equally unsurprisingly, what Barth says in his detailed treatment of theological anthropology in *Church Dogmatics* is consistent with and sometimes reminiscent of the *Protestant Theology*. At the outset, in treating of 'Man as an Object of Theological Knowledge', Barth proclaims that '[a]nthropology has sometimes disguised itself as cosmology and theology' (21). The problem of problems is: 'Who am I who am now undertaking to give an account of what God and the world mean to me?'

---

and reconciliation, see paragraph 15 of *Church Dogmatics* I/2, 122-202. We are somewhat prepared for this in the first half-volume, I/1, 409.

27. Quoted in Ronald Grimsley, *Jean-Jacques Rousseau* (Brighton: Harvester, 1983) 3.

28. *Church Dogmatics*, III/2 (Edinburgh: T & T Clark, 1960) 231-42.

29. Gunton alludes to Barth's discussion here in *The One, the Three*, 32.

30. However, note also Barth's coupling of medieval mysticism with the humanistic Renaissance in *Church Dogmatics* I/1, 34 and the connection between Franciscan Pneumatology and that Renaissance in I/2, 251. See too the connection in I/2, 289-90 between the Renaissance and Buddeus and the later reference to the Middle Ages and the Renaissance in the same volume, 335.

'Theology itself', said Barth, 'has only to be unsure about its foundations and its truth, and this uncertainty has only to mount to a crisis like that which marked the age of Schleiermacher' to guarantee the crisis of Feuerbachian 'theology as anthropology' (21).[31] In Nietzsche's thought, humanity attains an unprecedented description. At the end of his literary life, Nietzsche bore the title 'Antichrist' and pitted himself as Dionysus against the Crucified. 'That everything should finally become a formal crusade against the cross, is not immediately apparent, but has to be learned and noted from a reading of Nietzsche. Yet it must be learned and noted if we are to understand him' (237). In a well-turned phrase Barth observes that Nietzsche 'resolutely and passionately necessarily rejected, not a caricature of the Christian conception of humanity, but in the form of a caricature the conception itself' (231). So '[w]ith the discovery of the Crucified and His host he discovered the Gospel itself in a form which was missed even by the majority of its champions, let alone its opponents, in the 19th century' (242). Barth also highlights Nietzsche's attack on Christianity as essentially an attack on Christian morality. It is the attack of one who is posing as a new man, the man of 'azure isolation', as Nietzsche says with reference to the eponymous hero of *Thus Spoke Zarathustra*. Barth interprets Nietzsche as man alone, man without his fellow-man and this determines the location of his treatment of Nietzsche in the theological anthropology of the *Church Dogmatics*.

I noted that Barth's rehearsal of the story of anthropology from the Renaissance through Leibniz beyond Hegel to Nietzsche bears comparison with his account in *Protestant Theology*. If Buddeus can scarcely be accused of a 'crusade against the cross', he is, on the account offered in *Church Dogmatics*, very sadly, though inadvertently, complicit in it. Our exploration of whether reason versus revelation is more fundamentally a question of moral self-sufficiency versus reconciliation is furthered if we close our historical investigation by attending to Nietzsche. Along with Polanyi in *Personal Knowledge* and Barth in *Protestant Theology*, Colin Gunton identified the epistemological malaise to which revelation succumbed, but he was also interested in the advent of atheism and of nihilism, accounting for them as something that flowed – at least in significant part – from epistemological breakdown. [32] Barth did not focus on atheism in *Protestant Theology* and did not studiously delineate a movement from the demise of revelation to inchoate atheism.

31. See the connection between Feuerbach and rational orthodoxy that Barth makes in *Church Dogmatics* I/2, 7.

32. See, as a whole, both *Enlightenment and Alienation* and *The One, The Three and The Many*.

However, a short chapter on Feuerbach did feature in that volume, where Barth described Feuerbach's relationship to theologians such as Schleiermacher, Tholuck and the Hegelians in terms reminiscent of his description of Wolff, the neologians and Schleiermacher in relation to Buddeus and rational orthodoxy. Was not Feuerbach drawing the just conclusion, on his theological predecessors' premises, that anthropology is the secret of theology?

In describing Nietzsche's opposition to Christianity as an opposition to the cross of Christ and to Christian morality, Barth is unquestionably correct. If in the intellectual history of Europe moral sense ever claimed the protection of Christianity while rejecting redemption through the cross, in Nietzsche any moral sense remotely tainted with Christianity must be abolished along with that cross which casts its dark shadow over European morality. Turning to Nietzsche, we come to the end of the line whose trajectory we are examining. This way of putting it is meant to be provocative in two ways. The lesser provocation is that 'line' and 'trajectory' connote a far more organised project than I have essayed. My treatment has been episodic, not systematic. The greater provocation is the interesting one. How is the line to be understood on the Barthian account of it if the terminus and inner secret of European moralism is Nietzschean immoralism? With Nietzsche, it would seem that the moral garment of the aggressor has dropped off and reconciliation in history is nakedly assailed. But the supposition coursing through my account has been that reconciliation in history is Christian teaching in conflict with self-respecting, independent moral sensibility. If it turns out that Nietzsche radically assaults that moral sense, can any associated attack of his on reconciliation in history really be plausibly understood as the efflorescence or telos of the moral sense of which I have generally spoken, the one that he now attacks?

The terms in which I couch this question skip over the prior question of whether the result of my own sorties into modern European intellectual history coincides entirely with that of Barth. I have not committed myself for or against Barth's association of, for example, Leibniz and Rousseau. Moreover, Nietzsche has entered on the scene at this point just because he completes our report on Barth's interpretation of intellectual history. Of course, we have met him before. We must now let him speak on his own terms and see where exactly he fits into our account.

Chapter 4

The Verdict of Nietzsche

Dionysus Against the Crucified

In describing Nietzsche's thought in terms of a crusade against the cross, Barth did no more than echo Nietzsche himself. 'Have I been understood? – *Dionysos against the Crucified*.'[1] So ends *Ecce Homo*, Nietzsche's sketchy but calculated account of his writings and his vocation, completed shortly before his mental collapse in January 1889, an event from which he never recovered. *Ecce Homo* is often read as betraying the signs of Nietzsche's derangement. It probably does, but that does not of itself disqualify the material substance of his account of his authorial goals, and a perusal of his earlier writings indicates that even if there is in *Ecce Homo* exaggeration or occasional twisting of the tale, it does not disqualify the account overall. The opposition between Dionysus, whose divine energies Nietzsche lauded right at the beginning of his published literature, and the Crucified is nuanced in two ways. Firstly, as Nietzsche in rather startling fashion dissociates Jesus from Christianity in a work

---

1. *Ecce Homo*, 'Why I Am A Destiny', 9. From now on, I follow the practice of placing references, where possible, in the body of the text. All the following quotations from *EH* come from this chapter, so I indicate in the text only its section number, not page number. As a rule, my exposition of Nietzsche does not depend on the felicity of the translation of particular words; consequently, I have felt free to use translations other than those in the standard critical English-language edition of Nietzsche's works published by Stanford University Press.

written at about the same time, 'the Crucified' must be taken as a symbol of staurocentric Christianity and not straightforwardly identified with the historical Jesus.[2] Secondly, Nietzsche partially identifies himself with the Crucified a few pages before the end of *Ecce Homo*.[3] Here, Nietzsche is castigating 'the good', who 'crucify him who writes *new* values on new law-tables' (4).[4] Nietzsche identifies himself with and aspires to pioneer this project of revaluation. At the very heart of his intellectual and literary enterprise at the end of his life was the ambition to create and write new values in the hope of inspiring others to do the same. 'The good . . . sacrifice the future *to themselves*, they crucify the whole human future!' (4) Thus, in *Ecce Homo*, Nietzsche connects reference to 'the Crucified' with his campaign against morality. Of himself, Nietzsche says that '[n] o one has yet felt *Christian* morality as *beneath* him', a morality that 'has hitherto been the Circe of all thinkers' (6).[5] What defines Nietzsche, what sets him 'apart from all the rest of mankind' is that he has '*unmasked*' Christian morality (7). In introducing this point, Nietzsche says: 'Have I been understood?', the exact same form of words he uses before his concluding declaration: '*Dionysos versus the Crucified*'.[6] The conclusion of *Ecce Homo* exemplifies Barth's point about Nietzsche's concern with the cross and Christian morality.

Amongst the other places in his literary corpus where the cross is also mentioned, we should pick out the 'decisive chapter' in Nietzsche's *magnum opus*, *Thus Spoke Zarathustra*, the manifesto that declares the

---

2.   For Nietzsche on Jesus, see *A* 29-35. This is one reason why *Der Antichrist* might be translated as 'The Anti-Christian' rather than 'The Antichrist'. However, there are other reasons for translating it as 'The Antichrist', notably on the basis of passages where the Greeks are brought into the question in 'Attempt at Self-Criticism' in *The Birth of Tragedy and Other Writings* [*BT*], eds. Raymond Geuss and Ronald Speirs (Cambridge: Cambridge University Press, 1999) 5; cf. *EH*, 'Why I Write Such Excellent Books', 2. Of course, even if we opt for 'Antichrist', the bare word 'Christ' is ambiguous between the Christ of Christianity and the Jesus, called the Christ, of history. I agree with those who, like Michael Tanner in his introduction to *A*, judge that Nietzsche meant to retain the dual meaning in the German.

3.   After his mental collapse, Nietzsche could even sign a letter as 'the Crucified': Ronald Hayman, *Nietzsche: A Critical Life* (London: Weidenfeld & Nicolson, 1980) 335.

4.   Cf. Nietzsche, *Thus Spoke Zarathustra*, trans. Graham Parkes (New York, NY/ Oxford: Oxford University Press, 2005) 3.26.

5.   Circe is an enchantress who features in Classical literature and mythology, including in Homer's *Odyssey*.

6.   See too the beginning of section 8. It is not a form of words peculiar to *EH*; see, e.g., *OGM* 3.1 and *A* 49.

imperative, if not the whole substance, of his revaluation. [7] This chapter is almost twice as long as any other chapter in *Thus Spoke Zarathustra*, and the second longest chapter of that work is more or less twice as long as any of the others.[8] Furthermore, in *Ecce Homo* Nietzsche spends over twice as long in recounting *Thus Spoke Zarathustra* as he does in describing any of his other works. This 'decisive' chapter is titled: 'On Old and New Law Tablets' (3.12). 'When I came to human beings', says the eponymous Zarathustra at its beginning, 'I found them sitting on an old conceit: all of them believed they had long known what good and evil were for the human being'. 'Zarathustra' is so named after the historical figure more familiarly known to most of us as Zoroaster, 'that Persian in history' who 'was the first to see in the struggle between good and evil the actual wheel in the working of things . . . Zarathustra *created* this most fateful of errors, morality' (*EH*, 'Why I Am A Destiny', 3). After *Thus Spoke Zarathustra*, Nietzsche produced a book titled *Beyond Good and Evil*, of which he said that 'it says the same things as my *Zarathustra*, but differently, very differently'.[9] *Beyond Good and Evil*, described in *Ecce Homo* by its author as 'in all essentials *a critique of modernity*' ('Beyond Good and Evil', 2), is sub-titled 'Prelude to a Philosophy of the Future', and however we interpret its relationship to *Thus Spoke Zarathustra*, it certainly shares with that work the desire to promote a post-Christian anthropological vision that, to Nietzsche's mind, must underlie any fruitful project of moral re-evaluation.

Given Nietzsche's general reputation for subtlety and complexity, never mind any philosophical elusiveness that attends *Thus Spoke Zarathustra* in particular, a judgement to the effect that the basic idea of the chapter 'On Old and New Tablets' is simple seems to belong in that territory where the ultra-naïve abuts upon the ultra-absurd. Nevertheless, it is a judgement that can generally be sustained in a generalization that is not vacuous. What Nietzsche proposes in this chapter is that morality, long culturally regarded as objectively binding and divinely given, is not

---

7.   Nietzsche describes it as the 'decisive chapter' in *EH*, 'Thus Spoke Zarathustra', 4. Strictly, it is of the crucified rather than the cross that Nietzsche speaks in *EH* itself.

8.   The second longest chapter, 'On the Superior Human', is found in 4.13, but that (fourth) book of *TSZ* was a subsequent addition by Nietzsche to his original volume.

9.   *Selected Letters of Friedrich Nietzsche* [*SL*], trans. Christopher Middleton (Chicago, ILL/London: University of Chicago Press, 1969) September 22, 1886. Nietzsche also regarded the two works that immediately preceded *TSZ* as 'commentaries' on it 'written in advance of the text', cited in Graham Parkes, 'Introduction' to *TSZ*, xi.

really so. It is a human invention. Nineteenth-century Europeans should have become aware of this. Sadly, they are usually retarded in this respect and fail to heed the imperative that we become creators of value. The *Übermensch* leads the way.[10] It is a way that avoids the cross, putting it behind us.

> 'O my brothers, I dedicate and direct you to a new nobility: you shall become for me progenitors and cultivators and sowers of the future . . . Your will and your foot, which wills beyond you yourselves – may those constitute your new honour! . . . Not that a spirit they call holy led your ancestors to much-praised lands that *I* praise not: for where the worst of all trees grew, the Cross – about that land there is nothing to praise' (3.12.12).

Thus spoke Zarathustra.[11] He was speaking rather mildly at this juncture; Nietzsche could identify the nadir of Richard Wagner's art as the point when, as a 'decaying and despairing decadent', he 'suddenly sank down, helpless and broken, before the Christian cross. Did no German have eyes in his head or pity in his conscience for this horrid spectacle?'[12]

CHRISTIANITY ON THE SURFACE

Before publishing *Thus Spoke Zarathustra*, Nietzsche had produced a trilogy of 'free-spirited works' in the first of which, *Human, All Too Human*, he had opened his campaign of direct public attack on Christianity.[13] Although Nietzsche was later to say that '[o]ne could,

10. If the term *Übermensch* must be translated, the familiar 'Superman' is best avoided. Something like 'Overhuman' probably has to do, although it lacks the connotations of 'beyond' alongside 'above'. 'Über' is a common affix in *TSZ*.
11. See too the telling and illuminating reference to the cross in 4.6.
12. 'How I Broke Away from Wagner', *Nietzsche Contra Wagner* [*NCW*] in *The Portable Nietzsche*, trans. Walter Kaufmann (New York, NY: Viking, 1954). Nietzsche is referring to Wagner's opera, *Parsifal*. Bryan Magee judges this work more Buddhist than Christian in *Wagner and Philosophy* (London: Penguin, 2000) 276-85. Be that as it may, *Parsifal* delivered Nietzsche a nasty blow because he had once so exalted Wagner. For a slightly different critique of the cross in a Dionysian light, see Nietzsche's material published under *The Will to Power*, ed. Walter Kaufmann (New York, NY: Vintage, 1968) 1052.
13. At the back of the original edition of *GS*, Nietzsche wrote that his book 'marks the conclusion of a series of writings . . . whose common goal is to erect *a new image and ideal of the free spirit*'. The original *Human, All Too Human*, published in 1878, was subsequently expanded to include two supplements – *Assorted*

with some freedom of expression, call Jesus personally a "free spirit"', the free spirit and Christianity are described at this early stage as antitheses: 'To test whether someone is one of us or not – I mean whether he is a free spirit or not – one should test his feelings towards Christianity.[14] If he stands towards it in any way other than *critically* then we turn our back on him' (*HH* II.2.182). In all three of these 'free-spirited' works – *Human, All Too Human, Daybreak* and *The Gay Science* – there is a concentration of passages that deal specifically with Christianity. Plenty is said about Christianity elsewhere in these works and, quite emphatically, it would be completely wrong-headed to think that we can fully or even adequately understand what Nietzsche thinks about Christianity just by looking at the passages where he explicitly talks about it. Nonetheless, we can without distortion at least get our bearings on his criticism of Christianity from the passages where he is explicit; the core or bald substance of his antagonism, even if not its depths and the breadths, will come to light by reporting on them.[15] So, skimming crudely along the textual surface, we turn to passages in the trilogy that preceded *Thus Spoke Zarathustra*.

Considered substantively, Christianity is intellectually incredible. In the chapter devoted to 'The Religious Life' in *Human, All Too Human*, Nietzsche refers to 'the errors of reason' (I.124; 133), having given non-religious examples of such errors since the beginning of his volume.[16] By the most elementary canons of philosophical reasoning, Christianity enshrines an epistemological absurdity (I.113). However, a corruption of heart as well as head was required to get Christianity under way

---

Opinions and Maxims and *The Wanderer and his Shadow* – the whole retaining the title of the original volume. His prior volumes, *The Birth of Tragedy* [*BT*] and *Unfashionable Observations* [*UO*], do not deal directly with Christianity although Nietzsche subsequently remarked of the first of these that its silence on Christianity was a sign of profound hostility ('Preface' to the 1886 edition of *BT* 5; *EH*, 'The Birth of Tragedy', 1). Thomas Brobjer plausibly finds this an unconvincing literary self-interpretation, 'Nietzsche's Changing Relation with Christianity' in Weaver Santaniello, ed., *Nietzsche and the Gods* (New York, NY: State University of New York Press, 2001) 155, n. 28.

14. It is not that Christianity and the free spirit later cease to be antithetical; rather, it is only later that Nietzsche separates Jesus from Christianity in this way, *A* 32.

15. As a matter of fact, what Nietzsche was saying about Wagner at the end of his authorship gets at the heart of what he was saying about Christianity in these early publications: see *The Case of Wagner* [*CW*] in *The Birth of Tragedy and the Case of Wagner*, trans. Walter Kaufmann (New York, NY: Random House, 1967) including the summary 'Epilogue' following the 'Second Postscript'.

16. The phrase 'errors of reason' itself is used early; e.g., I.27.

and its corruption is expressed particularly in its stance on humankind (I.114). Theological anthropology, soteriology and the doctrine of God are melded in rotten intertwinement. An early paragraph is eloquent. In contrast to the Hellenic,

> Christianity, on the other hand, crushed and shattered man completely and buried him as though in mud: into a feeling of total depravity it then suddenly shone a beam of divine mercy, so that, surprised and stupefied by this act of grace, man gave vent to a cry of rapture and for a moment believed he bore all heaven within him. It is upon this pathological excess of feeling, upon the profound corruption of head and heart that was required for it, that all the psychological sensations of Christianity operate: it desires to destroy, shatter, stupefy, intoxicate (I.114).

These are among the first words on Christianity that Nietzsche published in the first book that directly engaged with it, and it usually gets no better than that for Christianity according to Nietzsche. What irks him beyond endurance is the demeaning of human beings that underlies Christian notions of God and redemption, and these notions swarm over the whole range of Christian life and thought, spilling over into the life and thought of everyone infected by it, which, in Europe, means most life and thought *simpliciter*. Prosaically stated, nothing is more obnoxious in Christianity than its doctrine of sin. The sin-grace axis expresses and reflects both its dire spiritual sensibility in general and its miserable theological anthropology in particular. Nietzsche explains and analyses this in various ways, inquiring into and remarking on social and psychological origins, and it is these ways rather than his declaration of bare revulsion towards Christian soteriology and anthropology that distinguish Nietzsche's authorship. For my purposes, however, these can be left out of account and the account domesticated. It suffices to identify the bullseye of his target. Of course, the cross, that grim announcement and public spectacle of decrepit, lost human vagrancy, stands at the centre of Christian anthropology and soteriology.

What Nietzsche has said about Christianity at a relatively early point in the first volume of *Human, All Too Human* is supplemented in both parts of the second volume. In one of these we read that '[i]t was Christianity which first painted the Devil on the world's wall; it was Christianity which first brought sin into the world' (II.2.78).[17]

---

17. There is an early reference in II.1.8 to 'erect[ing] the Cross against the dreadful background of the impossibility of human knowing' before the brief

This same note is struck early in the second of the three free-spirited volumes, *Daybreak*. Nietzsche's discussion of Christianity occupies the second part of the first of its five books, but before he has got there he has referred to that Christian invention, 'the repellent flaunting of sin' (I.29), and after he has got there he refers to the 'gloomy propylaea of Christian salvation' (IV.321).[18] The trademark intellectual baselessness, psychological falsity and anthropological venom of Christianity are all exposed in *Daybreak* and in this connection we note that critical discussion of Pascal is prominent in the first book. Finally, in the third volume of the trilogy, commonly translated under the old-fashioned and now inappropriate title, *The Gay Science*, there is also a section on Christianity, but it is delayed longer than in *Human, All Too Human* and *Daybreak* and is briefer.[19] Nonetheless, it contains some of the most well-known or telling things that Nietzsche said on the subject, including the aphorism: 'What decides against Christianity now is our taste, not our reasons' (3.132). It is in *The Gay Science* that we encounter the famous passage on the death of God (3.125). The question of sin is prominent in this part of *The Gay Science*: 'The Christian decision to find the world ugly and bad has made the world ugly and bad' (3.130). 'The founder of Christianity thought that there was nothing from which men suffered more than their sins. That was his error' (3.138). A section is devoted to the origin of sin, wherein Jews and Christians are contrasted with the Greeks and Prometheus (3.135).

To reiterate: I am obviously just skating along the surface here, but swift reconnaissance of the surface at least informs us about what Nietzsche regarded in his earlier authorship as the unacceptable core content of Christianity. 'You name it . . . Christianity has . . . produced it: profound self-dissatisfaction, guilt, soul torment, self-contempt, self-hatred, habitual shame, despair, and sickening submissive obeisance.'[20] Christianity, as Nietzsche later puts it, has '[o]nly *bad* ends: the poisoning, slandering, denying of life, contempt for the body, the denigration and

---

discussions in II.1.92-98, and there is a later one (224) before II.1 has run its course. (See too 225.) II.2 more or less ends with reference to Christianity (350), which has been discussed several times in II.2 before that.

18. The 'propylaea' is a kind of large archway fashioned in Classical architecture. It is the same word in the German.

19. Reading *GS*, we might get the impression that Nietzsche incorporated his concentrated remarks on Christianity into the middle of the book. The impression is somewhat misleading, as the fifth book was added only later to the original *GS*.

20. Williams, *The Shadow*, 124. I listed at this point pertinent passages in *D* in particular.

self-violation of man through the concept of sin' (*A* 56). Of course, much of this had been said by others long before.[21] Nietzsche thought that Christianity presupposed 'that all men are great sinners and do nothing whatever except sin' (*HH* II.2.156). Logically, '[i]f man is sinful, through and through, then he may only hate himself' (*W* 10 [128]). (Pascal crops up in this connection too.) Christianity is 'the religion of antiquity grown old', advancing 'a general uglification of man' (*HH* I.247; II.1.224; *D* I.71-72). Enough said.[22]

The Anti-Natural and the Antichrist

What has the question of morality to do with sin, cross, soteriology and anthropology? According to Christianity, sin includes flagrance of God's moral law and if the idea of sin is an obstacle to spiritually healthy life and thought, the idea of moral law, and therefore of morality itself, naturally comes up for review. *Human, All Too Human* included an early chapter 'On the History of the Moral Sensations', which preceded the discussion of Christianity in the following chapter ('The Religious Life'), from which I have quoted. *Daybreak* was sub-titled: *Thoughts on the Prejudices of Morality* and the third book of *The Gay Science*, which features the passage on the death of God, opens with the words: 'After Buddha was dead, they still showed his shadow in a cave for centuries – a tremendous, gruesome shadow. God is dead; but given the way people are, there may still for millennia be caves in which they show his shadow. – And we – must still defeat his shadow as well' (3.108). A number of elements coalesce to shape that minatory shadow, but no element shapes it more than does Christian morality.

---

21. See the reference to Thomas F. Bertonneau's essay in 'Celsus, the First Nietzsche: Resentment and the Case against Christianity' in Williams, *The Shadow*, 125.

22. It is sometimes said that Nietzsche's opposition is rather to the church and contemporary Christianity than to authentic Christianity. See, e.g., Helmut Thielicke, *Modern Faith and Thought* (Grand Rapids: Eerdmans, 1990) 106, n. 44 and *The Evangelical Faith*, volume 1 (Edinburgh: T & T Clark, 1974) 249-59. It is not an either/or and Barth is closer to the mark in observing that Nietzsche attacks the real thing. Nietzsche does say that '[m]odern human beings live in this vacillation between an intimidated or hypocritical Christian morality and an equally cowardly and inhibited turn to antiquity', 'Schopenhauer as Educator' in *Unfashionable Observations*, trans. Richard Gray (Stanford, CA: Stanford University Press, 1995) 2. That is indeed an attack on contemporary forms. But just as Nietzsche favours a proper return to antiquity, so he opposes a proper Christianity that he believes is entailed in choosing antiquity.

When it comes to morality, Nietzsche holds that people have commonly erred with respect to both form and content. With respect to form, they have erred in positing a transcendent moral order. There is none. Nor is there an immanent one. 'There are absolutely no moral phenomena, only a moral interpretation of the phenomena' (*BGE* 4.108).[23] Nietzsche claimed that he was the first to formulate the proposition '*that there are no moral facts at all*'.[24] Morality is a human creation and Nietzsche was later to write a book *On the Genealogy of Morality*, offering some explanation of how this came about.[25] The content of the moral practices stemming from Christianity is also errant. However, in this connection, we should take note of a statement cited too infrequently in the secondary literature on Nietzsche's moral thought: 'It goes without saying that I do not deny – unless I am a fool – that many actions called immoral ought to be avoided and resisted, or that many called moral ought to be done and encouraged – but I think the one should be encouraged and the other avoided *for other reasons than hitherto*' (*D* II. 103).

To what, then, is Nietzsche opposed in the content of Christian morality? Well, the two great doctrines sanctioned and nurtured by European morality are 'equal rights' and 'sympathy with all that suffers' (*W* 37[8]). 'The increasingly spreading morality of compassion' ranks 'as the most uncanny symptom of our European culture turned uncanny', and the answer to the question: '*Where lie your greatest dangers?*' is: 'In compassion' (*OGM*, Preface, 5; *GS* 3.271). Nietzsche lays down the marker early in the cause of the Antichrist that '[a] ctive sympathy for the ill-constituted and weak – Christianity' is 'more harmful than any vice' (*A* 2). Compassion has its worthy rival as a moral curse. Before getting to *A* and to that part of it which alludes to the 'poison of the doctrine "*equal* rights for all"' . . . more thoroughly sowed by Christianity than by anything else', readers should have read in *Twilight of the Idols* that 'Equality', a principle 'which the theory of "equal rights" merely expresses, is of the essence of decline' (*A* 46; *TI* IX.37).[26] However, neither compassion nor equality take us to the root of the matter. Rather, Christian advocacy

---

23. This is a key Nietzschean proposition: see too *WP* 258.
24. *Twilight of the Idols* [*TI*], trans. Duncan Large (New York, NY/Oxford: Oxford University Press, 1998) VII.1.
25. This is one translation of the title: both the first and last words in the German title, *Zur Genealogie der Moral*, allow alternative possibilities of translation.
26. 'Equality of souls before God' is also a major indictment of Christianity in the section that climaxes *A*. See also 'On the Tarantulas', *TSZ* 2.7. Key components of Nietzsche's social and political philosophy come to light in these attacks.

of compassion and assertion of equality constitute growths on the soil of the foundational rot, which is this: Christianity is anti-natural. This criticism fuels the blast that brings to its climax the work that, along with *Ecce Homo*, more or less climaxes Nietzsche's authorship: *The Antichrist*.

> I *condemn* Christianity, I bring against the Christian Church the most terrible charge any prosecutor has ever uttered. To me it is the extremest thinkable form of corruption. . . . The Christian Church has left nothing untouched by its depravity. . . . Wherever there are walls I shall inscribe this eternal accusation against Christianity upon them – I can write in letters which make even the blind see. . . . I call Christianity the *one* great curse, the *one* great intrinsic depravity, the *one* great instinct for revenge for which no expedient is sufficiently poisonous, secret, subterranean, *petty* – I call it the *one* immortal blemish of mankind (62).

Its revenge is revenge against 'the natural'. It is an advantage to stay with *The Antichrist* because in the course of his discussion there of the natural, which exposes the grounds of Christianity's moral failure, Nietzsche also highlights the opposition between Christianity and Renaissance, something he had also voiced back in *Human, All Too Human* (I.237), so he is touching on a question that has been of conspicuous background interest to us in this volume even before arriving at Barth's observations on Nietzsche and the Renaissance.

The conclusion of Nietzsche's *The Antichrist* flows from his recitation of an historical story that culminates in pitting the Renaissance against Christianity. The Renaissance was the '*Revaluation of Christian values*' (61) and Nietzsche had conceived of *The Antichrist* as the first volume of a multi-volume work to be written under that title. It was the Germans who prevented the Renaissance from ousting Christianity, most notably in the figures of Luther, Leibniz and Kant. The philosophical theology or theological philosophy of the latter two effectively confirmed and definitely did not cancel the Lutheran Reformation's cancellation of the Renaissance. Thus, Leibniz's relation to the Renaissance is viewed entirely differently from the way in which Barth views it; Leibniz is a case of betrayal, not of fulfilment. Leibniz placed his philosophy at the disposal of Christianity where the impulse of the Renaissance was to negate it. In pitting Christianity against the Renaissance, Nietzsche finishes *The Antichrist* where he started it. 'The European of today is of far less value than the European of the Renaissance', he said near the beginning (4).[27] 'The Germans have robbed Europe of the last great cultural harvest of *Renaissance*', he said near the end. 'The Renaissance – an event without meaning, a great *in vain*! – Oh these Germans, what they have already cost us! In vain – that has always been the *work* of the Germans. – The Reformation; Leibniz; Kant and so-called German philosophy' (61).

Nietzsche's historical remarks accompany a contrast between human types. Christianity has willed the creation of 'the domestic animal, the herd animal, the sick animal man' (3). This willing was no contingent affair, an efflux of its religious course but not essential to the religious character of Christianity. On the contrary, it is actually definitive of it. The Renaissance ideal is strength and virtù, which is 'virtue free of moralic acid' (2).[28] Christianity 'has waged *a war to the death* against this *higher* type of man' and 'taken the side of everything weak, base, ill-constituted', thus making 'an ideal out of *opposition* to the preservative instincts of strong life' (5). This is '*depravity*': 'I call an animal, a species, an individual depraved when it loses its instincts, when it chooses, when it *prefers* what is harmful to it' because 'life itself' is 'instinct for growth' (6). Life is will to power. Christian opposition to the natural, that is, to the actual, takes its deadly moral toll in its sympathy for the sick and the weak. 'Nothing in our unhealthy modernity is more unhealthy than Christian pity' (7). This moral error is grounded in 'the will to lie', as Nietzsche puts it at the end of *Ecce Homo*, of which Christian morality is 'the most malicious form . . . it *denies* the very foundations of life' ('Why I Am A Destiny', 7).

The obnoxious anti-natural conception that herein blights the human and cultural landscape triumphed in Europe with the triumph of Christianity. How did Christianity attain this conviction – a conviction theologically constitutive of, not historically contingent to, it? Pondering the Jewish origins of Christianity, Nietzsche describes 'the Jews' as 'the most *fateful* nation in world history: their after-effect has falsified mankind' and its issue is Christianity (24). Nietzsche refers at this point to his book of the previous year, *On the Genealogy of Morality*. In the volume preceding that one, *Beyond Good and Evil*, Nietzsche had written as follows:

---

27. There is an even earlier reference: see section 2.
28. See also *W* 10[45]. For a brief statement of the a-moral connotations of virtù and its robust Renaissance character, see Keith Ansell-Pearson, *Nietzsche contra Rousseau: A Study of Nietzsche's Moral and Political Thought* (Cambridge: Cambridge University Press, 1991) 41.

The Jews – a people 'born for slavery', as Tacitus and the entire ancient world say, 'the chosen people among peoples', as they themselves say and think – the Jews have achieved that miraculous thing, an inversion of values, thanks to which life on earth has had a new and dangerous charm for several millennia: – their prophets melted together 'rich', 'godless', evil', violent', 'sensual' and for the first time coined an insult out of the word 'world'. The significance of the Jewish people lies in this inversion of values . . . the *slave revolt in morality* begins with the Jews (5.195).

Nietzsche spells this out in the first essay *On the Genealogy of Morality*. Impotent in the face of their enemies, the Jews took revenge by lambasting as evil and extolling as moral the opposite of what exists in actual, flourishing human life, namely 'powerful physicality, a blossoming, rich, even overflowing health along with whatever is required for their preservation: war, adventure, hunting, dancing, war games and in general everything that includes free and cheerful activity' (1.7). This is natural life. Resentfully, the Jews moralise it negatively. 'The slave morality begins when *ressentiment* [Nietzsche studiously uses the French] itself becomes creative and gives birth to values' (1.10). The moral values of Christianity, inscribed in its Jewish roots, constitute vengeance against life.[29]

In *The Antichrist*, Nietzsche offers an exercise in Old Testament criticism. He traces the decomposition of Israel as a case of internal social and political anarchy combining with the effect of the external pressure of Assyria to produce the reversal of an earlier Jewish conception of Yahweh as a God of power.[30] It is a reversal that directs us to 'the *denaturalizing* of natural values', featuring a concept of God and of moral world-order that stand as the antitheses of natural life and not as its expression (25). Then, on 'a soil *falsified* in this way, where all nature, all natural value, all *reality* has the profoundest instincts of the [priestly] ruling class against it, there arose *Christianity*, a form of mortal hostility

---

29. A social philosophy, embracing the theoretical question of justice and the practical question of slavery, a philosophy embedded in Nietzsche's outlook at this point, can be traced through his work from its published beginnings. E.g.: 'There is nothing more terrible than a class of barbaric slaves which has learned to regard its existence as an injustice and which sets out to take revenge, not just for itself but for all future generations', *BT*, 18.

30. Nietzsche finds greatness in the Old Testament prior to this reversal: see *BGE* 3.52.

to reality as yet unsurpassed' (27). Despite his shortcomings, Jesus personally is exempted from the corruption that Nietzsche identifies as Christianity: 'The word 'Christianity' is already a misunderstanding – in reality there has been only one Christian, and he died on the Cross' (39). Disgustingly, the apostolic perversion of his teaching, springing from the Judaic roots of Christianity, sustained an 'instinctive hatred *for* actuality', which constituted 'the driving element, the only driving element in the roots of Christianity' (39). Jesus died; how could this be explained? It was explained in the most repulsive way, namely, as a sacrificial death for sin (41). Then comes resurrection, and human life beyond the grave becomes a prominent belief. Nothing as totally unhinged from reality has been inflicted on human sensibility.[31]

The upshot was that the clean, wholesome, strong acceptance, affirmation and celebration of the natural in the cultures of Greece and Rome were negated by Christianity:

> The whole labour of the ancient world *in vain*: I have no words to express my feelings at something so dreadful . . . reality . . . *All in vain!* Overnight merely a memory! – Greeks! Romans! nobility of instinct, of taste, methodical investigation, genius for organization and government, the faith in, the *will* to a future for mankind, the great Yes to all things . . . reality, truth, *life* . . . (59).

In the first essay *On the Genealogy of Morality*, Nietzsche had written that there was no greater event in history than the struggle between two opposing sets of value-systems described under the rubric: 'Rome against Judea, Judea against Rome' (1.16). The Imperium Romanum and 'God on the cross' are locked in combat at the end of *The Antichrist* too (58). It is a strife of the exquisite noble with the anti-natural ignoble. In *The Antichrist*, Nietzsche declared that Christianity, not content with 'robb[ing] us of the harvest of the culture of the ancient world . . . went on to rob us of the harvest of the culture of *Islam*', which 'owed its origins to manly instincts' and said 'Yes to life' (60). From there, Nietzsche moved to the 'harvest of Renaissance', the *revaluation of Christian values*', the celebration of what is noble. Luther destroyed it. Nietzsche is reproducing late in *The Antichrist* one of the basic notions

---

31. Of course, Paul is a particular target for attack here. See also the discussion in *D* 1.68. For coverage of this, see Morgan Rempel, *Nietzsche, Psychohistory and the Birth of Christianity* (Westport, CT/London: Greenwood Press, 2002), although he seriously overestimates the extent to which Nietzsche understands Paul.

that he adopted in *On the Genealogy of Morality* where we read that the '*ressentiment*-movement we call the Reformation' stifled the Renaissance (1.16). From there, Nietzsche sets a smart pace to the shrill, denunciating crescendo of *The Antichrist*.

The philosophies of Leibniz and of Kant do not threaten Christianity. On the contrary, they are complicit in its ugly perpetuation. According to *Ecce Homo*, Leibniz and Kant were the 'two greatest impediments to the intellectual integrity of Europe' ('The Wagner Case', 2). Nietzsche does not always speak unfavourably of either Leibniz or Kant (*GS* 5.357). Yet, what we cannot do is to take Nietzsche's words at this point in *Ecce Homo* the less seriously because he was on the verge of mental collapse. So it is with *The Antichrist*. In it, Nietzsche focusses his energies in a blaze of incandescent fury on *German* impediment to cultural progress, but he has long castigated his compatriots on the grounds that, intellectually, Germany is at the heart of Europe's trouble.[32] German philosophy as it is carried on by its two representatives, Leibniz and Kant, is the perpetuation of theology, clinging to the fabrication of a transcendent reality and a moral world-order.

I mentioned earlier that Nietzsche's contrast between the heritage of the Renaissance and of Christianity, a contrast often focused on Renaissance and Reformation, is also advertised in his earlier works. In this respect, as in the case of salient elements in his substantive criticism of Christianity, *The Antichrist* stands in continuity with them. Thus we read in *Human, All Too Human*:

> The Italian Renaissance contained within it all the positive forces to which we owe modern culture: liberation of thought, disrespect for authorities, victory or education over the arrogance of ancestry, enthusiasm for science and the scientific past of mankind, unfettering of the individual, a passion for truthfulness ...indeed, the Renaissance possessed positive forces which have *up to now* never reappeared in our modern culture with such power as they had then. All its blemishes and vices notwithstanding, it was the golden age of this millennium (I.237).

---

32. Nietzsche's worries about Germany go back to his very early days and his enchantment with Greece, an enchantment he never lost, just as he never abandoned the early sense that Germany had squandered its legacy. As a schoolboy, he came (and who can blame him?) under the spell of Hölderlin's *Hyperion,* which dramatically switches mood and tone in its concluding scathing denunciation of Germans: F. Hölderlin, *Hyperion and Selected Poems*, ed. E.L. Santner (New York, NY: Continuum, 1994).

Nothing in this passage (including in the original German) specifies further what Nietzsche means by '*now*' (the italics are his) so it presumably refers mundanely to the immediate present.[33] It is 'the climax of this millennium and what has happened since then is the grand reaction of all kinds of herd instincts against the 'individualism' of that epoch' (*SL*, October, 1882).[34] As we have already learned from his later work, the sickening reality is that the Reformation killed it all off best it could, and that best was very effective. Nietzsche continues:

> In contrast to it there stands the German Reformation: an energetic protest by retarded spirits who had by no means had enough of the world-outlook of the Middle Ages and greeted the signs of its dissolution, the extraordinary transformation of the religious life into something shallow and merely external, not with rejoicing, as would have been appropriate, but with profound ill-humour.[35]

This delayed the Enlightenment, which might 'perhaps have dawned somewhat sooner than it did and with a fairer lustre than we can now even imagine'. While his personal association with the Enlightenment must be treated with at least a degree of caution lest we conclude that Nietzsche is just a species of Enlightenment rationalist, we should nevertheless note that at this juncture of his authorship Nietzsche associates himself with the 'children of the Enlightenment' (I.55), whether or not the association really holds.[36] Anyway, when the Enlightenment did arrive it was squashed by Germans, and the bitter lament on this account that Nietzsche incorporated into the conclusion of *The Antichrist* is found also in these earlier works.[37]

---

33. At this point in the book and at this juncture of his authorship, Nietzsche emphasises the significance of the sciences (*Wissenschaften*), which he has introduced early (e.g., I.26).

34. That Nietzsche *regards* the Renaissance as a comprehensive phenomenon of great reach is indicated, e.g., in his description of one of his heroes, Napoleon, as 'one of the greatest continuators of the Renaissance', *GS* 5. 362.

35. For one of Nietzsche's rants against Luther, see *GS* 5.358. This section is called '*The peasant rebellion of the spirit*', Luther being 'the "most eloquent" and immodest peasant Germany ever had', *OGM* 3.22. However, 'Luther's service is perhaps nowhere greater than in having had the courage of his *sensuality*', *OGM* 3.2.

36. *HH* was dedicated to Voltaire: see Erich Heller's 'Introduction' to an earlier edition of Hollingdale's translation of *Human, All Too Human* (Cambridge: Cambridge University Press, 1986) x.

37. See, e.g., the explicitly titled section on 'German hostility to the Enlightenment'

Germans: Luther, Leibniz, Kant. Luther has been mentioned but not featured in this volume and we began our story later than his day. Despite the interest in Leibniz that arises from Barth's account, nothing much is to be gained from tracing Nietzsche's hostility towards him. Nietzsche's position on morality or the cross can be described without bringing Leibniz into the equation beyond what has already been reported. As far as I can judge, other things Nietzsche has to say about Leibniz are not particularly illuminating for my purposes.[38] As a matter of fact, in *Ecce Homo*, a third German philosopher is indicted in addition to Leibniz and Kant, the two philosopher-criminals who philosophically secured the theology of Luther and the German Reformation: Arthur Schopenhauer. Tracing Nietzsche's constructive and critical dialogue with Schopenhauer over the years of his authorship would yield a remarkably comprehensive, though not exhaustive, account of Nietzsche's philosophy. However, I am not giving such an account, so we must leave Schopenhauer out of the story despite the promising connection we find portended in Nietzsche's remark that what first drew him to Schopenhauer was 'the ethical air, the Faustian odour; Cross, Death, Grave and so on' (*SL*, October 8, 1868).

That leaves us with Kant. Schopenhauer responded to him and Kant responded to Leibniz. Kant is potentially such a relevant figure for our purposes, not to mention a towering presence in his own right, that, once he pops up on our radar, we scarcely need a justification for bringing him deliberately into our story.

THE SINS OF KANT

If any major modern thinker appears at first blush to exemplify both the primacy of matters epistemological in modern engagement with Christianity and the collision between autonomous moral sense and traditional construal of Christian belief in reconciliation in history, it is surely Immanuel Kant.[39] Yet, as for epistemological primacy, Nietzsche's

---

in *D* III.197.

38. The passage in *GS* that I mentioned above where Nietzsche speaks more favourably of Leibniz (and Kant) is preceded by laudatory comment on Leibniz (*GS* 5.354). Apologies to Martin Heidegger that 'my purposes' do not comprehend his engagement with Leibniz in 'The Word of Nietzsche: "God is Dead"' in *The Question Concerning Technology and Other Essays* (New York, NY: Harper & Row, 1977) 53-112; see 74 (cf. 98) on Leibniz.

39. On the latter issue, see especially, in the context of his overall argument, Kant's averment that 'The Gradual Transition Of Ecclesiastical Faith Toward The Exclusive Dominion of Pure Religious Faith Is The Coming of The Kingdom

conviction was that a moral programme underlies the drive to knowledge that superficially motored philosophy. This was mentioned in the introduction to this volume and Kant looks like a candidate we should consider as a prestigious exemplar this principle. As for moral sense and Christianity, Nietzsche detected collusion rather than collision between Kant and the tradition. In the opening of his essay famously addressing the question: 'What is Enlightenment?', Kant ascribed to moral and spiritual weakness – that is, to lack of courage and to laziness – the widespread failure to use one's own reason to free oneself from what is a 'self-incurred tutelage'.[40] As far as this goes, it accords comfortably enough with Nietzsche's own thoughts and, in his relatively early work, Nietzsche was prepared to credit Kant with appearing 'honest and honourable in the best sense' even though he was 'insignificant . . . lack[ing] breadth and power' (*D* V.481).[41] However, Nietzsche developed into a strident opponent of Kant's moral and intellectual impulse and philosophical performance, whose substance and purport he deemed woefully mistaken. Nietzsche concluded that it lacked 'intellectual integrity' (*TI* IX.16). This is rather mildly put: Kant is, in fact, the 'most stunted conceptual cripple ever' (*TI* VIII.7). What did Kant succeed in doing to incur the wrath of Nietzsche?

We have arrived at Kant on the wings of *The Antichrist* and two adjacent sections early in that work (10-11) tell us where Nietzsche has arrived intellectually in relation to Kant. Kant discovered or devised a 'secret path' back to an old ideal, restoring two things: 'the concept "*real world*"' and 'the concept of morality as the *essence* of the world'. These are basically theological ideas: 'The Protestant pastor is the grandfather of German philosophy'. They are also the 'two most vicious errors in existence'. In propounding them, Kant joins Luther and Leibniz as threats to German integrity. The basis of Kant's moral error is the setting up of an external and impersonal standard. Instead, I ought to be devising my own morality. Choice should be accompanied by joy in choice, neither of which is possible as long as morality is something given. 'What destroys more quickly than to work, to think, to feel

---

of God', *Religion Within the Boundaries of Mere Reason* in Immanuel Kant, *Religion and Rational Theology*, trans. Allen W. Wood and George Di Giovanni (Cambridge: Cambridge University Press, 1996) 146-153.

40.   Immanuel Kant, 'What Is Enlightenment?' in *Critique of Practical Reason and Other Writings in Moral Philosophy*, trans. and ed. Lewis White Beck (Chicago, ILL: University of Chicago Press, 1949) 286-292, quotation from 296. The political context of Kant's remarks is often overlooked when they are quoted.

41.   Later, too, in the Preface of *OGM* (5), Nietzsche notes in his favour Kant's disdain for compassion.

without inner necessity, without a deep personal choice, without *joy*?
. . . It is virtually a *recipe* for *décadence*.' The decline and decadence that
characterise Kant's philosophy are an expression 'of the final exhaustion
of life'. Nietzsche sums up the indictment: 'The erring instinct in all and
everything, *anti-naturalness* as instinct, German *décadence* as philosophy
– *that is Kant!*', the 'fatal spider'.

If Kant's spiritual pedigree features the Protestant pastor, he is even
more firmly soldered to a more universal figure, namely the priest. With
his concept of 'practical reason', Kant

> designed a reason specifically for the case in which one was
> supposed not to have to bother about reason, namely when
> morality, when the sublime demand 'thou shalt' makes itself
> heard. If one considers that the philosopher is, in virtually all
> nations, only the further development of the priestly type, one is
> no longer surprised to discover this heirloom of the priest, *self-
> deceptive fraudulence* (*A* 12).[42]

This is not the only occasion in *The Antichrist* on which Kant and
the priest are associated (55). Earlier, the priest and the idealist were
associated. 'It is necessary to say *whom* we feel to be our antithesis – the
theologians and all that has theological blood in its veins' (8). Nietzsche's
target here is the 'idealist' – the one who 'assumes, by virtue of a higher
origin, a right to cast strange and superior looks at actuality'. The priest
plays the same decadent game. Kant is, indeed, 'a *crafty* Christian,
when all's said and done', exhibiting decadence and declining life in his
division of the world into the real and apparent (*TI* 3.6).[43] However, no
indictment can be greater than to associate Kant with the specific craft
and craftiness of the priest.

What precisely does Nietzsche have in mind? Nietzsche's discussion
of the priest is prominent in *The Antichrist*. It follows a relatively
sustained discussion in the third and final essay *On the Genealogy of
Morality*, which features the case of 'the ascetic priest'.[44] The question

---

42. 'To assert the existence as a whole of things of which we know nothing
    whatever, precisely because there is an advantage in not being able to know
    anything of them, was a piece of naiveté of Kant, resulting from needs, mainly
    moral-metaphysical' (*WP* 571).
43. See also in *TI* VI.3 Nietzsche's reference to 'the thing in itself' as the *horrendum
    pudendum* – that dreadful, shameful thing – sported by metaphysicians.
44. Before he got to that discussion, Nietzsche had opined that Kant's 'categorical
    imperative smells of cruelty' (2.6).

addressed in the third essay is: 'What Do Ascetic Ideals Mean?' and its morose guiding passion is the lamentable sickliness of European humanity. Nietzsche approaches his question in various ways, and Kant crops up in more than one context, one instance of which is via the more specific question: 'What does it *mean* when a philosopher pays homage to the ascetic ideal?' (3.6).[45] 'At first', says Nietzsche, 'the philosophical spirit always had to disguise and mask itself in the *previously established* types of the contemplative human being', one of which is the priest (10). This meant that '*the ascetic ideal* long served the philosopher as a form of appearance'. Enter the ascetic priest who, 'until the most recent times . . . has given us the repulsive and gloomy caterpillar form in which alone philosophy was allowed to live and crawl around'.

In tackling the ascetic priest, Nietzsche is trying to understand at least three things: the inner meaning of his asceticism; how life conceived as will-to-power can be channelled into life-denying asceticism; and how this phenomenon has affected European humanity. Inwardly considered, asceticism is an attempt to master life itself; it uses the energy available in its 'power-will' to block sources of energy; its effects have been vast and devastating.[46] '*The ascetic ideal arises from the protective and healing instinct of degenerating life*' (13) and this degeneration greatly preoccupies Nietzsche in his last works. He craves life in its strength and this is the ferocious opposite of what the ascetic priest exemplifies and dispenses. The priest shepherds the sick; that is his role. The whole hamartiological apparatus of developed Christianity is constructed to this end. As long as Kant held on to his transcendental ideas and entertained the prospect of an unknowable real world other than the actual world, he was beholden to the life-denying philosophy of the ascetic priest.[47]

Yet the connection between Kant and the priest is made stronger in *The Antichrist* where the relatively measured and analytic, though passionate, investigation of priestly asceticism in *On the Genealogy of Morality* is replaced by an attack that takes its trajectory from the specifically Jewish priesthood. In the third essay *On the Genealogy of Morality*, Nietzsche had spoken highly of the Old Testament in comparison with the revolting New (3.22). In *The Antichrist*, Nietzsche distinguishes between

---

45. The following references are all to this third essay in *OGM*.
46. While 'power-will' is cumbersome and I availed myself of the phrase 'will-to-power' in describing Nietzsche's enquiry, the translator rightly uses 'power-will' instead of 'will-to-power', because the German is '*Machtwillens*' and not '*Wille-zur-Macht*'. 'Energy' ('*Kraft*') is a different word.
47. The remarks in 3.12 and 3.25 should be associated in the context of Nietzsche's overarching convictions about the ideal and the actual.

the early religion of Israel and its subsequent priestly corruption. Priests devised a guilt-based salvation-mechanism and a moral world-order that features God punishing people for disobedience. For Nietzsche, the moral world-order is a lie and where philosophers adopt it, they have 'seconded the Church' (26). The priest is 'the most dangerous kind of parasite, the actual poison-spider of life' (38). He 'has a life-interest in making mankind *sick* and in inverting the concepts "good" and "evil", "true" and "false"' (24). 'Kant too, with his categorical imperative was on the same road' as the priests who perpetrated a moral lie (55).[48] These are the associations that enable Nietzsche to include Kant along with Luther and Leibniz in the denunciation of Christianity that concludes *The Antichrist*.

We should not overlook the significance of joy, a subject that Nietzsche introduces in connection with Kant. Before the observations on joy quoted earlier from that section of *The Antichrist* in which Nietzsche calls Kant 'a fatal spider', Nietzsche says that 'Kant's categorical imperative should have been felt as *mortally dangerous*! . . . The theologian instinct alone took it under its protection! – An action compelled by the instinct of life has in the joy of performing it the proof it is a *right* action' (11). In *Daybreak*, Nietzsche had opined that in the demand Kant made 'that duty must *always* be something of a burden . . . there is concealed a remnant of ascetic cruelty' (IV.339). Although Nietzsche would have been familiar with the fact that Kant thought through the danger of so relating morality to happiness that the one was ordered directly to the other, reference should be made to the first set of his remarks in *Twilight of the Idols* on the 'Four Great Errors', following a brief section on 'Morality as Anti-Nature'. The first error to tackle is the error of 'confusing cause and consequence'.

> There is no error more dangerous than that of confusing the *consequence with the cause*: I call it the real ruination of reason. . . . *Every* proposition which religion and morality formulate contains it; priests and moral legislators are the originators of this ruination of reason. . . . The most general formula underlying every religion and morality is: 'Do this and that, stop this and that – then you will be happy! Or else'. . . . Every morality, every religion *is* this imperative – I call it the great original sin of reason. . . . In my mouth that formula is transformed into

---

48. Kant was 'a fanatic of the formal concept "Thou shalt"', *W* 10[11]. This is not the only place in which Nietzsche describes Kant as a 'moral fanatic': see *WP* 382.

its inversion – *first* example of my 'revaluation of all values': a well-balanced person, a 'happy man' *has* to do certain actions and instinctively shies away from others. . . . In a formula: his virtue is the *consequence* of his happiness (*TI* VI.1,2).

I have omitted reference to Nietzsche's evocation of the physiological basis of this felicitous behaviour because my concern is the gulf between him and Kant, especially Kant's prescription for moral felicity. If Kant is anywhere in the orbit of Christianity in his attitude to joy, he is in deep trouble with Nietzsche because the clash between Nietzsche and Christianity on this point, as on most others, is not cushioned. 'Hatred . . . of joy in general is Christian' (*A* 21).[49] Contrast Homer and the pre-Homeric poets who exhibit a 'joy in the actual and active *of every kind*' (*HH* II.1.220). Contrast also Zarathustra. The song that originally concluded *Thus Spoke Zarathustra* (the fourth book was a later addition) is a song of love for Eternity but also and equally and at the same time a song of joy. 'Joy – deeper still than misery . . . all joy wants Eternity . . . wants deepest, deep Eternity!' (3.15).[50] Zarathustra aspires to be a yes-sayer and not just a no-sayer.[51] The task of Zarathustra is set out early in these terms: '*I teach you the Overhuman*' now that God is dead (*TSZ*, 'Zarathustra's Prologue', 3). 'Of Old and New Tablets' lays bare the heart of Nietzsche's teaching, although it does not include everything that is closeted away in or emanates from that heart. It is a kind of Sermon on the Mount whose first principle is that we should get on with shattering such old law tablets as those to whose style Moses got us accustomed on another mount. *That* is where the healthy connection between joy and moral law begins. Seriously and properly undertaken, the destructive task is a super-human, overhuman task.[52]

---

49. Nietzsche draws ironical attention to the fact that the founder of Christianity was reputedly 'the bringer of glad tidings', *A* 35.
50. Note the sentiment uttered close to the conclusion of the third book of *TSZ*: 'If that joy in searching is in me that drives my sails on to the undiscovered, if a seafarer's joy is in my joy . . . how should I not lust after Eternity?' (3.16.5). This was almost right at the end of the original *TSZ*. A kind of joy attends the end of book 4 too (4.20). Tyler Roberts remarks that 'Nietzsche figures two modalities of desire: suffering desires life, though not its own, and joy desires eternity', *Contesting Spirit: Nietzsche, Affirmation, Religion* (Princeton, NJ: Princeton University Press, 1998) 35. I am not sure if Roberts gets the first modality right, but he is certainly right on the second.
51. '[A]ll in all and on the whole: some day I want only to be a Yes-sayer!' (*GS* 4.276).
52. Surely the nimble light-heartedness of the free spirit is a kind of prelude to

While the figure of the *Übermensch* does not explicitly feature in the works that succeeded *Thus Spoke Zarathustra*, Dionysus does – Dionysus, god of authentic joy in actuality, a joy that has pain at its heart.[53] In his name or in the name of him in whom Dionysus became incarnate, that is, Zarathustra, the task of dismantling Christianity proceeds (*EH*, 'Thus Spoke Zarathustra', 6). Concluding the précis of his books that constitutes the spine of *Ecce Homo*, Nietzsche explained 'Why I Am A Destiny'. '*Revaluation of all values*: this is my formula for an act of supreme coming-to-oneself on the part of mankind which in me has become flesh and genius' (1). The 'formula for a destiny *that has become man . . .* stands in my Zarathustra – *and he who wants to be a creator in good and evil has first to be a destroyer and break values*' (2).[54] It is all about the 'self-overcoming of morality through truthfulness' (3). *That* is what constructive moral philosophy is all about. It is the opposite of what Kant's moral philosophy is all about. In his transgression, Kant is not alone (*D*, 'Preface' 3).

Application

Nietzsche's observations on Kant bear in two respects on the way in which my account of Nietzsche and my earlier reading of Western intellectual and cultural history can mesh. Firstly, in previous chapters I have stirred up a contest between the realms of epistemology and of morality, both viewed in light of their encroachment on traditional Christian convictions about revelation and reconciliation. If we insist on implicating Nietzsche in that contest in the terms in which I have described it, there is no doubt on whose side he enlists. Such is his disdain for the vagaries of Christian theological epistemology, the ridiculous irrationalism of faith, that he might baulk at being implicated in the contest, scorning the whole undivided Christian scheme of things. The whole Christian business, revelation and reconciliation, reason and moral attitude, is ridiculous and offensive in one go. It would certainly be wrong either to play down Nietzsche's objection to the damaging foundations of Christian theological epistemology or to saddle him

---

eternal joy. The great exemplar of the former is Laurence Sterne, author of *Tristram Shandy* (*HH* II.1.113).

53. However, the shadow of the *Übermensch* surely enwraps the messianic and haunting end of the second essay in *OGM* (2.24), followed only by the brief and telling reference to Zarathustra (2.25).

54. Nietzsche adds: '*Thus the greatest evil belongs with the greatest good: this, however, is the creative good.*'

with false antitheses imported on the basis of a set of authorial concerns articulated independently of Nietzsche's own work. Nonetheless, the foregoing account indicates where Nietzsche's sympathies lie in a reading of intellectual history.

Kant's critical philosophy, with its strictures on our knowledge of things-in-themselves, his *Critique of Practical Reason* and *Religion within the bounds of Reason Alone*, may *prima facie* seem to crown a claim that, if epistemological considerations are not outstanding above all others in the dismantling of traditional Christian claims for revelation by the end of the Enlightenment period, they are certainly second to none. Nietzsche approaches matters differently.

> Deeply distrustful of the dogmas of epistemology . . . I noticed . . . that no epistemological skepticism or dogmatism had ever arisen free from ulterior motives – that it acquires a value of the second rank as soon as one has considered what it was that *compelled* the adoption of this point of view. Fundamental insight: Kant as well as Hegel and Schopenhauer – the skeptical-epochistic attitude as well as the historicizing, as well as the pessimistic – have a *moral* origin (*WP* 410).

Just as Pascal used 'moralistic' scepticism to open out the possibilities of faith, so Kant used English epistemological scepticism to cater for the 'moral and religious needs of the Germans' (*WP* 101).[55] According to Nietzsche, moral sense trumped reason in Kant's philosophy in the sense that rational limitation was in the service of a moral philosophy that conceptually adumbrates moral sensibility. To anyone who supposes that the Christian view of redemption was qualified, modified, reduced, truncated or abolished by Kant's moral sense, Nietzsche's message is: 'Think again'. Christianity neatly, nicely and loathsomely creeps back under Kantian protection. A theologically conservative – or even religiously non-committal – protest that Kant has diluted in bucketfuls the Christian doctrine of redemption is met by the Nietzschean assurance that poison remains poison even if the outward decoration of the vessel changes, and if poison remains in the body its destructive effects persist. Of course, the blame for the continuation of Christianity's triumphant nihilism – and Christianity's demeaning of the human is the

---

55. 'Christians today like to set up Pilate, with his question 'What is truth?', as an advocate of Christ, so as to cast suspicion on everything known or knowable and to erect the Cross against the dreadful background of the impossibility of knowing' (*HH* II.1.8).

ultimate nihilism – is not be laid at the feet of Kant alone, but Kant does significantly share the blame for keeping Christianity on a victorious track.

Nietzsche may be doing Kant an injustice. However, when his judgement about the moral roots of Kant's enterprise is set alongside the account offered in the preceding chapters, we have on board one more advocate of the following hypothesis: that the Western rejection of the claims of revelation in the name of reason historically exemplifies what Nietzsche took to be the case in philosophy, and which the Augustinian tradition has taken to be the case theologically, that is, the governing role of moral will in philosophy of religion. The epistemological then lies at least one layer above moral depths. If Nietzsche's take on Kant were completely wayward, we should rightly ask exactly what his engagement with Kant contributes to the overall argument of this book. It was not completely wayward. It may have been wayward in many respects and many of Nietzsche's formulations might be disregarded.[56] But he was generally right on the moral roots of Kant's enterprise. The author of an impressive study on Kant observes that 'from the beginning, Kant regarded the philosopher as having the primary task of confirming and even grounding the moral man's view of the world', epistemological theory being in the service of moral freedom.[57] Kant consciously assigns to reason a moral vocation. It is what Nietzsche makes of that, not this basic and broad description of Kant's enterprise, which is controversial.

The second respect in which my account of Nietzsche and my earlier reading of intellectual history mesh emerges when the question of the relationship between autonomy and morality comes up. For Nietzsche, Kant superbly exemplifies the claim that you cannot have both autonomy and morality. "Autonomous" and "moral" are mutually exclusive' (*OGM* 2.2).[58] It is either one or the other. Nietzsche maintains

---

56. One would not guess on the basis of Nietzsche's account that, as Gordon E. Michalson puts it in his fine study of *Fallen Freedom: Kant on Radical Evil and Moral Regeneration* (Cambridge: Cambridge University Press, 1990), for Kant, '[i]n some profound and awful sense, I am opaque to myself, considered as a moral agent' and that the problem of evil 'brings Kant closer and closer to the insight that reason is not fully self-governing, but is subject to forces too murky to specify', 141.

57. Richard L. Velkley, *Freedom and the End of Reason: On the Moral Foundation of Kant's Critical Philosophy* (Chicago, ILL/London: University of Chicago Press, 1989) 30. It is less the statement itself than the exposition of it in this volume that is so illuminating.

58. On this, see Keith Ansell-Pearson, 'Nietzsche on Autonomy and Morality: the Challenge to Political Theory', *Political Studies* 39.2 (1991) 270-86. In the

that Kant's ambitions are incoherent in attempting to posit both a moral order and a self-determining will. We are in even greater trouble if self-legislative reason is judged to be operating properly only when it is putatively divorced from natural inclinations.[59] It is in connection with the collision between autonomy and morality, as Nietzsche perceives it, that we can approach the question that I anticipated at the end of the last chapter arising from a juxtaposition of Barth's remarks on Nietzsche as the revealer of the inner nature of post-Renaissance humanism and my preceding analysis of moral self-sufficiency and reconciliation in history. The question was: how could a destroyer of morality be the culmination of a moral critique?

Nietzsche points the way to the answer, even if we reject Nietzsche's way of answering it and, indeed, reject the whole of his philosophy. In principle, the moralism that drove opposition to reconciliation in history might be a cloak for an autonomy that will outgrow and discard the moralism in time. In that case, moralism would be a contingent form of opposition to reconciliation in history, subservient to an autonomous impulse that can dispense with the form, just as the Romanticism of Barth's Rousseau lays bare the inner secret or telos of the rationalism that he externally opposes and overthrows. This is obviously not how Nietzsche himself would see it, ranging moralism, as he does, on the side of traditional Christianity and in opposition to, not cloaking, autonomy. The alternative perspectives here paraded before us are, to a large extent, accounted for by different views of what we are calling moralism. If we were to join Barth, we should regard moralism as antithetical to Christianity; if we were to throw in our lot with Nietzsche, we should regard moralism as enslaved to it. The disagreement here is not just disagreement over the inner nature of the moralism that appeared in post-Reformation Europe. It is disagreement over the nature of Christianity. We have heard enough from Nietzsche on Christianity to realise that what he takes Christianity to be is very distant from what Barth takes it to be. Nietzsche's Christianity, lacking in any appreciation of the goodness of creation and the exaltation of humanity that launches its Scriptures, is a joylessly craven affair, lived out before a spidery God. It is not the Christianity of Barth. Nor, indeed, of the New Testament.

---

context of Nietzsche's wider thought, the conceptual contrast is less qualified than we might be tempted to suppose from its context in *OGM*.

59.   Nietzsche connects questions of autonomous self-direction with a critique of the proposition that 'the moral law' is 'supposed to stand *above* our own likes and dislikes', *D* II.108.

Disagreement over the placing of moralism is not one that we need to pursue, let alone to adjudicate. Before embarking on pursuit, we should have to do better than just to flail around the terminology of moralism and autonomy and should need to adumbrate a conceptual analysis of them, else the weapons of dispute would be ineffectually blunt instruments. They do not need to be sharpened for we do not need to decide whether the moral underpinning of Kant's philosophical thought, for example, reveals that he is on the side of the angels or on the side of the Antichrist – whether the moral tendencies of a Kant or anyone else demonstrate tacit (or, for that matter, explicit) allegiance to autonomous, anti-Christian impulse or to Christian, anti-atheistic impulse. We do not even have to recognise that the issue is rightly described by means of those alternatives. We might regard both Barth's conviction that European moralism is the mask of anti-Christian autonomy and Nietzsche's conviction that the same moralism is the lackey of Christian religion as equally extreme and equally mistaken. Strictly, we do not need to decide. All along, our interest has been in the relative positioning of the epistemological and the moral, in revelation and reconciliation.

Of course, it was Rousseau and not Kant whom we picked up in Barth's analysis. Rousseau both heavily influenced Kant, whom Nietzsche regarded as 'a moral fanatic à la Rousseau' (*WP* 101), and bitterly antagonized Nietzsche because he believed in a moral world-order.[60] Nietzsche forces Rousseau to the same either-or as Kant must face. Either autonomy or morality.[61] And we could ask the same kind of either-or question in relation to Rousseau as we asked in relation Kant: who is right – Barth, who sees Nietzsche as exposing the inner telos of counter-Christian Rousseau, or Nietzsche, who sees Rousseau as his crypto-Christian antipodes? The question needs no more to be answered than it did in the case of Kant, but it profits us to attend briefly to Nietzsche's criticism of Rousseau.[62]

---

60. For a strong reading of Rousseau's well-known and long-established influence on Kant, see Velkley, *Freedom*. '[A]s a defender of the life of theoretical inquiry, Kant assigns to it, even more clearly and dramatically after studying Rousseau, the primary task of justifying the moral view of the world', 31.

61. Robert Pippin, who from the very first chapter of *Modernism* has shown his sensitivity to the nuances of autonomy, indicates 'what could be called the "German" version of autonomy' propounded by Nietzsche, 80.

62. Barth and Nietzsche appear to be broadly agreed on the connection between Renaissance, Stoicism and Rousseau (*HH* II.2.216), though note Nietzsche's reference to the 'mythical Rousseau' here. On the 'eighteenth century of *Rousseau*', see *WP* 62.

Nietzsche was 'contra Rousseau' (*D* III.163).[63] Nietzsche's opposition to Rousseau is nothing if not profound: when he uttered five 'Nos' in a notebook entry in 1887, the only named personal antagonist was Rousseau (*W* 10 [2]).[64] In 'Schopenhauer as Educator', written near the beginning of his published authorship, Nietzsche said that the modern age had set up three images of the human being, one of which, the man of action, was promoted by Rousseau. In *Twilight of the Idols*, written near the end of his published authorship, he called Rousseau the 'first modern man' (IX.48).[65] What makes him modern is also what makes him despicable; he wanted to 'return to nature' and establish an egalitarianism that the French Revolution celebrated – 'there is no more venomous poison in existence' than the doctrine of equality – and in this form he depicted the moral human being. Rousseau gets things upside-down: 'Not the corruption of man but the extent to which he has become tender and moralized is his curse' (*WP* 98; cf. 382). Rousseau is a 'moral tarantula' – and he bit Kant (*D*, Preface, 3). When Nietzsche proceeds to accuse Rousseau of *ressentiment* and observes that he has 'something German' about him 'in the worst sense', it is clear that our dear Jean-Jacques is seriously down amongst the low-life.[66] To say that 'everything that stems' from him is 'false, contrived, windy' and 'overblown' sounds risibly anodyne by comparison.[67]

63. See also *WP* 98-101. Rüdiger Bittner's editorial comments in Nietzsche, *W*, xi-xii and Kate Sturge's comment on translation in the same volume, xli, well alert the reader to the editorial shortcomings of the arrangement of Nietzsche's unpublished material in *WP*. This does not make Kaufmann's edition and Kaufmann and Hollingdale's translation unusable; it is just that it must be used critically and cautiously. For a helpful study of Nietzsche and Rousseau, see Ansell-Pearson, *Nietzsche*. See too his *An Introduction to Nietzsche as Political Thinker* (Cambridge: Cambridge University Press, 1994).

64. We read here a comprehensive indictment of Rousseau, who falls foul in so many respects that Nietzsche regards as critical. Yet we should not forget that, at an earlier stage, Rousseau is one of the eight thinkers mentioned with whom Nietzsche has 'had to come to terms when I have wandered long alone'. From these thinkers 'I will accept judgement, to them I will listen, when in doing so they judge one another', *HH* II.1.408. This is from the 'Descent into Hades', which concludes the first book of the second part of *HH* as we now have it.

65. For the allusion in 'Schopenhauer as Educator', see *UO*, p. 200. In *TI*, Rousseau is not just the 'first modern man', he is also the 'idealist and *canaille* in one person'. Along different lines, note Polanyi's acknowledgement of the epoch-making significance of Rousseau, *Knowing and Being*, 5.

66. These accusations are proximate to each other in *TI* IX.3 and IX.6. In the chronological order of contagion, it is the Germans who catch his disease from Rousseau, *WP* 92.

67. *TI* IX.6. Nietzsche makes both this comment and his comment about

Nietzsche believed that Rousseau did not merely abhor developed civilization (*W* 10 [53]), he also 'needed moral "dignity" in order to stand the sight of himself, sick as he was with unbridled vanity and unbridled self-contempt' (*TI* IX.48). The man made in Rousseau's image 'despises himself and yearns to transcend himself' (*UO*, 'Schopenhauer as Educator', 4). He longs for the 'good, natural man' as Nietzsche definitely does not (*W* 7 [46]). He must invent his 'good nature' to flee from his torments (*D* I.17). Where Barth perceives self-assertion, Nietzsche perceives self-loathing.[68] Rousseau combines 'self-contempt and heated vanity' (*WP* 98).[69] Barth is not aiming to produce a psychological evaluation of Rousseau. In principle, he could allow that the philosophical expression of hubris (or, to revert to his own vocabulary, absolutism) is grounded in self-loathing. If we take our bearings from the detection by post-lapsarian humans of their own shame (Genesis 3:7), we naturally encounter the question of whether we are to understand post-lapsarian, as opposed to pre-lapsarian, hubris as having its source in self-loathing.[70]

These remarks are not gratuitous. From a theological point of view, a question that is not only deep and complex but also extremely important emerges here if we take the Genesis account as providing a theological norm or abiding theological contribution. Was Nietzsche's hubris, whether he rightly detected self-loathing in Rousseau or projected it onto him, itself rooted in self-loathing? He was certainly extremely sensitive to the psychological ramifications of shame and extremely sensitive as a person. [71] In what is surely one of the most self-revealing things he wrote, Nietzsche concludes the third book of *The Gay Science* with eight answered questions, the last three of which are distinguished by the repetition of a single concept in the answer. '*Whom do you call bad?* – He who always wants to put people to shame. *What is most human to you?* – To spare someone shame. *What is the seal of having become free?* – No longer to be ashamed before oneself' (273-275). 'Shame, shame,

---

Rousseau's Germanness in the context of an attack on George Sand.

68. Nietzsche also finds in Rousseau 'self-intoxication': *HH* II.2.221. Note Nietzsche's interpretation of Rousseau in physiological terms, *D* V.538.

69. See too *WP* 100 on 'the absurd vanity of the weak man', which Rousseau exemplifies, and the description of Rousseau's mental state in this section.

70. That Adam and Eve's awareness of their nakedness entailed shame in 3:7 is inferred from Genesis 2:25. It is surely a short step to infer self-loathing from shame in this connection.

71. Williams, *The Shadow*, chapter 1. It is worth noting an observation Nietzsche made just before taking up professorial appointment in Basel as a young man: 'One is honest about oneself either with a sense of shame or with vanity', *SL*, 46.

shame', says Zarathustra '– that is the history of the human!' (*TSZ* 2.3). God in Christ '*had* to die: he saw with eyes that saw *everything* – he saw the depths and grounds of the human, all its veiled disgrace and ugliness. His pitying knew no shame: he crawled into my filthiest corner. . . . He saw *me* always: on such a witness I wanted to take revenge – or else not live myself' (*TSZ* 4.7).[72]

So speaks the murderer of God in *Thus Spoke Zarathustra*. Zarathustra 'was chilled to his very marrow'.[73] Here, we must firmly shut the doors of psychological analysis that are swinging open unbidden. Not that Nietzsche would have us shut those doors; for him, psychological analysis is a crucial component in philosophizing. 'Psychological observation can 'hit the bullseye . . . of human nature' (*HH* I.36).[74] Nor should theologians shut those doors; on the contrary, we shall understand actual human beings through psychological analysis far better than by merely deploying block and blanket concepts. However, psychological analysis is not for here and not for now. The question of Nietzschean self-loathing, like that of Cartesian dissociative identity or the fabric of Kantian moralism, must be parked. This is not to hide behind snide and craven insinuation. It is to acknowledge that my stated remit is the world of ideas.[75]

Because both Barth and Nietzsche were interested in Rousseau, it is at this juncture rather than in connection with Kant that I make a concluding point I could have made earlier. In the fifth book of *The Gay Science*,

---

72. I have – almost unpardonably – wrenched this from its literary context in which alone we shall appreciate the power of Nietzsche's drama.

73. The older Hollingdale translation of *Thus Spoke Zarathustra* (London: Penguin, 1969), first translated in 1961, uses the word 'chilled' both here and at the beginning of the next section (called 'The Voluntary Beggar', but not enumerated 4.8, as it is in the Parkes edition). This captures the continuation of Zarathustra's physical state. In using 'freezing' instead of 'chilled' at the beginning of the next section, Parkes is acknowledging the fact that the German phrase (*fror ihn*) differs from the earlier word (*fröstelte*), but the price we pay is that we lose sight of the root connection between the German words.

74. Nietzsche's partiality for the French *moraliste* tradition is philosophically important for him (*HH* II.2.214).

75. Psychologically, alongside the question shame – and, as phenomenological analysis would show, connected with it – the question of the relation of the attitudes of compassion and disgust in Nietzsche invites reflection. Having said in *GS* that his greatest danger lay in compassion, Nietzsche remarks in *EH* that '[*d*]isgust at mankind, at the "rabble", has always been my greatest danger' (49). In *OGM* 3.14, Nietzsche refers to 'the two worst epidemics that may have been reserved for us – against the *great disgust with human beings*! against the *great compassion for human beings*!'

Nietzsche asks the question: 'Where might science get the unconditional belief or conviction on which it rests, that truth is more important than anything else, than every other conviction?' (344). In answer, and in later work, he develops the notion that the valorisation of truth in Christianity (and in Plato) fostered a 'will-to-truth' and this turned against Christianity itself because the will-to-truth exposes the untruth of Christianity. 'This is how Christianity *as dogma* perished, by its own morality' (*OGM* 3.27). But, he immediately, says, 'this is also how Christianity as *morality* must now perish – we are standing at the threshold of *this* event'. Nietzsche continued to explore this. 'Among the forces cultivated by morality was *truthfulness*: this eventually turned against morality' (*WP* 5). As far as Nietzsche was concerned, this is not only applicable to Christianity but also to Rousseau, however little either was aware of it. For Nietzsche, if Christian truthfulness contains the seed of self-destruction by virtue of the fact that truthfulness entails the demise of Christianity, a moralism that celebrates autonomy will also contain the seed of self-destruction by virtue of the fact that autonomy entails the demise of morality. In relation to the second axis of this take on autonomy and morality, I do not immediately hear any dissent from Barth.

CONCLUSION

What exactly has the argument advanced in this volume achieved? Would we have emerged in the same place with regard to epistemology, morality, revelation and reconciliation if we had had trained our sights on, for example, Hobbes, Spinoza, Hume and Mill instead of on Descartes, Locke, Rousseau and Nietzsche? Even if we were to return a positive answer to that question, does my thesis accomplish anything more than a description of the relative roles of epistemological and moral factors in the formation of modernity, thus requiring further steps to demonstrate the further thesis that moral considerations trump all rival ones? Could modernity be analysed in terms of questions of theodicy, the rejection of immaterialism or the significance of pre-Adamites – just to give examples – so that matters putatively more basic than the moral came to light?[76]

The answer to these questions is a resounding: 'Perhaps, perhaps not and perhaps'. I have aimed to provide only a window or an angle on modernity. Not everyone and everything is visible through it. Other

---

76. The sprawling but vivid and instructive study by Frank E. Manuel and Fritzie P. Manuel of *Utopian Thought in the Western World* (Oxford: Blackwell, 1979) also, if sometimes indirectly, suggests a way of adding to this list.

windows may afford wider vistas. The substance of my contentions has been dictated by the *ad hominem* or *ad homines* nature of its argument and approach. It is theological adherence to Polanyi's observations on Locke and the modern mind that has set us off on the trail; it is this trail that has led us to where we have now arrived; its course has been selective and the end of the trail is not an absolute terminus on a certified high road. It is to theology that we should now turn, specifically to Colin Gunton. In doing so, we need to think beyond epistemology.

Chapter 5

From a Theological Point of View

According to Colin Gunton

The introduction to this volume included a remark about the substance of Colin Gunton's *Enlightenment and Alienation*. He described it as the 'intellectual ancestor' to his Bampton Lectures, *The One, the Three and the Many*, which was his crowning and most detailed investigation of the question of modernity.[1] It was in *Enlightenment and Alienation* that Gunton turned to Polanyi's observations on Locke, and I shall fill out and expand the brief comments made on it in the introduction before moving onto the Bampton Lectures. In the course of my discussion hitherto, I have alluded to other pertinent essays by Colin Gunton, but these two books are the principal contributions to the subject at hand. Therefore, while I may refer in passing to others from his pen, I shall not be delving systematically or comprehensively into his authorship as such. These two books are products of the late twentieth century and such is the effect of technological advance on our consciousness of time that what is of yesterday seems to be in the distant past. Consequently, one must unfortunately make a deliberate point of saying that interest in Gunton's work remains alive in this millennium.[2] Even if this were not

---

1.   For the reference to intellectual ancestry, see *The One, the Three*, 113, n. 1.
2.   A decade ago, at least three books appeared within the space of a year: Lincoln Harvey, ed., *The Theology of Colin Gunton* (London/New York: T & T Clark, 2010); David A. Höhne, *Spirit and Sonship: Colin Gunton's Theology of*

the case, his contributions remain noteworthy and helpful today in their own right. Although I highlight those aspects of his thought that are most relevant to my enquiry, this should not result in a distorted account of these two volumes. My enquiry in this volume will gain in depth only if I attend to Gunton's interest in epistemology in the context of his wider concerns.

In my introduction, I made reference to Gunton's ambition in *Enlightenment and Alienation* to explore the alienation characteristic of our time, for which trends of *thought* (I deliberately italicise that word) are causally responsible, and also to his averment that the Enlightenment encouraged a cast of mind whose first alienating characteristic 'is the tearing apart of belief and knowledge' (5).[3] This is the point at which Polanyi and Locke are mentioned. The second mark of alienation 'follows from it' and this is 'an exaggeration of the part played by the mind in the organization of its knowledge' (5). Here, we meet Kant, a figure more prominent in Gunton's two books than will appear from my following account, a thinker who, '[i]n a sense . . . made reason into God' (61). His resolution of the dualism of sense and reason that developed in the wake of Descartes' philosophy 'brings us to the heart of modern alienation' (25). It is a morally momentous dualism, for the 'divorce of the natural and moral universes is perhaps the worst legacy of the Enlightenment and the most urgent challenge facing modern humankind' (25). We should be doing an injustice to Gunton if we failed to note the social concern, encompassing the environment – theologically, God's creation – that underpinned his project. His ultimate aim in writing was practical. He was implacably opposed to the Enlightenment and any historically preceding drive to control the world. Like Polanyi, who made positive use of Augustine on this point, he wanted to make faith the basis of understanding. Unlike that of Polanyi, Gunton's faith is faith in a triune God. By contrast, unmoored from Trinitarian faith and situated in the

---

Particularity and the Holy Spirit (Burlington, VT/Farnham, England: Ashgate, 2010); Bradley G. Green, *Colin Gunton and the Failure of Augustine: The Theology of Colin Gunton in Light of Augustine* (Eugene, OR: Pickwick, 2011).

3. *Enlightenment*, 2. From now on, page numbers to these two volumes are usually placed in the text. Gunton does not actually define alienation when he starts talking about it, although he refers to Christians having 'alienated themselves from their own sources of life' (3). It is a general sense of being alienated from our world and from each other – an estrangement, we might say, though Gunton does not use that term – that Gunton apparently has in mind when he starts out his discussion. Although I summarized some of the argument of *Enlightenment* in my introduction, I am crafting it a bit differently here as my two accounts serve slightly different purposes.

broad Cartesian heritage, Gunton contends that Lockean reason and Kantian autonomy alike inhibit intellectual and spiritual health.[4] The kind of creation of values we witness in the work of Jean-Paul Sartre emanates from the errors that have developed along this trajectory (64).

Speaking as a theologian, Gunton was greatly and understandably exercised by the responsibility that theology bore for this historical development. He had no doubt that theology, along with philosophy, was well and truly implicated in it. How so? By adumbrating a doctrine of a God who is omnipotent and the necessity of whose existence is demonstrable. This generates a reaction. 'The scene, then, is set for the process we see taking place in Kant and Sartre, the process of the exclusion of God from the scene and his replacement by man' because humans feel crushed by the weight of omnipotent necessity, feeling neither free nor responsible, and philosophies of radical autonomy are a reaction to that (68). Theology is thus not only implicated, it actually bears a significant measure of responsibility for the philosophy that followed in its train. On the surface, it might look as though Gunton was more interested in theological *ideas* than those whom we tend today to call 'theologians', because it was theology in the hands of a philosopher that did the damage. 'The crucial part in the process was played by Descartes' (68). However, in his intellectual development, Gunton consciously made the move to thinking of such figures as Descartes and Locke as theologians.[5] Whichever way it is plotted on our disciplinary map, Cartesian doubt methodologically placed God in the intellectual hands of the doubting self. Consequently, the God who, according to the canons of methodological correctness, now emerged from human thought could easily morph into being merely a product of my thought. Atheism, including that of Nietzsche, issued from this process. Now, 'the idea of God is in itself alienating and dehumanizing' (69).

Here Gunton was indebted to the work of Eberhard Jüngel. The theological remedy to the problem at hand is a Christ-centred view of God, humankind and the world. The moral consequences of post-Cartesian developments are dire indeed.[6] For Gunton, the form taken by the Cartesian elevation of the mind, philosophically distinguished from

---

4.   Locke, in fact, got into hot water over his belief or unbelief in the Trinity.
5.   P.H. Brazier, ed., *Revelation and Reason: Prolegomena to Systematic Theology* (London: T & T Clark, 2008) 132-33, where Locke is also described as 'a religious thinker'. This source has to be treated with considerable caution and reserve overall; Gunton did not express and would not have expressed himself in print as he does in this transcribed series of lectures and responses.
6.   At this point, Gunton invoked the work of Michael Polanyi on Marxism (78-83).

the activity of the senses, issues in a morally devastating epistemology. Kant is just as bad as Descartes, but philosophically he inherited a problem that Descartes did much to conjure up, and Descartes resolved his own epistemological quandary with the aid of a mistaken notion of God.

It would be wrong to give the impression that epistemology eclipsed every other concern in *Enlightenment and Alienation*. 'Adam', says Gunton, 'as representative alienated man, did aspire to a kind of Kantian and Sartrian autonomy and self-assertion' (95). This does not immediately strike the ear as a diagnosis that picks out epistemology as the cause of the malaise of alienation, certainly not in the form of a skewed philosophy of perception in relation to mind. The three parts of *Enlightenment and Alienation* deal respectively with perception, freedom and (biblical) interpretation. Following Coleridge's lead, Gunton observes that 'there is a sense in which none of the problems is more important than the others' (85).[7] It would be unjust to ferret out and seize on epistemology so as to pull apart tendentiously what Gunton has joined together. Nonetheless, his preoccupation with the significance of the question of perception in modernity – the dualism of sense and reason, of perception and mind, about which he says much to which I have not alluded – at the very least makes epistemological questions second in importance to none in his analysis and, if we are disposed to press the question, they do seem to have actual priority.[8]

We do not have to press the question with regard to *The One, the Three and the Many*. Although it is not blatantly obvious from the beginning, epistemology was also at the heart of Gunton's concerns in these Bampton Lectures. In the fourth chapter, Gunton announced: 'Thus we come to what has long underlain the topics of this book, the epistemological dimension of the question of modernity' (106). Unsurprisingly, at the point at which he says this (the final chapter of the first part of the volume) he remarks that the foregoing chapters are evidence that 'the interest' in the volume 'is not focused on the problem of knowledge alone' (106).[9] As in *Enlightenment and Alienation*, in *The One, the Three and the Many* Gunton

---

7. Coleridge, the 'presiding genius' of *The One, the Three* (15), was second to none in diagnostic and constructive importance in the argument of *Enlightenment*. If anyone has primacy there, including over Polanyi, Coleridge does (85). It is because this is an exercise in quarrying Gunton's analysis selectively and not surveying his investigation dispassionately that Gunton on Coleridge is largely absent from my account.

8. In the case of Locke too, the question of the relation of mind to the world is bound up with the issue of belief and knowledge, *Enlightenment*, 5.

9. On the substantive and structural significance of this (fourth) chapter in his book, see early comments, 5.

developed the claim that theology bears a heavy burden of responsibility for the lamentable state of intellectual and cultural affairs that developed in the modern West. Specifically, the theology of creation occupies the limelight. 'Creation' and 'culture' are both mentioned in the sub-title of the volume, which is about the former even more than about the latter. The roots of the modern crisis with respect to the latter lie in a failure in Christian theological thought in relation to the former. It is a three-fold theological failure: a failure to (a) counter Platonizing suppression of the plurality and diversity of creation; (b) uphold the interpretation of the *imago Dei* in relational as opposed to rational terms or to interpreting it as opposed to the possession of other fixed characteristics; and (c) establish and sustain a continuity between human and non-human creation. [10] These failures helped to shape a culture of disengagement, the culture of modernity. Subscribing to Charles Taylor's dictum that '[i]t is of the essence of reason . . . that it push us to disengage', Gunton described disengagement simply as 'standing apart from each other and the world and treating the other as external, as mere object' (14).

Not unexpectedly, the finger is pointed early at Descartes, who initiated the destructive deracination of social order from the soil of metaphysical order. God is now displaced as the focus of the unity and meaning of being. And not unexpectedly, behind Descartes there is some bad theology going on. William of Ockham is near the bottom of the business. Denying the existence of universals, Ockham landed us with a world of discrete particular existences related neither to each other nor, as far as their intrinsic nature is concerned, to their creator. Central to Gunton's task is his desire both to correlate the struggles of the ancient with the struggles of the modern world in trying to figure out the metaphysical relation of the one to the many and also to indicate what is distinctive about the modern struggle. Ockham gave us a formless 'many' and robbed us of a relevant 'one', so the modern rational mind now had to take on the job of bestowing unity on an order in which God is marginalized. It accomplished its task to the point of effectively displacing God. This is the upshot of the modern struggle. The unity forged by reason has turned out be very dangerous. Even when religion supplies the principle of unity, the divine 'one' is oppressive enough in theology and life as long as the divine 'three' is neglected. The non-theistic 'one' extra-theologically generated out of rational human thought is worse still, its valorisation lending itself to totalitarianism, though Gunton grants that

---

10. For Gunton's positive contributions, see *Christ and Creation* (Carlisle: Paternoster, 1992) and *The Triune Creator: a historical and systematic study* (Edinburgh: Edinburgh University Press, 1998).

totalitarianism is complex. Where homogeneity is not demonic like this, it is crass, like Coca-Cola. The path of modern disengagement leads to such termini as these. 'Homogeneity is the spectre at the whole banquet of modernity, not merely in some of its courses' (44). Consequently, an amorphous modern 'many' reacts to a stifling modern 'one' and rises up against it. Either the many is suppressed or the one is fragmented and neither outcome is beneficial.

Ockham is near rather than at the bottom of the business because behind his bad move lie at least two figures who promoted the industry of making bad moves.[11] The first is Plato, for whom the particular lacked the significance it really does possess and, on top of this, whose concentration on human rationality translated in the hands of theologians who followed his lead into an interpretation of the *imago Dei* in unbiblical terms of rationality.[12] Those acquainted with Gunton's literature can expect no prize for guessing who the most eminent of those theologians is. It is the second figure, Augustine. What he should have done was to correct Plato. What he did was to welcome and incorporate him into Christian theology. Theology and the world needed Irenaeus instead. 'Irenaeus's triune God is one who creates by his will a particular world to which particularity is integral' (54). Augustine's God creates out of an arbitrary will; his world is not Christologically or pneumatologically formed and moulded in the Irenaean (and biblical) fashion. Gunton offers a thesis: '*The root of the modern disarray is accordingly to be located in the divorce of the willing of creation from the historical economy of salvation*' (55; his italics).

Ockham's isolated particulars featured at the expense of treating particularity as a relational phenomenon. Gunton tracked Blumenberg's argument that Ockham's denial of universals entails the eventual displacement of God because not only are Ockham's remaining particulars intrinsically unrelated to God, they also do not constitute any encouragement for a rational supposition that a Creator is required to explain their existence. The upshot is that God is ontologically disconnected from creation in that there is no correlation of any kind between God and creation. The ontologies of the divine and of the human are separated. God holds creation together by sheer will. In the end, nothing will be lost intellectually if God exits the intellectual stage because what Ockham assumes is God's creation is taken by irreligious successors to be perfectly

---

11. However, when it comes to displacing 'the centre of meaning and truth from the divine to the human creator', Ockham is at the very 'source . . . of the worst of the problems of modernity', Gunton, *A Brief Theology of Revelation* (Edinburgh: T & T Clark, 1995) 47-48.

12. Plato is not all bad for Colin Gunton; see 14-16.

self-explanatory. In darkening counsel like this, Ockham worked in the
shadow of Augustine. What a sombre shadow! Modernity rebelled against
the thought of a monistic God in accordance with whose arbitrary will
humans were placed in the world, their particularity crushed underneath
the undifferentiated unity of divine being and their understanding stifled
by the predestining arbitrariness of divine will.

Bad theology, then, has been historically efficacious. The 'distinctive
shape of modernity's disengagement from the world is derived from its
rebellion against Christian theology' (16). Epistemology suffers grievously
at the hands of theology. Gunton's observation on the centrality of
epistemology, reported earlier, is made in the chapter on 'The rootless will'
and the will has been a central concern of his before that. After Ockham,
'[t]he scene is . . . set for a contest of wills', a contest 'between the God who
appears to impart particularity only to that which is a function of his will,
and therefore to deprive particularity' of intrinsic meaning, and 'the human
will which appears to achieve independence only in the kind of arbitrary
self-assertion which appears to be the mark of divinity' (58). Displacement
means replacement; human subjectivity replaces the transcendent, displaced
God. God is not just abandoned; the predicates traditionally his are now
arrogated to his human creatures. The elevation of human reason is the
first step in this process. Godlike, it knows as God knows. The second step
is more sinister: human is now substituted for divine *action*. As Edward
Craig put it, 'we are being said to be not so much like God as a replacement
for God' (111). A faulty doctrine of God, especially God as Creator, has
much to answer for. The 'chickens truly come home to roost when the
attributes of the rejected deity are transferred to a multiplicity of individual
and unrelated human agents' (122). Healthy created particularity, which
a sound theology of particularity would have promoted and protected, is
forfeited and exchanged for innumerably socially diverse and conflicting
particulars. With regard to the wider epistemological scene, the historical
outcome is relativism and the denial of religious truth-claims. Therewith,
we are landed well and truly in the modern soup.

Disaster could have been averted had Augustine's Platonism not firmly
elbowed out Irenaeus' trinitarianism. Augustine's own trinitarianism went
as far as to advance a sense of the unknowability of God, thus piling on
epistemological haplessness every which way. As Gunton puts it elsewhere,
Augustine's particular way of understanding the Trinity lacked 'the
conceptual equipment to avoid a final collapse' into various heresies whose
entertainment ultimately re-established 'that deep-seated problematic
about the knowledge of God with which we now so anxiously wrestle.'[13]. In

13. 'The History. Augustine, the Trinity, and the Theological Crisis of the West' in

The One, the Three and the Many, when Gunton is occupied with a difficulty faced specifically by post-Kantians trying to propound a knowledge of God that stands the test of scepticism, atheism and agnosticism, he is keenly aware that Augustine's ontological and epistemological foundations are all wrong, the former on account of the way that he interprets the divine essence, the latter on account of his neglect of the divine economy. The whole is the product of misguided Platonising. The goodness of creation was demoted because of the perceived inferiority of the sensible world; its diversity was obscured because of interest in the created reflection of eternal, intelligible forms; its relational nature was marginalized because it wrongly interpreted the *imago Dei*.

'The divorce of the human from the world' is 'perhaps the most disastrous outcome of the modern project' (211). Dramatically, or at least pithily, stated, Gunton sought 'the roots of the modern crisis of culture . . . in an inadequate exegesis of the opening chapters of Genesis and the other biblical focusing of creation' (2). Historically, bearing down heavily on the exegesis is the dread Augustinian deity – Trinitarian in name but monistic in countenance. Belief in God as triune properly entails that the one and the many are ontologically equally ultimate. Belief in the triune God as creator enables creation to be the scene of a rationality we can apprehend, rather than being the deposit of arbitrary will. That is because the Word that unified creation from its inception has been manifested within that creation in Jesus Christ, and the Spirit who establishes us as relational beings in the world is the very one who binds Father and Son in a perichoretic unity at the ground of the world. That is why we should have drawn on Irenaeus and not on Augustine. Where Augustine understands creation theologically as an act of divine will absent any significant role for Son and Spirit, Irenaeus understands creation as a work undertaken by God's two 'hands', Son and Spirit, and their economic role in redemption unites palpably and indissolubly the orders of creation and salvation. [14] Trinity and cosmos are integrated as profoundly as can be. Theologically, nothing is more important.

The sorry tale does not end with malformed theology and epistemology. There is a crisis of language, too, sceptically unhinged from attachment to worldly objectivity. In connection with it, Gunton emphasised that 'the present situation has much to do with the development of certain patterns

---

The Promise of Trinitarian Theology (Edinburgh: T & T Clark, 1991).

14. Irenaeus is ubiquitous in *The One, the Three*, as he is elsewhere in Gunton's authorship. His importance is flagged up from the beginning of this volume (2). Yet, in the course of a discussion that promotes him, note Gunton's observation that he does 'not wish to idealize Irenaeus' (53).

of thought' (113). I shall be considering critically the place he gives to thought, although my remit in this volume constrains me to pass by the matter of language. What I particularly wish to explore is the way in which Gunton connects Christian theology and epistemological trouble. However, it would be remiss of me not to report first on the theological remedy that he concocts to cure our condition. We should not overlook the fact that his concerns in the Bampton Lectures remained as profoundly social and political as they were in their 'intellectual ancestor'. In particular, in these Lectures, Gunton talked darkly of totalitarianism prior to making a firm connection between it and epistemological malaise: 'Out of modern rationalism by a strange development there emerge both a Heraclitean flux and its *alter ego*, the totalitarian state that rushes in to fill the social and political vacuum' (112). For him, then, conceptual reconstruction is no academic or theological luxury. Where theology injured, there theology must heal. What bad theology did, good theology must undo. It needs to put back together God and the world for humans' sake.

The exercise of doing so takes the form of a Trinitarian resolution of the problem of the one and the many, a problem that Gunton has highlighted in the ancient world, but which appears with a distinctive turn in the modern world that has displaced God. Here, constructively, is where his essay is innovative. Essentially, its programme is to adumbrate a scheme of 'trinitarian transcendentals'. 'My concern is to develop a trinitarian analogy of being (and becoming): a conception of the structures of the created world in the light of the dynamic of the being of the triune creator and redeemer' (141). To achieve this, Gunton drew on Samuel Taylor Coleridge. Coleridge developed a concept of 'idea', a concept that is ontologically grounded and whose function is to regulate thought. The Trinity is the 'idea of ideas', that is, it is an idea – the supreme idea – that ought to govern and regulate our thought, including ideational thought. The Trinity is not a characteristic or mark of all being in the sense in which the search for the *vestigia trinitatis* was carried on from the time of the Fathers onward. Rather, what marks all being is the 'transcendental' and transcendentals are analogically grounded in ideas. Gunton's relatively abstract conceptuality – his notion of the Trinity as an idea that grounds transcendentals – is enfleshed as follows:

> The doctrine of the Trinity is in the first instance a way of characterizing the being of God, that is, of saying something of the kind of being that God is. It is thus idea rather than transcendental, for it is as a making known of something of the character of the source of all being, truth, goodness and beauty

that the doctrine of the Trinity is important. But although it is not transcendental, not a mark of all being, it yet generates transcendentals, ways of looking at universal features of the world of which we are a part and in which we live. The expectation is that if the triune God is the source of all being, meaning and truth we must suppose that all being will in some way reflect the being of the one who made it and holds it in being (145).

In its being, the world exhibits marks that derive from rather than directly correspond to the being of God as Trinity. The idea of God as Trinity generates transcendentals that correspond to it and that illumine the nature of reality. In this context, Gunton deploys the familiar trinitarian notions of perichoresis, substance and hypostasis. We pause with perichoresis just to show something of how Gunton proceeds in constructive theology. Perichoresis, to all appearances a 'speculative' concept, to all appearances 'useless' outside the strict domain of inner-trinitarian relationships, is actually a fruitful notion that embraces movement, recurrence, interpenetration and unity-in-variety.[15] It provides us with a perspective on the world, a world we should perceive as an order of things dynamically related to each other in time and space. The world 'is perichoretic in that everything in it contributes to the being of everything else, enabling everything to be what it distinctively is' (166). For example, Prigogine and Stengers observe that physics 'now recognizes that, for an interaction to be real, the "nature" of the related things must derive from these relations, while at the same time the relations must derive from the "nature" of the things' (172). Gunton observed that this 'is a statement of created, analogous, perichoresis'. He followed a similar strategy in elucidating the transcendental quality of 'hypostasis' and 'substance'; indeed, he picked out the significance of his innovation in relation to '*hypostasis*' (6). It all illustrates that 'the crucial and concrete realities of our world are the particular things – substances – which are what they are in virtue of being wholes that are constituted indeed of parts but in such a way that they are more than simply the sum of the parts' (201).

This is the theological remedy in a world where the history of attempts to understand the relation of the one to the many is dominantly a history of failure. The material substance of transcendental trinitarianism is not our quarry, but its remedial status is.

---

15. While in systematic theology, perichoresis normally has primary reference to the inner-trinitarian life of God, it was also historically deployed in patristic times to refer to the relationship of divine and human natures in Christ.

QUESTIONS

While the following concentrates on questions and disagreements, its
intention is not to exude a sense of comprehensive demurral. There was
much to be grateful for in this theologically statesmanlike essay, as in the
more slender *Enlightenment and Alienation*. The author's qualities as an
independent as well as a constructive thinker were on fine display in the *The
One, the Three and the Many*. Much in it is persuasive. The root theological
conviction that informs Gunton's analysis – viz., that in a world created by
the triune God, we may plausibly suppose that transcendentals will feature
– surely has much to commend it.[16] The general case for saying that the
relational nature of deity generates a correlative conceptual imperative
about how we understand both specifically human and wider cosmic
being is helpfully made. Colin Gunton executed the theological task *vis-
à-vis* modernity with the concern, dignity and sobriety appropriate to it.
He limned the contours of an elegant scholasticism.[17] An expository and
critical account of *The One, the Three and the Many* essayed independently
of the context in which I am considering it would discuss much that will
not be discussed below and convey a sense of its richness that has not
been conveyed above.

But what should we make of *The One, the Three and the Many* in the
context of our specific enquiry? Truth to tell, Gunton was not a reliable
commentator on the history of thought. This is clear if we step back to
Enlightenment and Alienation and read what he apparently assumes there
about Locke in connection with observations that he makes elsewhere.[18]

---

16.   This general theological instinct, though it can be played out in very different
      ways, has very recently been saluted by Alister McGrath, who remarked that
      '[f]or the Christian theologian, one attractive possibility is to see a Trinitarian
      "big picture" as having the intellectual and imaginative capacity to function . . .
      as meta-rationality', *The territories of human reason: science and theology in an age
      of multiple rationalities* (Oxford: Oxford University Press, 2019) 225.
17.   The reader who interprets this remark as a none too subtle slight on Colin
      Gunton's work may upbraid me with the gnomic Barthian warning: 'Fear of
      scholasticism is the mark of a false prophet', *Church Dogmatics* I/1, 279.
18.   See both *Revelation and Reason*, 43-49, and another text that must be treated
      with similar caution and for the same reason, *The Barth Lectures*, ed. P.H. Brazier
      (London/New York, NY: T & T Clark, 2007). In the former text, Gunton's
      description of Locke's 'rational' concept of reason compounds the problems
      with his wider exposition of Locke. In the latter text, it is most wrong-headed
      to say that Locke 'tended to play reason against revelation' before adding the
      inaccurate statement that he 'made revelation an inferior source of knowledge',
      53-54, although at least we can see what he is getting at with that second
      statement. (He later calls Lockean faith a 'second-rate form of knowledge',

In relation to the history of theology in particular, he also stood on very shaky ground. His treatment of Augustine has particularly drawn fire. He is scathing: 'I don't like Augustine. I think he is the fountainhead of our troubles.'[19] It is important to bear in mind that this remark was not designed for publication, but John Webster was surely right to interpret it as more than a matter of casual apostrophising.[20] Augustine is arraigned on the most solemn of charges. *The One, the Three and the Many* begins by quoting William Morris: 'Modernism began and continues, wherever civilization began and continues to *deny* Christ' (1), and these words are also quoted later (175). Augustine is profoundly, if unwittingly, complicit in the denial. Bradley Green has devoted a monograph to *Colin Gunton and the Failure of Augustine*. To my mind, he succeeds in showing that Gunton simply misreads Augustine at several points central to his (Gunton's) own discussion, although full allowance must be made for the fact that Gunton is also capable of striking a tentative interpretative note.[21] It certainly would have been a sad irony had Augustine deployed a doctrine of the Trinity as a weapon to help in combatting the fragmented incoherence of Classical culture only to sully it in helping to produce the fragmenting incoherence of modern culture.[22]

While adjusting his account of Augustine's thought would have entailed a radical revision of the way in which Gunton formulated his thesis, it would not necessarily have entailed its abandonment. It might still be the case that Augustine's thought, while innocent of the charges that Gunton laid against it, was so misappropriated in the Middle Ages that putative Trinitarian modifications of Platonism on Augustine's part dropped out of theological sight, leaving us with the naked villainy of Ockham. However, Gunton's historical theology is also controversial when we loiter for a moment in the days of Ockham. Consider Gunton's claim that '[t]he theological voluntarism and absolutism of the late Middle Ages generates a rejection of God and the transfer of his powers to man' (57). (Of course, this medieval theological voluntarism is supposed to derive from Augustine.) So depicted, God leaves humans without freedom and this opens the door

---

145.) Apparently, he was unmoved by my account of Locke, *Revelation and Reason*, 45.

19. *The Barth Lectures*, 97.
20. So John Webster in his essay on 'Gunton and Barth' in Harvey, ed., *The Theology of Colin Gunton*, refers to Gunton's Augustine as the '*fons iniquitorum*, from whose balefully inadequate Trinitarianism Barth never managed to extricate himself', 17-31, quotation on 23.
21. See *The One, the Three*, 72, n. 48; 120.
22. See, in general, Cochrane's account of Augustine in *Christianity and Classical Culture*.

to rebellion. I earlier noted that, in making this judgement, Gunton drew on the work of Hans Blumenberg. Yet, members of the theological guild have to reckon with Wolfhart Pannenberg's criticism of Blumenberg's analysis. Pannenberg found that Ockham (and Scotus) greatly *weakened* the absolutism of Augustine's double predestination and were far removed from any anti-human tendency. The force of Pannenberg's criticism extended beyond the matter of double predestination, on which Gunton did not focus. Gunton frequently drew Ockham into the picture, beginning with his *prima facie* endorsement of Blumenberg's account (28). A later reference to Ockham shows how important a figure he was in Gunton's account (46). On Pannenberg's interpretation, the theological voluntarism of the late Middle Ages was as interested in human as in divine freedom. He concluded that '[m]odern times did not come into being as the result of an act of human self-assertion against the absolutism of the Christian conception of God'.[23]

For our purposes, it does not matter whether Gunton or Pannenberg was historically right on divine absolutism and we should bear in mind that Gunton did not accept the whole of Blumenberg's thesis (85).[24] Certainly, the analysis I have attempted in this volume would have been helpfully deepened by an investigation of the claim that revolt against medieval theological voluntarism lies or largely lies behind modern human self-assertion. Such an investigation would have illuminated an important dimension of the opposition to divine reconciliation in history. Whatever the outcome of that analysis would have been, there is no doubting the historical importance of the role played by mistaken theological ideas.

---

23. *Christianity in a Secularized World* (London: SCM, 1988) 9. Amongst contemporary or recent theologians, Pannenberg would have made a good conversation partner in this volume, had space permitted it. His germane contributions over the years go back to an early essay on 'Types of Atheism and Their Theological Significance' where he explores the fact that '[t]he presupposition of contemporary Western atheism lies in the development of modern natural science and its mechanistic picture of the world, especially in eighteenth-century France', and yet he emphasised 'presupposition, no more than that'. When he gets on to Feuerbach, a major player, he reflects on 'man as an absolutely self-empowered being', a vision enabled but not produced by the scientific revolution. For all this, see *Basic Questions in Theology*, ii (London: SCM, 1971), 184-200, citations from 184-85 and 192.

24. See too Pippin, *Modernism*, 27-28 on Blumenberg. Pippin makes the important observation that '[o]n the assumption of modernity's self-defined legitimacy . . . the suspicion of a merely self-defined assertion of the will, in more traditional terms, a sceptical suspicion, will always be looming on the horizon', 25. In *The One, the Three*, Gunton more than once made favourable reference to Pippin's volume, though to an earlier edition of it.

Speaking generally, there is no need to quarrel with Gunton at that point and, when fundamental ideas of God and humankind are in view, we dare not underestimate their importance and the devastation that error can produce. Gunton's strictures on William of Ockham must be taken very seriously.[25] Only constraints of space, necessary boundaries to my discussion, have marked this out as forbidden territory.[26]

Yet, it is precisely in tandem with an appreciation of the theological solemnity and skill his proposal displays that critical questions about Gunton's theological response to modernity surface. Suppose that we grant *ad hominem* that theological error on creation contributed to the making of modernity, whatever the complicities of Augustine and Ockham (or, for that matter, Plato) in the whole business. What surely strikes the reader of *The One, the Three and the Many* is the weight Gunton attaches to mistaken *ideas* in his diagnosis of the malaise of Western thought.[27] What he did with the human will in this respect is illuminating. He accorded centrality to the role of will in modern formation and he was right to do so. However, in situating the significance of the *concept* of will within a worldview, we must not obscure its *existential* human centrality, and this tends to happen in Gunton's work.

As a way into this, it is worth pondering his treatment of divine unity. Although he was certainly cautious, somewhat uncommitted and certainly not simplistic, Gunton gave a sympathetic hearing to the claim that there is a connection between a strongly unitary view of deity and a unitary view of society that in the worst cases courts totalitarianism. Augustine, of course, is the main figure responsible for the appearance in Western thought of this unitary view of deity. How was Gunton reading Scripture here? Allow as much as possible for the view that there are intimations of the Trinity, or at least, of divine plurality in the Old Testament, in order to honour Colin Gunton's conviction that a theology of trinitarian plurality is constructively and remedially vital. Nevertheless, the social

---

25. See in this connection an important study by Michael Allen Gillespie that connects Ockham, Descartes and Nietzsche, and that both agrees and disagrees with Blumenberg, *Nihilism Before Nietzsche* (Chicago, ILL/London: University of Chicago Press, 1995).

26. It is also regrettable that we cannot explore the connection between Augustinian anthropology and scepticism: see Harrison, *The Fall of Man*, e.g., 11.

27. 'Ideas' here is used in the ordinary-language, not Coleridgean, sense. On this too, see Bradley Green, *Colin Gunton*, 170-73. Green indicates here that he is sympathetic to a cognate line of criticism that I took in my discussion of Gunton's volume in the first edition of *Revelation and Reconciliation*. See also Green, 'Colin Gunton and the Theological Origin of Modernity', 165-79, in Harvey, *The Theology of Colin Gunton*.

system of ancient Israel, directly or indirectly expressing the imperative to love one's neighbour as oneself, as well as the imperative to love God, was grounded in the nature and unity of the one Lord God of Israel. As the classical prophets preached the oneness of God, so they called for relationships in which the weakest and feeblest of Israelites – each an individual, particular creature – should be treated with the compassion of God. Theirs may not have been the post-apostolic Augustinian oneness, but Israel's vocation to care for the vulnerable particular is grounded in the *nature* and *ways* of the one God, understood as holy and merciful in character. If a post-apostolic Augustine should have learned one thing from that New Testament which lay between him and the witness of Old Testament Israel, it is that the more clearly the divine nature and ways are presented, the more manifestly the rebellious will breaks the cover of its concealment. When the workers in the vineyard note the coming of the son, the hostility encountered by the prophets of Israel is replicated and intensified (Matthew 21:33-38). When the human creature sets his or her will in opposition to God, whether with Adam or against Jesus, it is not on account of theological misunderstanding or misrepresentation, still less one much corrigible by theologically sound trinitarianism.

The post-apostolic Augustine certainly did learn the above lesson. Up to a point, Gunton owned the general perspective adopted here. 'Christianity is indeed offensive to the natural human mind; and yet', he added, 'it is often made offensive by its representatives for the wrong reasons' (1).[28] True; but the proportions in his account were not quite right. In his account, 'the wrong reasons' were over-rated. Suppose we agree on the need for an Irenaean corrective to Augustine if we want to repristinate and advocate a biblical trinitarianism along orthodox theological lines, accepting that both Irenaeus and the Cappadocians provide a healthier orthodoxy than did Augustine. Still, how can we maintain that the will to displace God is ever *in large measure* provoked by theological error on the matter of the divine will in a theologically erroneous scheme?[29] Sound trinitarianism is not going to make much of a headway against the kind of perspective offered by Nietzsche, e.g., on '*The greatest advantage of polytheism*' in *The Gay Science* (3.143). Of

---

28. I do not demur from Bradley Green's remarks on Gunton's *The Actuality of the Atonement*, as found in 'Colin Gunton and the Theological Origin of Modernity' in Harvey, *The Theology of Colin Gunton*, 173. Note also Gunton's observation that the church 'lives from the atonement' in *The Actuality of the Atonement: a Study in Metaphor, Rationality and the Christian Tradition* (Edinburgh: T & T Clark, 1988) 194.

29. See, e.g., *The One, the Three*, 119-23.

course, it depends on how large 'large' is. Certainly, we must oppose and try to revise a theology that makes divine oneness oppressive and the divine will inhibitive. Getting God and humankind right is important; not to do so is damaging; and in another context I should want not only to underline and emphasise this as strongly as possible but also to warn against the dangers of underestimating the fateful consequences of theological error. What Gunton does not adequately take into account is scriptural testimony to the fact that when we get God right, the rebellious human will is as heatedly active as ever. Do Gunton's words not ring strange on the biblically-attuned ear when he says that *after* Augustine's mistakes 'the scene was set for a contest of wills' (58)? Under optimal earthly conditions, right there in the garden, when neither genetics nor the environment were to blame, humans rebelled. (Very broadly speaking, I read Genesis 1-3 theologically rather than literally here.) A contest of wills erupted when, in the salient respect, the scene was everything but set for it – a scene pregnant with the prospect of continuously harmonious concord beyond the most blissful imagination. In 'a theological assessment of our era' (11), how can this not be underlined in an analysis of modernity? How can 'the *root* of the problem' (my italics) be theological (129-30)?

Bearing this in mind, what might at first blush look like a finical quibble turns out to be a little more than that. I refer to the following: 'Modern fragmentation is the result of seeing human life in terms of the competition of unrelated and arbitrary wills' (123). Or: 'Underlying much modern dogma there is the implicit belief that the prime reality is the human will' (219). Or: 'Without a philosophy of engagement we are lost' (15). Agreed. But the emphasis in these sentences is on people *seeing* life in terms of the competition of wills rather than on the actual competition of wills or on *belief* in the prime reality of the will rather than on its existential prime reality. On the back of the momentum generated by these considerations, we must ask: why an emphasis on a *philosophy* of engagement rather than on engagement? Theological beliefs can underlie existential attitudes but the biblical witness is rather adamant on the fact that it is also the case that existential attitudes underlie beliefs. Of course, this simplistic contrast between beliefs and attitudes is *ad hoc*; both the concepts in question and the substantive matter itself are complex and obviously call for proper differentiation and analysis. I presume that the point is clear without undertaking that analysis. The point is that there is room to wonder seriously whether Gunton wrongly appraises the texture of modernity and hence, to change the figure, approaches the healing task with the wrong implements.

Doubtless, a philosophy of engagement is required to counter disengagement, but if balance and proportion are not right in our appraisal of modernity, the quality of cultural engagement that a philosophical theology of Trinitarian transcendentals promotes will be overestimated. Doubtless, too, '[t]he development of a theology of the human and created – and fallen – particularity is one of the most urgent tasks of our time' (73) and a Trinitarian resolution is called for at this point, but there is a danger of overestimating how far theological concepts will go in healing. Colin Gunton wanted theological remedy to be practical and he was unquestionably sincere in his allegiance to Kierkegaard's observations in *Two Ages* when he reports on Kierkegaard's behalf that '[w]e talk about relationships instead of living them and "count . . . each other's verbal avowals of relation as a substitute for resolute mutual giving in the relation"'.[30] But his treatment of Augustine and will, even if Augustine has theological blood on his hands, meant that he insufficiently cleared himself of the suspicion that he believed that intellectual theological construction is, in principle, able to counter successfully the force of rebellious human will or, if we descend into banal formulation in the interest of expository caution, able to achieve much more than it really can.

If this were an essay on the question of theology, I should wish to nuance and refine this critique. The question of theology has arisen here largely because attitudes to theology and to epistemology are connected in Gunton's work. It seems either a stratospheric generalisation or a ludicrously bland truism to say that theology and epistemology are connected in Gunton's work by their orientation to the intellectual sphere, but it actually has a pointed application in this context. Where there is imbalance in our attitude to theology of the kind manifested by Colin Gunton, the question of epistemology is correspondingly exaggerated. Gunton's positioning of epistemology in his investigation of modernity is not quite right. Epistemological questions are unquestionably significant; no one doubts that the questions of meaning and of relativism in relation to truth, which Gunton described as mounted on the epistemological issue, are intellectually and culturally central. However, to argue in exactly the vein he did that bad theology has often generated epistemological error is to exaggerate the relative places of both theology and epistemology. For sure, the diabolical theology of the serpent seduced Eve into perceptual error and when perception goes wrong in this form and on this scale, then we do indeed enter an epistemological morass. Correspondingly, in

30.   *The One, The Three And The Many: An Inaugural Lecture in the Chair of Christian Doctrine*, printed at King's College, London, 1985, 5.

Enlightenment and Alienation, Gunton gave perception prominence in his account of the generation of the epistemological problem in Western thought. Nonetheless, mysterious as is the nature of human constitution, what stands out in the account of the human part in the Eden affair is that neither Eve nor Adam had a will strong enough to resist seduction. The twisted theology of the serpent was not *the* cause of the errant epistemology of its prey, because the latter is brought on by the misdirection of desire and the failure of will so that acquiescence in bad theology is a function of willing wilfulness. Eve misjudged what she saw because she misjudged whom to heed but hers was no more innocent misjudgement than it was innocent misperception. Misdirected desire skewed perception; skewed perception galvanised the will to misdirected action; will was the expression of desire at the level of decision. Epistemic error functioned to mediate between desire in contemplation and will in action.

This all comes to light in God's confrontation with the pair and the revelation that they are blameworthy and not innocent. All this is in Eden. Augustine and his epigones may have been theologically wrong, but Gunton would concede both that they were not guilty of diabolically sheer evil and that the victims of their putative theological error were not just innocent accomplices. Does not the innate disorder of post-Edenic human will mediate between putative theological error (for example, on creation) and ensuing epistemological error (for example, on methodical doubt)? If Gunton knew this in principle, he did not clearly enough demonstrate it in practice.[31] We can apply to him, *mutatis mutandis,* Michael Polanyi's words: 'It is not enough to show how a logical process, starting from an inadequate formulation of liberty, led to philosophic conclusions that contradicted liberty. . . . If ideas cause revolutions, they can only do so through people who will act upon them.'[32] We could finish the sentence another way and say: 'who will to act upon them'.

Of course, Gunton would not have denied this and, of course, he believed in the responsibility of individual perpetrators – Descartes and Kant alongside Augustine and Ockham – for any errors involved. A question stirred up by his exposition is: why were the putative intellectual faults of the medievals visited on them by moderns and not corrected by appropriating an internally healthier strand of the biblical or Christian

---

31. An exploration of what is entailed in David A. Höhne's contrast between Gunton and Bonhoeffer suggests the possibility of a parallel line of criticism: *Spirit and Sonship,* 69.

32. *The Logic of Liberty,* 103. Cf. Cochrane's observation that '[i]t is a truism to say that ideas have no legs; by themselves they do not march', *Christianity and Classical Culture,* 61.

tradition? Gunton explained early on that he was not offering 'primarily a genetic or causal account' of the 'modern condition', a 'neutral description of how and why modernity came about. . . . To be sure, causal influences will be suggested and analysed', he added, 'but the centre of interest is to be found in the kinds of attitudes, ideologies and forms of action that are characteristic of the era we call modernity' (4-5). Throughout his volume, he remained alert to the need to be sensitive on the question of historical causation. [33] It might be pedantic to try to keep count of when Gunton was and when he was not analysing his material in causal terms, and he steered clear of adopting an explicit logic of the history of ideas.[34] He felt no need to distinguish between arguing that Augustinian ideas are *conceptually* incapable of resisting epistemological crisis and claiming that they were an *historically* significant contribution.

The force of Gunton's analysis is somewhat abated as long as we do not know more precisely how Augustine's ideas reached their destiny, reaped their deserts, on his reading of Augustine. It is one thing to say that Augustine's Trinitarian theology is unsound and logically capable of generating a crisis in religious epistemology; it is another to ask about the conditions under which this logical possibility was historically actualized. Whatever someone *might* do with ideas, what historically *was done* depends on something other than just the ideas themselves. Gunton accused Augustine of harbouring a Trinity that floated free from the currents of divine economy in time, but he himself did not sufficiently fortify himself against the danger of floating conceptual relationships that drift free from historical currents in Western time. Whether we are speaking of historical genesis or contemporary forms of unbelief, causes have to be distinguished from reasons, motives for intellectual endeavour disentangled from concepts deployed in its course. With respect to Augustine, suppose, for the sake of argument, we lament an overdose of Platonism, chafe at introspection, resist predestination, regret the insufficiency of Christological control in the construction of this theism and so forth. Why did all this breed religious agnosticism rather than

---

33. See, for example, his citation of Amos Funkenstein's warning against confusing 'after' with 'because' when connecting the Christian doctrine of creation with the rise of modern science (109); cf. Green's citation of Gunton's remarks on Augustine and historical causality, *Colin Gunton*, 55.

34. Unlike Michael Buckley, whose study *At the Origins of Modern Atheism* (New Haven, CT/London: Yale University Press, 1987) he admired. For Buckley's studied approach to this question, we should pick up the discussion at p. 333. I am inclined to agree with Bradley Green's implicit reservation about David Cunningham's Hegelian interpretation of Gunton in this connection, *Colin Gunton*, 39.

constructive religious criticism? Those who stand theologically in the broad Augustinian heritage in their commitment to the heart-springs of thought and action will surely require a modification of Gunton's account of Augustine's villainy, even if they are dissatisfied with Augustine's trinitarianism and understanding of God as Creator. If Nietzsche and Dooyweerd are agreed on anything in this world, it is worth heeding them, and they are agreed on the heart-springs of thought.[35] Is all this not bound to put pressure on the suggestion that the Augustinian soul transmigrated into the atheistic body or, to switch philosophical allegiance, became the form of the atheistic body through the gland of a false trinitarianism?

While Gunton was aware of the perils of being sweeping, he swept too much and swept questionably. In practice, though perhaps not at all in principle, Gunton got close to acquiescing in Polanyi's belief that 'human thought represents the highest level of reality in our experience.'[36] It surely does not; human prayer attains a higher level and Gunton just as surely believed that. His practically excessive regard for conceptual thought and his overestimation of epistemological questions are of a piece. Both excesses threaten to put the conceptual formulations of conscious mind in the driving seat of human life, which is something of an irony given Gunton's strictures against an intellectualist interpretation of the *imago Dei*.

Gunton made some surprising concessions to Polanyi. He quoted, with apparent approval, Polanyi's description of his aim in *Personal Knowledge*: 'The principal purpose of this book is to achieve a frame of mind in which I may hold firmly to what I believe to be true, even though I know that it might conceivably be false (135)'. Gunton let this go uncritically without subjecting it to a theological test and elsewhere owned the statement.[37] He quoted Calvin on faith: 'a firm and certain

---

35. For a quick route into Herman Dooyweerd on this, see *In the Twilight of Western Christendom* (Nutley, New Jersey: Craig, 1972).
36. *The Study of Man*, 71. 'The craving to understand actuates the whole mental life of man' (84).
37. *Revelation and Reason*, 25. Cf. 'I Know That My Redeemer Lives: A Consideration of Christian Knowledge Claims' in Gunton, *Intellect and Action: Elucidations on Christian Theology and the Life of Faith* (Edinburgh: T & T Clark, 2000) 61. Actually, Polanyi had a poor understanding of Christianity. His comment that 'Christianity sedulously fosters, and in a sense permanently satisfies, man's craving for mental dissatisfaction by offering him the comfort of a crucified God' in *Personal Knowledge*, 199 is completely adrift, as is the association of Christianity with '[a] fiduciary philosophy' that 'does not eliminate doubt, but . . . says that we should hold on to what we truly believe,

knowledge of God's benevolence toward us, founded upon the truth of the freely given promise in Christ, both revealed to our minds and sealed upon our hearts through the Holy Spirit' (135, n. 8). It is little short of astonishing that, apparently not intending a British understatement, he remarked that Calvin says this 'not meaning quite the same thing' as Polanyi when the latter opines that 'all knowledge derives from a kind of faith'. Calvin and Polanyi most certainly do not mean the same thing. Whatever overlapping meanings there are, Polanyi's ruminations on faith in general epistemology, however religious faith may be assimilated to that, connect faith and knowledge in a way quite different to the way in which Calvin did, who was concerned specifically about Christian faith.

Did Gunton's concentration on the relationship of antiquity to modernity cause him to narrow his gaze too much to a point where the basic substance of biblical teaching on faith and will was not prominent enough in his field of vision? It may seem singularly perverse to speak of Gunton narrowing his gaze in a work of such wide scope. He certainly concentrated hard on the relationship in question. He observed that '[i]t is widely agreed that the two poles of the thought of Protagoras, the first and greatest of the Sophists, were theological agnosticism . . . and epistemological and moral relativism' (106). There are signs that, in his ruminations on the duo of theology and epistemology, and his concomitant ruminations on moral crisis, Gunton effectively collapsed moral and epistemological relativism. If that was the case, it was a mistake; it is one thing to associate them, quite another to assimilate the one to the other. It is both interesting and noteworthy that he approvingly quoted Charles Taylor early in his book: 'Descartes' ethic, just as much as his epistemology, calls for disengagement from world and body and the assumption of an instrumental stance towards them' (13).[38] It is interesting on more than one score. For one thing, partial as he was to aspects of Taylor's analysis, Gunton did nothing with Taylor's contrast between Descartes and Montaigne though, admittedly, we should not expect him to do everything.[39] For another, although we should not

even when realizing the absurdly remote chances of this enterprise, trusting the unfathomable intimations that call upon us to do so', *Personal Knowledge*, 318. There is sustained error in the discussion on 'Religious Doubt' in that volume (279-86) and it is not surprising that the last sentence of *Personal Knowledge* is wrong! Chapter 10 of Polanyi's *Meaning* is revealing, although Mitchell reports Torrance's caution about the rendering of Polanyi's thought by his authorial collaborator, Prosch, in *Michael Polanyi*, 119.

38.   These are the words that precede those I earlier mentioned Gunton had quoted in Taylor's work: 'It is of the essence of reason . . . that it push us to disengage.'

39.   He picks Taylor up again in 203, n. 36.

rush to translate Gunton's approval of Taylor in this respect into a flat statement that he (Gunton) also thought that ethics mattered as much as epistemology in the formation of modernity, Gunton's treatment of Descartes elsewhere certainly makes that statement plausible. Likewise, his stance on Kant would support such a claim. If this interpretation of Gunton goes through, then it is regrettable that he did not clarify his position and that he treated epistemology as he did.

What *did* Gunton do with Descartes elsewhere? When Taylor observed that Descartes' ethic calls for disengagement, he had particularly in mind 'an instrumental stance' on Descartes' part towards body and world. Seizing on this phrase, Gunton naturally glossed it in terms of using 'the other as an instrument, as the mere means for realizing our will' (14). Since this includes the human other and not just the otherness of the world or body, this is a most grave indictment of Descartes. However, it is 'the world' that Gunton apparently had foremost in view and our 'technocratic attitude' towards it. Referring again to Taylor, Gunton regarded the treatment of 'matter as merely the intrinsically meaningless object of our instrumentality' as originating in a tradition that began with Descartes (207). Given that the scandal of our treatment of the created order so weighed on Gunton's mind, we are scarcely going to encounter an indictment of Descartes more serious than this. The Cartesian will looms as darkly as, if not darker than Cartesian epistemology here. It is difficult to read Gunton without judging that he was open to reading Descartes' epistemology as a product of Descartes' will. If he was, it both usefully integrates the different things he had to say about Descartes and conforms to some of the judgements about the centrality of the Cartesian will that I rehearsed in the first chapter of the book. However, the surmise cannot be a confident one, for Gunton did not in either *Enlightenment and Alienation* or *The One, the Three and the Many* explicitly relate epistemology to will in Descartes in this way. Had he done so, perhaps exploring the proposition that thinking *is* willing for Descartes, it would have gone some way to reduce the distance between his and my interpretation of modernity. As it stands, my judgement remains that he overrated epistemology.

Gunton applied the descriptive 'Cartesian anxiety' to the Cartesian question about certainty (135) and it is a salutary reminder of our responsibility to see pride of will as only one side of the modern and, for that matter, ancient coin. On at least two occasions in *The One, the Three and the Many*, Gunton made reference to Babel. The first was when 'individual mind and will' displace 'the characteristically monistic God of medieval antiquity' in an attempt 'to wrest from God the prerogatives of absolute freedom and infinity . . . in effect a new Babel' (124). The second was also in connection with monism and with talk of 'the warring Babel' that emerges from a 'fragmented' rather than a 'relational . . . plurality' (187). If Babel and Descartes enter our field of vision at one and the same time, perhaps it is the thought of technology or technocracy that will connect them. 'The building of a massive structure that presumes definite technical discoveries and mathematical skills, as well as the common will of a group of people who think it necessary to erect the building . . . in essence anticipates the possibility of a development that would be realized only in the technical age in a way that would affect the whole of humanity.[40]

According to Gunton, under the influence (pre-eminently) of Descartes, the human mind became the locus of certainty, but it cannot sustain its ambitions and such knowledge as it thinks it possesses becomes fragmented in late modernity or postmodernity. So the unity of the Babel enterprise is shattered. Gunton's reference to 'anxiety' was appropriate in this connection. The builders of Babel declared: 'Come, let us build ourselves a city and a tower with its top in the heavens, and let us make a name for ourselves, lest we be dispersed over the face of the whole earth' (Genesis 11:4). In this connection, von Rad aptly observed that the desire for fame and anxiety are the driving forces of culture.[41] Stepping further back behind it all, in *The Concept of Anxiety*, Kierkegaard gave an intricate exposition of anxiety in relation to original and originating sin. On any account of the opening chapters of Genesis and in any sustained account of the Christian Scriptures, matters epistemological are demonstrably so hedged about with other matters that they should not be so plucked out or re-contextualised in an account of modernity that we forget where they were originally embedded.

So What About Epistemology?

Perhaps the case for making some extremely bland, general and cursory remarks on epistemology as we draw this chapter to a conclusion dies a death of the thousand qualifications portended by this adjectival cluster. Nonetheless, not to make any remarks seems to border on dereliction of duty, and conscience makes cowards of us all.

In the New Testament, faith and knowledge, or believing and knowing, are not sharply distinguished. Peter's confession to Jesus – 'We have believed, and have come to know, that you are the Holy One of

---

40.   Claus Westermann, *Genesis 1-11: A Commentary* (Minneapolis, MN: Augsburg, 1984) 554.

41.   *Genesis: a commentary* (Philadelphia, PA: Westminster, 1961) ad loc.

God' (John 6:69) – does not substantively reflect peculiarly Johannine epistemology even if its report reflects peculiarly Johannine interests and the formulation is distinctive. According to its testimony in the Hebrew Bible, Israel came to know God through its religious experience. Awareness of God through the world is involved, to which the Wisdom literature, including the Psalms, bears witness, but the centre of Israel's experience is compounded of divine revelation in divine speech and in externally visible action. If experiences of hearing God speak had not been joined by seeing anything remarkable in the way of events, there would have been nothing to validate the experience of God having spoken – the equivalent of concepts without percepts would have been empty. If remarkable things in the way of events had been seen but without any accompanying word from God, they should have been unintelligible – percepts without concepts are blind.[42] In the New Testament, this pattern is maintained but Jesus is now the earthly embodiment of God. He speaks, he acts and, in a solemn revelation of God, he suffers. The resurrection is the hinge on which the New Testament witness turns; it is act interpreted by word.

If we track the New Testament witness, the content of divine revelation is not derived from reason. In one respect, this is true by definition but, more to the point, it cannot be so derived any more than any beliefs about anything that has happened in history originate in reason. Reason's role with regard to historical claims is adjudicatory, not initiative; in that sense, historical truths are not 'truths of reason'. We do not have to agree with Locke that reason comes to its work with an empirical *tabula rasa* to agree that he is correct on the general point that reason is not the *source* of religious (Christian) truth but has a role to play in the *assessment* of biblical testimony. The New Testament writers themselves strongly encourage assessment of their testimony in evaluating their witness. Luke undertakes to write his Gospel in order for Theophilus to have an ordered eye-witness basis for teaching already received (Luke 1:1-4). In light of a familiar atheist objection that Christianity celebrates blind faith, we might with – I hope – pardonably slight exaggeration say that Luke wrote his Gospel in order to confute that idea and to make sure that Theophilus did not fall prey to blind faith. When, according to John's witness, Jesus pronounced blessed those who believed without seeing, he clearly meant believing without seeing with one's own eyes (John 20:29). The eyes of others, the eyewitnesses, are the basis of their belief and, therefore,

---

42. I am borrowing, of course, from one rendering of Kant's phraseology about concepts without percepts being empty and percepts without concepts being blind.

indirectly the basis of ours. When Paul offered to supply witness names, addresses, mobile phone numbers and assorted web links to Corinthian doubters that Jesus had been raised from the dead, he was displaying a consistent attitude (1 Corinthians 15:5-8). 'Basis' is important; a basis for faith is not the same as the vital faith itself.

If theologians eager to stay close to the Bible wish to interpret and respond to modernity on matters epistemological, two questions immediately and naturally arise. Firstly, how did the biblical witness become discredited in the course of Western history? Secondly, how can it be made credible again? Those who implicitly or explicitly emphasize moral self-sufficiency in responding to the former question should by no means neglect the range of intellectual considerations put forward by sceptics and unbelievers. If thinkers, whether favourably or unfavourably disposed – or avowedly noncommittal – towards the New Testament exercise historical reason in an attempt to evaluate critically the New Testament testimony, there should be no *a priori* theological objection to that, no barrier erected at its entryway to make it a no-go area. At the same time, Christians will, along with others, though with some distinctive reasons, query the proposition that historical reason is scientifically neutral, certainly where self-involving matters are at stake. The great 'masters of suspicion' – Marx, Nietzsche and Freud – will go along with them there, for all their complicity in 'rationalist' rejections of Christianity. And, of course, all concerned will realise that questions about the intrinsic accessibility to historical reason of cardinal features of the New Testament testimony immediately arise when we actually embark on its testimony as a whole; its testimony is the proper subject of critical historical investigation regardless of any *a priori* ideas we have about the suitability of historical reason for the task of investigating the kind of material we find in the New Testament.

Historians of thought who are shaped by the contours of biblical testimony will thus look out for at least two germane things: firstly, the movement of Western will or desire in a direction away from Christianity and, secondly, the intellectual conditions for critical doubt about the Bible. The former is a cultural shift. On the individual level, according to biblical testimony, humans are innately disposed to rebellion, rejection, distaste or vacillation in relation to God. Historically surveying European culture, it is not surprising if the late Renaissance or the Italian Renaissance become the object of our scrutiny if we scan the horizon for signs of theologically or religiously restless will and desire. Nor is it surprising if the Renaissance or at least the late Renaissance should occupy a place of interest in relation to the second question, the changed intellectual conditions. It would not be surprising if both things under consideration belonged to the discernibly identical stage of history. Reventlow's analysis has much to commend it.[43]

What would have been the correct theological response to incipient late Renaissance murmurings about Christianity? Those of us who are faced today with the demanding task of working out how to respond to anti-Christianity in our time will find this question a trifle comic, laced with a rather naïve presumption about the wisdom of hindsight. Perhaps that is a tad too cynical. So we might agree to ruminate on whether response should have begun with dogma instead of doubt or with broadly cognate Barthian affirmation of revelation instead of a rationalist apologetic. It is a little late in the day to begin an essay on epistemology in this volume, but let no one accuse this author of failing to sustain his slow descent into blandness.[44] It is possible at one and the same time to take seriously both the fundamental nature of the heart's spiritual or religious orientation or disposition and the empirical investigation of the Gospel witness, to take seriously both a scepticism about the universality of reason and the project of a rational defence of Christian belief. Assuredly, the question of God, whether or not God is believed in, is self-involving – we have an interest in its determination. It would be foolish to ignore Pascal's reasons of the heart and their alternatively distorting or purgative effect on reasons of the head. However, inasmuch as reasons of the head are involved at all, the case for believing the Gospel witness should be made. Speaking very generally, we should both claim that reason does not function as it should and describe what it would do if it were to function more as it should.

As for scepticism about the universality of reason, there is no need to affirm or deny it inflexibly from a strictly theological point of view. Of course, much depends on what 'reason' is supposed to comprehend. In categorical affirmations or denials of its universality, there is an element of judgement involved, based on wide-ranging intelligence on what is either known or claimed to be known across many spaces, times and

---

43. I am not sure whether Gunton discusses the Renaissance much in the course of all his writings. To all appearances, he is at best non-committal on whether it lies at the 'root of the modern world's abandonment of Christianity', and actually seems to discourage that belief: 'Christ, the Wisdom of God: A Study in Divine and Human Action' in Stephen C. Barton, ed., *Where Shall Wisdom be Found? Wisdom in the Bible, the Church and the Contemporary World* (Edinburgh: T & T Clark, 1999) 252.

44. Mandy Rice-Davies, who earned public notoriety in connection with a political scandal in the United Kingdom in the last century, reportedly described her life after it as 'a slow descent into respectability'.

cultures. Reason is historicised, but, in principle, it may be awakened
to uniform rational substrata that pervade geographical spaces and
historical times , if not universally, at least much more extensively than
is publicly apparent. Lacking the acquisition of such intelligence, I can
give *my* reasons – better, the church can give *its* reasons – for believing
the Gospel account, irrespective of whether you say: 'But they can
never be more than *your* reasons' or say: 'Reasons which validly hold
for you ought to do so only if they hold for *anyone* willing to reason'.
An Academic scepticism that nothing can be known is fairly met with
a Pyrrhonic scepticism that indicts the Academic proposition on the
ground of its self-refuting or unwarranted dogmatism, and it is a moot
question whether we should try to unpick or whether, if we should, we
could succeed in unpicking what looks like the ensuing sceptical knot.
If we are inclined to be indifferent to the philosophic resolution of the
sceptical question, it is because we are aware that we can suspend belief
but not suspend action. [45] Either we are all impelled to act without any
beliefs that are immune from sceptical assault, in which case Christians
are, in principle, no more vulnerable than anyone else to the accusation
of intellectual vacuity, or we should ask those who have the capacity to
do so to give an account, open to scrutiny, of the basis of beliefs on which
they act, in which case Christians ought to take unhesitatingly to the
level playing field.

The foregoing discussion may generate the worry that *fides historica*
and talk of 'belief' are absorbing existential faith. This worry must be laid
to rest. If faith reaches the kind of assurance that led the New Testament
writers to think of it as a form of knowledge, this is not the automatic
result of empirical demonstration or an exercise in propositional
assent. There is a vital distinction between having intellectual reasons
for believing and the cause of psychological assurance. If we uphold
the significance of the former, we are attending to just one strand of
the matter, to the persuasion of mind as far as is possible and as far as
our capacities go. For the water of probabilistic reasoning to become
the wine of religious certainty, God the Holy Spirit must be causally
at work in particular illumination. This is not the 'enthusiasm' feared
by Locke because reasons can be given. But religious certainty does
not follow directly or causally from the operations of reason. Further,
Jonathan Edwards' observation: 'Reason's work is to perceive truth and
not excellency', opens up whole vistas in discussion of epistemology that
I cannot begin to describe.[46]

---

45. Pascal again, with his celebrated wager in light of scepticism, *Pensées* 2.II.
46. 'A Divine and Supernatural Light Immediately Imparted to the Soul by

To deny the possibility of a revelation from God that can assure us of its truth is to become subject to the strictures of those sceptics who argue that the denial is itself a piece of unwarranted dogmatism, even if affirming revelation is subject to the same criticism. Setting aside the general epistemological question of scepticism, can it be categorically denied that God can so reveal himself that someone, somewhere can with justification claim to know his truth? If the answer is 'yes, it can be categorically denied', what would account for that? It would be accounted for if there were no God to reveal himself. It would be accounted for if there were such a God, but that God did not want to reveal himself. It would be accounted for if there were such a God and that God wanted to reveal himself, but lacked the power to do so. In all three cases, reason would have to be given for those beliefs, else dogmatism underlies the denial that God can so reveal himself that someone, somewhere should with justification claim to know his truth. If the battle be fought on empirical terrain with respect to the historical grounds for Christian truth-claims or on scientific terrain with respect to the scientific case against Christian (or religious) truth-claims, then, let battle commence. But our commencing ought not to be taken as concession that human reason is neutral, universal or unbiased. We are merely saying that it has its place.

Here endeth the blandness.

BACK TO DESCARTES AND COMPANY

Was Locke or Descartes, then, at the bottom of the modern malaise? Here beginneth a new phase of blandness, mercifully brief in the form of a conclusion to this chapter. Locke was not. Some reason has already been given for that conclusion, but we might add that his epistemology, even if we cannot agree with its general thrust, was not necessarily a very damaging error on the scale we have considered. Locke may have assumed the universality of reason and argued for a philosophical empiricism in ways from which we should dissent, but by proceeding both to limit very strictly how far that reason could take us and to deploy empirical argument in relation to Christianity along lines generally continuous with those found in the New Testament, he absolved himself of any fundamental guilt.[47] With Descartes, things are a bit different.

---

the Spirit of God, Shown to be Both Scriptural and Rational Doctrine' in Jonathan Edwards, *Sermons of Jonathan Edwards* (Peabody, MA: Hendrickson, 2005) 87-105, quotation from 103.

47. The questions that, according to Locke, we should ask about historical witness are perfectly in order from the standpoint of the New Testament witness itself.

If serious religious conviction really is dependent on the strength of the structure that he built on universal doubt, there is good reason to sympathise with those who say that we are in trouble. Had Descartes shown Lockean interest in exploring the grounds of Christian belief or Pascalian sensitivity to the place of action in relation to doubt, we might worry less about his universal doubt. We might even grant it as an acceptable heuristic moment in epistemological exploration on the ground that he had eggs (i.e., methods of accessing knowledge) in other baskets. As it is, I believe that there is less scope for adducing mitigating circumstances for Descartes' epistemology than there is in the case of Locke. I have tried to indicate both what lies behind him, in the form of Montaigne and scepticism, and what lies beneath his reason, in the form of will. It is important to read Descartes in that light.

Colin Gunton was interested in reconciliation and redemption, as he was in revelation.[48] For him, the doctrine of revelation was a function of the doctrine of salvation, of the 'divine saving economy'. There are statements where he locates salvation in relation to revelation, soteriology in relation to epistemology in what is to my mind a theologically congenial way.[49] We shall not examine what Gunton's way was, but we shall conclude this work by turning to the question of reconciliation.

See *Essay*, 4.15.4.

48. E.g., *The One, the Three*, 217, n. 5; 230; 'Towards a Theology of Reconciliation' in Gunton, ed., *The Theology of Reconciliation* (New York, NY/London: T & T Clark, 2003); *The Actuality of the Atonement*.

49. *A Brief Theology*, 18 and 110-11, where revelation is a function of the 'divine saving economy'. Cf. *Revelation and Reason*, 33: 'Revelation . . . is part of the function of the doctrine of salvation.' At this juncture, he affirms in even more decisive terms that this is Barth's position.

Chapter 6

Towards Reconciliation

Can and should Christian theology today continue to maintain that God has both revealed and effected in history a way of reconciliation? Although a distinction and contrast between revelation and reconciliation has characterised my discussion hitherto, the objective has been to highlight the distinction and contrast between matters epistemological and those that turn on the implications of moral self-sufficiency or autonomy. Considered on their own theological terms, while revelation and reconciliation are obviously conceptually distinct, contrast is artificial because theologically they are closely associated when it comes to history. Conceptually, revelation in history need not entail reconciliation in history but, theologically, claiming the latter always involves claiming the former. News of reconciliation comes as revelation. As for the question posed in the first sentence of this paragraph, it may appear to be both vacuous and futile. Vacuous because the phrase 'a way of reconciliation' is very general and vague; until flesh is put on it, the question seems impossible to begin to answer. Futile because we broke off our history with Nietzsche and responding to the question therefore involves executing a leap from Nietzsche's time to our own, landing in the twenty-first century with no attention to the twentieth or to the opening years of our millennium.

Both objections can be parried. As for vacuity, a consistently general reference to an event of reconciliation in history has been sufficient to carry the argument so far and the relative generality of the reference is not adequate reason to dodge the question entirely in a volume professing interest in theology. As for futility, it is certainly true that the selective historical sorties essayed up till the time of Nietzsche would require a supplementary enquiry into the intellectual history of the years between Nietzsche and the present if our interest were in the theological *status quaestionis* in the culture and context of our time. That, of course, has not been our interest. Yet, Colin Gunton wrote the contributions I have discussed at the end of the second millennium, so although my more detailed historical interest stopped with Nietzsche, who died in 1900, engaging with Gunton has meant looking at arguments propounded in a literature written the best part of a hundred years after Nietzsche's death by an author thoroughly contemporary in his concerns. At all events, it is appropriate to conclude with some *ad hoc* theological remarks on the possibilities of belief in reconciliation in history with an eye on the contemporary scene but without studied engagement with third-millennial theology in its wider context.

I have noted the obvious fact that this volume has scarcely touched on what the notion of reconciliation in history involves in detail but, whatever it does involve, the notion has historically been explicitly or implicitly correlated to belief in an historical fall. Does that mean that, whatever we can positively do today with reconciliation in history, we have to cut it free from its historical moorings? For some time, it has been widely held that no belief in historical reconciliation that involves correlative belief in an historical fall can be credible today. If that is the case, we have a negative condition for what constitutes an acceptable contemporary theological offering.

However, belief in an historical fall still has both stout and informed defenders.[1] Presumably, at least four components need to go into a credible proposal that we adhere to belief in an historical fall if the ambition is to think biblically and scientifically at the same time. First, Genesis 3 must be read as depicting an historical fall but not in a literal form. In the Scriptures of the Old and New Testaments, spatio-temporal events are portrayed in a number of ways, such as in the form of chronicle, literal account, symbolism or parable. Genesis 3 need not exemplify one of those four forms, which are just general examples of variety, their literary genres being informally described. But Genesis 3 stands at the head of a

---

1.   See, e.g., R.J. Berry and T.A. Noble, eds., *Darwin, Creation and the Fall: Theological challenges* (Nottingham: Apollos, 2009); Hans Madueme and Michael Reeves, eds., *Adam, the Fall and Original Sin: Theological, Biblical and Scientific Perspectives* (Grand Rapids, MI: Baker, 2014).

canon that embraces variety of that kind in its depiction of history and it suffices here to note the broad biblical availability of a pictorial account of events that, by definition, belong to the temporal order.

Second, we should need to maintain that the theological point of Paul's appeal to Adam in connection with Jesus Christ is basically or entirely undisturbed by positing a pictorial representation for the fall in this way (Romans 5:12-14). Of course, the conviction that Jesus was a man in history who died on a cross and rose bodily from the grave does not depend on a corresponding literality in the Genesis account of the fall. It is widely believed that it does not depend on the historical, let alone the literal, nature of the Genesis account either. However, we are not asking at the moment the general theological question of what is required in the way of history in Genesis in order for Paul to make his point successfully, but specifically whether Paul's explicit claims are affected if it is claimed that the historical nature of the fall is described in pictorial terms in Genesis 3. Those who wish to stand in theological succession to the apostle would have to argue that neither the fact nor the significance of the death of Christ is threatened if Genesis is pictorial history.

Third, when, in Darwin's wake, we posit cosmic death and disorder as phenomena prior to the appearance of humans on earth, we need to make clear that this does not invalidate commitment to that transgression in history which has commonly gone under the name of 'the fall'. The feeding habits of the animal kingdom are not described in Genesis 1, but the fish, birds and land animals introduced there presumably go about their business in the way that we know them to do. Further, the appearance of a seductive serpent in the garden of Eden seems to flag up the possibility of disruption in the cosmic order independently of human agency. However, the whole account is very condensed (whatever its genre), thus observing a rule of silence, and here we need do nothing more than affirm that there is no obvious collision between a Darwinian and biblical picture of death and disorder. Of course, the Darwinian picture raises questions in the area of theodicy, and those questions are undeniably of central importance for theology, but we do not have to address them here, still less offer provisional answers.

Fourth, we should underline that human transgression against God is not in principle amenable to scientific investigation. Sin has neurological correlates, just as the appearance on earth of religious or creaturely awareness, or awareness of religious or moral accountability *coram deo*, had and has neurological correlates. But the substance of religious awareness escapes scientific perception and is not in its nature neurologically detectable. We are headed here into the thick of questions of mind-brain identity and the set of issues that swirl around the question of dualism and its rejection. The language of 'neurological correlates' inescapably lands us there. But even if we minimize the direct theological – as opposed to scientific or philosophical – stake in reaching a dogmatic decision on the range of questions surrounding physicalism, dualism and all points in between, belief in the human fall surely requires both an affirmation of its neurological implications and a denial of its direct scientific cognizance.

Of course, even if these four sets of claims are individually and jointly plausible and defensible *prima facie* as far as they go, the question is how far we can plausibly go in fleshing them out in concrete biological, philosophical or theological detail. The devil in these claims (whether or not envisioned in serpentine form) seems to lie in the detail. Are questions of monogenism and polygenism, of the co-existence of an Adam and an Eve, of their capacity to represent humankind – just to select quickly from the surface of the Christian tradition and the concerns of scientific anthropology – fiendishly difficult to answer in a way that satisfies Scripture, theology and science?[2] Undertaking to answer that question would be an invidious distraction from our discussion, so we cannot here put to the test the feasibility of a contemporary statement of a doctrine of reconciliation in history that embraces commitment to an historical fall. All that can be done is to indicate as I have in a cursory way the *prima facie* availability of certain lines of defence for its champions. We cannot go further here. Many will urge that we should not trouble even to go that far, on the grounds that in our third millennium we can retain belief in reconciliation in history along lines continuous with the centuries of Christian tradition, while denying both the theological necessity and the theological plausibility of believing in an historical fall. For an example of this outlook, we can take the influential contributions of Emil Brunner in the last century. In his treatment of theological anthropology, he denied the historicity of Adam and his fall.[3] In his treatment of Christology, his discussion of penal and expiatory elements in connection with the atonement issued in a defence of the salient elements of the Christian tradition on objective reconciliation in history.[4] And in the more general

2.   See the recent attempt by S. Joshua Swamidass, *The Genealogical Adam and Eve: The Surprising Science of Universal Ancestry* (Downers Grove, Illinois: IVP Academic Press, 2019) and also Kenneth Kemp, 'Science, Theology and Monogenesis', *American Catholic Philosophical Quarterly*, 85 (2011) 217-36.
3.   *Man in Revolt: A Christian Anthropology* (London: Lutterworth, 1939) 84-88.
4.   *The Mediator: A Study Of The Central Doctrine Of The Christian Faith* (London:

treatments that we find in the second volume of his *Dogmatics*, Brunner
held it all together, rejecting an historical fall and advancing an historical
reconciliation.[5]

In order to make our task manageable, let me proceed on the
assumption that Brunner's general strategy is admissible – whether or
not he was theologically right – insofar as defence of a reconciliation in
history does not require defence of an historical fall. The supposition
that a plausible account of the reconciling work of Christ can be
offered without commitment to an historical fall may be tested only
in the course of attempting the account. To add to the list of what is
off-limits in this chapter, it goes without saying that it is impossible to
attempt here a theological exposition of that work beyond what can be
accomplished in a small corner of this vast field. To look no further than
the West, dogmatics has long been an awfully fragmented affair. There
are no ecclesiastically universal dogmatic criteria for judging whether or
not Christian belief in reconciliation in history can be defended today in
anything like the form in which it was rejected in the West on the general
terms of my account. Reference to '*the* form' in which it was rejected
already deploys terminology in a very broad and comprehensive sense.
Theological understanding of reconciliation in history was articulated
between the seventeenth and nineteenth centuries in a variety of ways
that could and did conflict with each other. These ways have persisted in
the twentieth and twenty-first centuries and new ones have been added.
So, glossing over historical theology before and after Nietzsche, I merely
ask the verbally anodyne but substantively weighty question of what
Christian belief in reconciliation in history might positively look like
today.

The Logic of Incarnation

'Revelation is ordered to reconciliation in history' has been a pervasive,
if sometimes unarticulated, sub-text underlying much of the discussion
in this volume. Reconciliation in history involves revelation in history.
The Christian tradition has usually maintained that God has provided
a general revelation outside Jesus Christ and the scriptural witness to
him, although Barth demurred from the tradition. I shall now take some
inexcusably large and unbelievably brisk steps to get to that aspect of
reconciliation that I want to highlight, namely, forgiveness.

Lutterworth, 1934) chapters 17-21.
5.   *The Christian Doctrine of Creation and Redemption: Dogmatics, vol. ii* (London:
      Lutterworth, 1952) 48-52; 281-297.

The historical locus of revelation, along with that of reconciliation, has often been a stumbling-block to detractors of the Christian tradition, but where one sees a duck, another sees a rabbit, and what is humanly a stumbling-block may be divinely a stepping-stone.[6] From one point of view, it seems intolerably odd that a God alleged to be good and universally caring should confine revelation, except in its general nature, to a very narrow stream of human history. If it is protested that a discarnate God in heaven is beatifically removed from human suffering, it may also be protested that an incarnate God on earth excludes the majority of the world from the supposed privilege of knowing him. However, we cannot have it both ways. If the first protest is dismantled by positing the appearance of God on earth, the second protest can no longer be sustained. For how can God come closer to us on earth than by becoming incarnate in human form, if such is possible? To deny that such is possible would be arrant folly unless belief in God, more particularly, in a triune God, is arrant folly. Intellectual agonizing over the possibility of incarnation on the assumption that we are justified in maintaining its possibility only if we can give a metaphysical account of it is needless and no more productive than two-dimensional creatures agonizing over how to conceive of a three-dimensional universe from within their framework. This is a case where a relatively abstract statement such as the following secures all that we need: God is able to create a world in which he could become incarnate. There is such a thing as a generic human form and God has so designed it that it is a possible vehicle for his incarnation. It is a possibility of which we usually become convinced because we have become convinced of its actuality, not because an *a priori* conceptual investigation of divine attributes or perfections has established the possibility. A detailed metaphysic of the incarnation may be elusive, difficult or even impossible if this is taken necessarily to involve an account of the 'how', of the mechanics, of the way a single person can be both human and divine. Neither logically nor theologically does this difficulty or impossibility in the least affect the credibility of the foundational claim that God shaped humanity so that he could become incarnate in its form. To make commitment to the ontological possibility of incarnation dependent on metaphysical comprehension of its actuality is illogical, needless and foolish.

In the Christian tradition, to be human is to live on this earth once, occupying one space and time. If, then, God comes amongst us as one

---

6.   The image of the duck-rabbit is associated with Wittgenstein, *Philosophical Investigations* (London: Macmillan, 1953) 194, though he picked it up from Jastrow.

of our number, God too will live on this earth once in incarnate form, occupying one space and time. For this reason alone, the thought-experiment of wondering why, if God became incarnate once, God did or does not become incarnate in every generation, if his goal is to privilege us with his presence and the revelation of his presence, is completely unproductive. Such appearances would not be incarnations because, according to the Judaeo-Christian tradition, unlike the Hindu or some Buddhist traditions, humans are not the kinds of creatures who can be re-born on this earth through the generations. If to be human is to live only once on this earth, then multiple incarnations could not really be incarnations as Christianity understands incarnation. Further, if we nonetheless persisted in conducting a thought-experiment featuring multiple 'incarnations' of God across the generations, the reincarnate body could be only at one place at any one time. Thus, most of the earth would be deprived of the reincarnate presence at any one time. In that case, thought-experiments motivated by the desire to maximize the universality of divine presence would be little advanced even on the hypothetical possibility of multiple incarnations.

Although patterns of migration, urbanization, social mingling and biotechnology mean that the following is a skeletal statement subject to germane modification, let us take it as a truism that human individuals are born within a lineage, descent, ancestry; they belong to a people, a race, a culture. If, then, God resolved in love to enter into the human condition, the election of a people appears to be appropriate, if not necessary. It is neither here nor there whether we use the language of necessity or appropriateness at this point, for we are simply noting what is involved if God becomes human. However, if we operate within broad biblical parameters, the fact is that the people to whom the Son of God was born would have to be chosen by God so long as we are talking about incarnate entry into the world and not the random evolution of a particular human from the stock of *homo sapiens*. When talk of election is *per se* judged to be a distasteful or arrogant exclusivism on the part of the chosen people, the critic has got things precisely back to front. Only by election can love and humility enter human history by way of incarnation. The prophets of Israel emphasize as much as they emphasise anything that the people of God have nothing to boast about. To boast of election is perverse.

Theological questions of Bible and of mission have their proper place in the context of the fact that the very particularity of the incarnation demonstrates the utter, self-giving humility of God's love for the world. If an incarnation that is at first blush exclusive as a matter of logic and of definition turns out, in truth, to constitute the most inclusive possible divine action on behalf of the human race, then consistency with God's inclusive loving purpose dictates that it must be recorded and proclaimed. In the Scriptures of the Old and New Testaments, that is precisely what happens in known languages that are translatable and so can be disseminated. Thus, all those times and places necessarily lacking the presence of God incarnate are informed about the necessarily particular incarnation. Obviously, missionary proclamation proceeds along exactly the same lines. No one doubts that ecclesiastical attitudes towards Scripture and mission have frequently obscured or destroyed the witness of the church. Just so, the performance of Israel obscured and destroyed the witness of Israel, and Paul effectively warned the church that its history could risk repeating the history of Israel, inasmuch as failure is possible (Romans 11:13-22). However, this does not overthrow the divine plan of revelation by way of incarnate presence. In sum, the exclusiveness of revelation in history in the form of incarnation in history is a demonstration, not a negation, of God's universal love.

Theologically, we could now explore the possibility of understanding incarnation as *ipso facto* reconciliation in history. However, in the history of Western theological thought the central place in Christian talk of reconciliation in history has usually been taken by the cross, whether or not it has been connected as strongly as it should be with incarnation on the one hand or with resurrection and ascension on the other. Accordingly, we shall look at this point in the direction indicated by one strand in a theology of the cross.

THE LOGIC OF FORGIVENESS

If the title of the previous sub-heading did not jar, the title of this sub-heading might. And perhaps it should. 'Logic' usually has a cold and impersonal connotation. Unless we are of the company of Chesterton's 'great humanitarian French freethinkers' who 'could make mercy even colder than justice', and who would doubtless have disposed of forgiveness as they did of mercy, forgiveness is typically emotional and personal.[7] It is not only that the words 'logic' and 'forgiveness' have radically contrasting feeling-tones. It is also that plenty of people who approach the subject will intuitively suppose that forgiveness has no logic. Pardon on the political stage might have a logic and this might be taken as a social-cum-legal parallel to forgiveness but it is more naturally thought of as

---

7.   'The Secret Garden' in G.K. Chesterton, *The Penguin Complete Father Brown* (Harmondsworth: Penguin, 1981) 24.

clemency and not forgiveness. Forgiveness normally obtains in the case of personal relations and here 'logic' seems to be alien. [8] Emanating from the heart and directed to the other, forgiveness seems to function absent a logical calculus of moral action. Whether or not that is really the case, the word 'logic' is expendable for my purposes but I retain it anyway in the sense of an 'inner logic' of this or that phenomenon, the 'logic' taking its shape from the phenomenon in question and referring to the conceptual structure exhibited in giving an account of that phenomenon. Of course, talk of 'conceptual structure' may seem to fall foul of the phenomenon of forgiveness in exactly the same way as 'logic' seems to do. Yet, the most intimate of experiences have their morphology; poets and novelists excel in depicting it; and no discussion of them is possible unless a kind of rough conceptual structure is available to enable us to contemplate them. In what follows, it will be important to indicate one component of an elementary moral logic that is at work in forgiveness.

Why approach cross and reconciliation via the notion of forgiveness? It is principally because the existential nature of forgiveness makes it a candidate for exploring reconciliation since connecting theological concepts to human existence is a *sine qua non* for understanding those concepts as long as Scripture is our guide. The terms of the new covenant announced by Jeremiah, which accounts for the Christian language of 'New Testament', embrace forgiveness: 'I will forgive their wickedness and will remember their sins no more' (31:34). In the most sustained treatment in the New Testament of the new covenant in its connection with the death of Christ, the author twice quotes from that passage in Jeremiah (Hebrews 8:8-12; 10:15-17). The dramatic Pentecostal sermon early in the book of Acts shows that the question of forgiveness is not left behind after taking centre stage in the ministry of John the Baptist, herald of the Son of God among us (Acts 2:38; Mark 1:4; Luke 1:77; 3:3). Revelation in history is the revelation of what Jesus Christ does in history, and a major way of describing what he does is to say that he effectuated forgiveness. To state the obvious, reconciliation is required because of estrangement between God and humankind; it is enabled because God forgives the sin that caused and causes the estrangement. So it is in human affairs. Where wrongdoing is the cause of estrangement, forgiveness is the most powerful and perhaps the only force to bring about reconciliation. If we want to map onto each other the contours of a theological understanding of reconciliation on the one hand, and

---

8. It was a consistent weakness in Reinhold Niebuhr's oft-stated distinction between the logic of personal relations and the logic of group relations that he failed to reckon with the theologically peculiar nature of the church.

human experience of reconciliation on the other, forgiveness is a likely and promising domain for the attempt. In what follows I briefly indicate that in the inter-human case, forgiveness entails paying the price for the other's wrong and undertaking the other's burden. If this marks the phenomenon in the inter-human realm, it prepares us psychologically and emotionally for its appearance in the divine-human realm. That, in turn, allows the idea of reconciliation in history to appear on the horizon in what should be a favourable light.

In putting things summarily as I have done, the natural reference point in the history of theology is the thought of Horace Bushnell, reputedly the father of Liberal theology in the United States. Bushnell, in a frequently quoted phrase, referred to the atonement as 'the cost of forgiveness to God'. With him, we are back in the time of Nietzsche. The title of his work, *The Vicarious Sacrifice, Grounded in Principles of Universal Obligation*, sums up its argument precisely.[9] According to Bushnell, atonement is most felicitously conceptualized as vicarious sacrifice but the moral principles that govern the atoning work of Christ are none other than those that ought to govern regular morally exemplary human action towards others. Some years after its publication, Bushnell published *Forgiveness and Law*, where he re-worked the second part of the argument set out in the earlier volume. He did not renege on what he had previously said, but he supplemented and refined portions of his argument. He tells us what impelled him to do so. 'I was brought squarely down upon the discovery, that nothing will ever accomplish the proposed real and true forgiveness, but to make cost in the endeavor.'[10] What does the cost of forgiveness involve? In respect of the forgiving disposition and action that I should possess and follow towards fellow-human beings, Bushnell says: 'You have taken his sin upon you in the cost you have borne for his sake.'[11]

It is characteristic of Bushnell in each of these volumes both to repudiate the ways of understanding the atonement that characterize the Anselmian and penal traditions of satisfaction and substitution, and to retain as much as possible of that language, giving it fresh meaning in accordance with his interpretation of Scripture. 'Substitution' is one conspicuous instance of this and is frequently spoken of in *The Vicarious Sacrifice*. 'The whole Gospel is a texture . . . of vicarious conceptions, in which Christ is represented, in one way or another, as coming into our place, substituted in our stead, bearing our burdens, answering for us, and

---

9.   Bushnell, *The Vicarious Sacrifice* .
10.   *Forgiveness and Law* (London: Hodder & Stoughton, 1875) 10.
11.   *Forgiveness*, 44.

standing in a kind of suffering sponsorship for the race.'[12] Bearing the sin of the other and substituting for the other in the vicarious sacrificial activity of love encapsulates the cost of forgiveness. It is the heart of the atonement. Although it is also the heart of Bushnell's argument that principles that are inapplicable to the loving and forgiving activity of the human race should not be adduced in an account of the corresponding activity on the part of Jesus Christ, the gulf between Christ and the rest of humanity is vast. By comparison to the activity of Christ, ours is 'as an insect life fluttering responsively to the sun'.[13] The word 'life' reminds us that it is not only the cross but the whole life of Christ that exemplifies vicarious sacrifice, according to Bushnell.

If he does not interpret a reconciliation in history along the main lines of the traditions he inherited, it remains the case that history, for Bushnell, is most certainly as vital a scene of divine revelation as reconciliation is the vital goal of divine action. The vicarious sacrifice of Jesus in history is the revelation of God in eternity: 'What he does among us by his sacrifice is to have its value in revealing, under time, how by sacrifice and much cost above time' the divine loving energies were operating.[14] *Christus Victor* features too:

> What is wanted is a casting down of evil in beings still existing, still to exist. And nothing could do that but some trial scene or crucifixion today, that allows it to be seen coping with pure excellence or the suffering capacity of goodness without force. . . . There was . . . no other way of breaking down the prince of this world and the pride of evil bodied in his kingdom, but to let the eternal patience meet him as it well knows how. For this purpose too, in great part, Christ was incarnate.[15]

Love, vicarious sacrifice and forgiveness work in accordance with an eternal law and '[t]he glory of his incarnate mission is precisely this, and in this is the gain of it, that he unbosoms, in time, what love and obedience to law were hid in God's unseen majesty, or but dimly and feebly shown before.'[16]

---

12. *Vicarious Sacrifice*, 38.
13. *Vicarious Sacrifice*, 124.
14. *Forgiveness*, 60.
15. *Forgiveness*, 248.
16. *Vicarious Sacrifice*, 319. 'God has not only a character everlastingly perfected in right, but . . . by the same law, he is held to a suffering goodness for his enemies, even to that particular work in time which we call the vicarious

Does Bushnell give us a key to understanding a logic of forgiveness that contributes to a contemporary commendation of reconciliation in history?[17] He certainly makes an important contribution. Theologically, he may fall short of a sufficient biblical affirmation of the dimensions of atonement and reconciliation, despite his attempt to demonstrate his position exegetically.[18] The robustly conservative James Orr, for example, agreed not only that '[t]he world is full of the suffering of the innocent for the sins of others' but 'more than this, the world is full of substitutionary, of vicarious forces – of the *voluntary* enduring of suffering for the sake of others. This is the point in Bushnell's book on *Vicarious Sacrifice*, and it is true and good so far as it goes.'[19] However, it does not go far enough. Orr observed that where difficulty is felt with belief in the atonement, it does not lie at the point indicated by Bushnell's theology; it lies rather in the expiatory force of the suffering of the innocent (Jesus) for the guilty. Bushnell, of course, did not omit this inadvertently; he disagreed with Orr and the tradition exegetically and theologically on this point. Whatever our exegetical and theological judgements on this question, Bushnell's interpretation of the dynamics of the sacrificial cost of human forgiveness in terms of bearing the sin of and substituting for another is fecund. Orr was not alone amongst major theologians who welcomed Bushnell's insights as far as they went. John Oman, a weighty opponent of a substitutionary or penal theory of the atonement, observed that '[i]n a sense all friendship, which bears obloquy and suffers loss on another's account, is substitutionary.'[20] Let us, then, take our cue from Bushnell, without presuming that his theology of reconciliation is adequate overall.

Take the case of a woman who has no particular complaints against her husband and habitually indulges herself with other men or women,

---

sacrifice of Christ', 305-06.

17. For Bushnell, the biblical warrant for proceeding thus is that '[i]n the NT it will be observed that forgiveness by God and forgiveness by men are set forth mutually, one by the help of the other', *Forgiveness*, 35.

18. Yet, in relation to *The Vicarious Sacrifice*, Bruce Mullin writes: 'There was a surprising hardness in a number of places in *The Vicarious Sacrifice* which was rarely found in B's earlier writings on the atonement', *The Puritan as Yankee: a Life of Horace Bushnell* (Grand Rapids, MI: Eerdmans, 2002). See Mullin's discussion on 230-31, from which these words are taken. 'Where this new appreciation for the sternness of God came from one cannot know', Mullin remarks, pondering Bushnell on God as judge exercising punitive action. In relation to Horace Bushnell's earlier writings, one may not know, but his theological account comes as no surprise if Bushnell was trying to be biblical.

19. *Sidelights on Christian Doctrine* (London: Marshall, 1909) 135.

20. *Honest Religion* (Cambridge: Cambridge University Press, 1942) 117. Oman does not refer to Bushnell by name.

doing so with some abandon and obvious relish and doing so increasingly overtly. Assume that her husband receives her back into the privileges and communion of marriage as often as she seeks restoration to the relationship with a measure of penitence and a significant element of sincerity in her admission of guilt, as far as he can judge. Comes a day when, for whatever reason, her unfaithfulness strikes her with horror, its pain and guilt are unprecedently felt, and for the first time she understands properly the husband's suffering on her account. There is deep contrition and a restored relationship, one that is unbroken in future. Nothing can be done on her part to blot out or make up for the past but nothing can be done either about the fact that nothing can be done.

So much for the couple in question. The husband's wider family and friends express various degrees of dismay. With minimal or no sanctimoniousness, they assume what they take to be an unimpeachable moral stance. All along, one and all have argued that the husband should cut off his wife. They differ only in their judgement of the stage at which that should happen, the conditions of any restitution of the relationship, and the finality of the prospective breach. They disagree a little in their evaluation of the relative proportions of different aspects of the offence committed against him and on the detail of what constitutes a fitting moral response on his part, given the impossibility of redress. But they agree in their insistence that wrongdoing should neither be tolerated nor met with no more than pained protest and ready restoration. Failing to persuade him, they judge that he has forfeited all human dignity and self-esteem and, while not putting it this way, they effectively maintain that there exists a moral order that requires respect and adherence, something he ignores and flouts, if not in the same way as his wife has done. Their general knowledge of him makes it hard to level credibly an accusation against him of weakness, but he is clearly wrong-headed. Only when the relationship shows every sign of having settled down so that it will be inviolate in the future do they give up protestations. But they do not give up their moral philosophy. They resign themselves to the conclusion that, in this scenario, morality is demonstrably cheap and sin is demonstrably free. If, when the matter is concluded, either there is no penalty for wrongdoing or the wife does not or cannot pay it, then the moral order is vapid.

The husband lacks the moral philosophy, let alone the combative spirit to join issue. There is a tightly circumscribed area of agreement with his friends and wider family when all concur that it is impossible to think of how the wife can make an adequate restitution for her wrong, but there the agreement ends. Not only does he not see how that could be done – in his heart and head he knows that it could not – but he is not minded even to pursue the question of restitution, or not sure if he should. It is a concept that strikes him as somehow out of place, though he is informed by his interlocutors and half-informed by his own moral sensibility that restitution is a viable moral category. He puzzles over another aspect of the matter as well. It seems to him that his friends were not quite right in declaring that, in the event, no penalty was exacted for wrongdoing. He feels as though he has paid it and it has been heavy. In the pain of the knowledge of the deed, accompanied by the struggle to forgive and the torment of love still felt, in his consistent offer and his wife's eventual acceptance of forgiveness, the burden of his wife's misdeeds has fallen heavily and, it feels, directly on him. Accordingly, penalty for wrongdoing has not been evacuated from the moral order. On the question of justice involved in all this, his thoughts are fuzzy and he is not sure whether the question of justice has entered into the resolution anywhere. What he does know is that there was no other way for that relationship to be restored than the way that it was restored, that is, through forgiveness. Yet the end, that is, restoration, seemed both desirable and even in some way right, though the intrusion of the word 'right' is puzzling to him because it normally has a connection with justice.

Like Coleridge's ancient mariner, who himself had rather been through the emotional mill, our cuckold joins the humble throng that worships on Sundays. And when, one morning, attending to the reading of the Second Lesson, he hears about one who bore the sins of others, he thinks that he knows a bit about what that might mean. Perhaps he lacks as much theology as he does moral philosophy and has not quite discerned that Jesus' atoning sacrifice as described in that Lesson is not in every respect the same as what he himself has done or experienced. But as he listens to the sermon that follows up the reading, with its talk of one bearing the sins of many, Jesus taking on the sins of the world in space and time, it does not strike his spiritual sensibility, moulded in some agony, as palpably immoral. He may have no intellectual explanation for the Christian understanding of reconciliation and no effective defence against its detractors, but he does not recoil from it spiritually.

Although a different illustration could have made the point I am making and, obviously, the respective roles of husband and wife are reversible, the illustration has been selected and the gender roles duly apportioned because of its basis in the prophecy of Hosea. What is it an illustration of? It is not meant as a comprehensive explanation or theology of atonement along the lines that limn the soteriology of Horace Bushnell. The illustration is designed simply to identify, in the spirit of his theology, *a* constitutive element in the theology of atonement. It is limited, but surely important. It shows how the principle of one bearing the sins of another is, indeed, amenable to comprehension from within the framework of human experience. There is a moral philosophy to be worked out in this context if it is indeed the case that the act of forgiveness can be squared with or must be understood within a wider moral order. This was a matter of first importance to Bushnell himself. However we work it all out, what matters for my purpose is that the *principle* of paying a price, bearing another's sins, undergoing the penalty of another's wrongdoing – what Bushnell, Orr and Oman could all agree was a form of 'substitution' – is not going to be alien to a wronged person who has forgiven when he or she encounters this thought in a Christian account of atonement. He or she will come to see that, in Charles Williams's words, divine substitution is not a 'cold gift' but a 'warm splendor . . . waiting to enrapture' humankind.[21] If the Christian account of atonement remains offensive to such a person, it may either be because of an element or elements in the Christian understanding of it that are additional to what we have identified and/ or because Christian talk of atonement trades in *universal* human guilt before God, thus indicting *me*. What is not problematic is the principle of substitution as described.

Forgiveness reaches its term only when there is reconciliation; bearing the penalty of another's wrongdoing is not just a disposition, it is an act. The relation of an eternal God to historical time in Christian theology introduces its own set of considerations. What a foray into the logic of human forgiveness does is to put on the table of intellectual discussion the possibility of a reconciliation in history, if we bracket out a host of other questions surrounding Christian belief. It puts it on the table of intellectual discussion, but it is not first and foremost an intellectual matter. *That* will be evident to forgiver and forgiven alike. Theirs will be an inward, we might say spiritual, disposition towards a Christian account of reconciliation in history. It should be a positive disposition. To be rightly disposed in spirit is a gateway to understanding in mind. The mind is willing and not reluctant to consider substitution in the tradition because it has understood substitution in experience.

If granting forgiveness is painful, so is asking for it. Our speech mounts a hill of ascending difficulty. I might just about admit that I fell short, acted inadvisedly or foolishly; I might go further and apologise for something inappropriately said or done or for giving offence; but to ask forgiveness in

21. *Descent Into Hell*, 816.

so many words is a psychological as well as verbal step further. Pathology abounds, of course. Granting forgiveness may be the act of a weak soul unable to protect its own dignity, still less to uphold any relevant moral law. On the other side of the coin, requesting forgiveness may likewise be the act of a weak soul. Like Josef K in Kafka's novel, *The Trial*, I may feel responsible for everything (or for much), which might involve apologizing for everything (or for much) and asking forgiveness for everything (or for much). Into forgivenesses, whether given or received, go an assortment of ingredients and no single, universal, fare is served up out of the concoction. Moreover, I have described the scene in terms of individuals. Groups need separate treatment; nations may come up for consideration. The limits of my discussion should not detract from its point because my aim has not been to adumbrate a theology of forgiveness but to suggest how experience of forgiveness provides access to belief in reconciliation in history. To transplant Bushnell's words out of the framework of his theology and with the caveat that I have suggested this line of approach, not demonstrated this conclusion, I quote him: 'The offense of the cross – how surely is it ended, when once you have learned the way in which God bears an enemy. . . . The recoil you were in is over.'[22]

If incorporating the logic of forgiveness along the lines set out above enhances the prospects for thinking favourably today about Christian belief in reconciliation in history, it also brings to sharp relief the requirements for religious belief in general, rich in their epistemological import.[23] Friedrich von Hügel makes precisely this point. Approaching the religiously sensitive and pastorally delicate question of theodicy, he assumed his correspondent to be 'non-contentious and non-controversial; to be athirst for wisdom, not for cleverness; to be humble and simple, or (at least) to feel a wholesome shame at not being so; to be just *straight*, and anxious for some light, and ready to pay for it and practise it.'[24] Von Hügel proceeded to speak as follows about our knowledge of germane existences and realities:

> We get to know such realities slowly, laboriously, intermittently, partially; we get to know them, not inevitably nor altogether

---

22. *The Vicarious Sacrifice*, 55.
23. In light of my later reference to H. R. Mackintosh, *The Christian Experience of Forgiveness* (London: Nisbet, 1927), note his epistemologically relevant remarks in connection with which he brings on board Rudolf Otto, 195.
24. 'On the Preliminaries to Religious Belief and on the Facts of Suffering, Faith and Love' in *Essays and Addresses on the Philosophy of Religion* (London etc.: Dent, 1921) 98-116, quotation from 98.

apart from our dispositions, but only if we are sufficiently awake to care to know them, sufficiently generous to pay the price continuously which is strictly necessary if this knowledge and love are not to shrink but to grow. We indeed get to know them, – in proportion as we become less self-occupied, less self-centred, more outward-moving, less obstinate and insistent, more gladly lost in the crowd, more rich in giving all we have, and especially all we are, our very selves.[25]

John Baillie took up von Hügel's words in a powerful exposition of the claim that the determining conditions of religious belief are moral conditions, a position he took to be first presented forcefully in modern philosophy by Blaise Pascal.[26] Yet Baillie was writing of 'modern philosophy' the better part of a century ago. Surely, we shall protest, the world is not now as it was for von Hügel, Baillie, Oman, Orr and Bushnell. Who now has the kind of time and the kind of qualities that von Hügel picks out or the kind of disposition and sensibility that Bushnell expounds? If I have attached the persuasiveness of the logic of forgiveness to the moral conditions of religious belief and if my rhetorical question has any force, does that not reduce the effectiveness in our day of the appeal to the logic of forgiveness as I have attempted to sketch it above? Does it apply?

LIMIT AND SUPPLEMENT

There are certainly limits to the application of what has been presented above – limits with respect to its persuasiveness. Talk of forgiveness has little or no purchase on the experience of many people because, for whatever reason, such talk is either palpably foreign or practically vacuous. It is not just that the logic of forgiveness, as outlined above, has limits when it comes to interpreting atoning reconciliation in history, at least unless we subscribe to Bushnell's theology. It is that we seem today to be in a different world from his and those others whom we have brought on board in his train. In his day, Bushnell worried lest the quality of our lives were such that we could little use human forgiveness as a way of explicating that of God; he worried that forgiveness of the kind he had in view might be or become alien to our experience.[27] It is instructive to revisit Hugh Ross Mackintosh's treatment of *The Christian*

---

25. *Essays*, 104.
26. *The Interpretation of Religion* (Edinburgh: T & T Clark, 1929) 362-63.
27. *Forgiveness*, 51.

Experience of Forgiveness in this connection. Publishing in the inter-war years, some decades after Bushnell had produced his works, Mackintosh made favourable reference to Bushnell who, as far as he could tell, was the first to talk in terms of 'the doctrine of the atonement as the doctrine of the cost of forgiveness to God'.[28] He quoted Bushnell supportively on 'sympathy with the wrong-doing party as virtually takes his nature . . . making cost in that nature by suffering, or expense, or painstaking sacrifice and labour', lauding the examples Bushnell gave 'of the truth that one man can really pardon another only in so far as he takes the other's sin upon himself in the cost he personally bears on his behalf'.[29] This, Mackintosh finds, is 'an exceptionally attractive and rewarding path of approach'.

However, in a sentiment cognate to that of Bushnell, Mackintosh also refers to the dictum familiar in his day 'that the higher man of today is not worrying about his sins'.[30] We have moved further on since Mackintosh's day: what will the higher man or woman of our day make of Mackintosh on forgiveness? What prompts the question is particularly the following. Responding to the fact that many people aver that they do not understand what forgiveness means, Mackintosh says, without any qualification, that 'we know each of us from our experience of home that forgiveness can and does happen'.[31] Later, there is some sort of qualification: '[W]e take the life a Christian home, where young people grow up in trust, built into the very substance of their being, that there is forgiveness with God' but now he adds: 'just as there is with their mother'.[32] The father does not come into it. Mackintosh repeats and slightly expands the point: '[B]roadly speaking, the Church is made up of Christian homes. . . . When children are told of God's pardon of their sins, it is all interpreted for them by the familiar attitude of a loving mother in taking a naughty child who is sorry back to her heart and her confidence.'[33]

This portrays life on a distant and utterly remote planet in the eyes of most Westerners today. And yet. It remains that people do forgive and are

---

28. *The Christian Experience*, 185. How important this view is for Mackintosh is shown by his reference to it in the 'Preface' of his volume (xii). Mackintosh held that '[t]he certainty of forgiveness in Christ is, if not the sum, at least the secret of Christian religion', 6. On forgiveness as concrete, historical occurrence, see Mackintosh's remarks on the theology of Wilhelm Herrmann, 46 and for reference to Hosea, see 189, n. 1.

29. *The Christian Experience*, 186. The following words are on the same page.

30. *The Christian Experience*, 186.

31. *The Christian Experience*, 211.

32. *The Christian Experience*, 274.

33. *The Christian Experience*, 280.

called on to forgive. Beneath the thick, opaque veneer of estrangement from the world and the vocabulary of forgiveness, countless millions are struggling with the very issue of forgiveness in inter-personal relationships and, at the moment of intolerable pain, will, in their way and equipped with a different and halting vocabulary, catch something of Bushnell's concerns. That is why I have featured Bushnell and we still need to approach reconciliation in history by appreciating him at this point as long as we do not shirk the pastoral work of translation and explication. However, the limits of his help are as patent as the fact of it is firm. Since Mackintosh's description of the Christian home will be recognized by only a small minority in the churches, it is evident that the context in which we must now talk of forgiveness is informed by a new social dynamic. It is a matter of regret that space forbids the exploration of that dynamic. Instead, I shall cast around for a supplement to Bushnell's contribution. Bushnell could count on shared moral experience and shared moral language, at least to a sufficient extent to enable him to make the argument he did. Oman died in the year that the Second World War broke out (*Honest Religion* was published posthumously), by which time much had changed since Bushnell's day in that respect. Since then and up to our point in time, appeal to shared moral experience and moral vocabulary has a more tenuous basis, to say the risible least. Consequently, not only does the logic of forgiveness suffer from an attenuated appeal when it comes to reflection on reconciliation in history but also anything constructed on the assumption of shared moral experience is, again to say the understated least, liable to topple at a little puff of moral wind. There remains a constituency large enough to benefit from Bushnell, though it is a constituency not culturally formed by common moral experience but one that comes into being as a result of discrete individual experiences. For what is culturally common, we would have to look elsewhere.

Some will protest this line of argument; should we not respond in holy impatience to this search for a supplement to Bushnell by pointing out that we are getting tangled up in needless convolutions because we are ignoring Barth's warning against seeking out a 'point of contact' in theological reflection? As Dean Inge remarked somewhere, 'He who marries the spirit of this age will soon find himself a widower'. Should we, then, instead of supplementing what has been said so far, shepherd off the field all endeavours to approaching reconciliation other than those that take a more direct approach in the manner of the Bible? The New Testament speaks of a reconciliation in history only because it speaks of a resurrection in history, and the resurrection of Jesus from the dead is the hinge on which its witness turns. Therefore, it is the hinge on which the combined witness of Old and New Testaments turn when they are conjoined to form a single Christian Scripture. Should we not take Route 1 to reconciliation by proceeding directly from the New Testament kerygma to contemporary need?

It is no part of my programme to discourage travel on Route 1. Reconciliation in history is approachable through resurrection. The New Testament witness to the resurrection is the witness to an event in history, but it is a matter of dispute whether or not the putative event can in principle be captured in any way or to any extent by standard or, at least, permissible methods of historical reasoning. Considered on its own terms, the witness can be interpreted in only three broad ways, whether to their mutual exclusion or in some kind of combination. The New Testament witness must be either badly confused, wilfully misleading or substantially dependable. If we conclude the latter, belief in reconciliation in history also becomes plausible. Resurrection, on New Testament terms, seals reconciliation and illuminates not only the nature of the atoning death of Christ, but also his incarnation and life. Even if we generously permit a Bushnell to help us along, does not the discovery of his limits alert us to the fact that enquiry into resurrection was always the way to go for those who want to lay down secure paving on the road to proclaiming reconciliation in history?

Many will answer in the negative – that we have long known that such a road runs into a dead end if we accent *enquiry* into the resurrection. Do not arguments over the historicity of the resurrection accounts belong to a theological and cultural past we should not try to retrieve? Weighty voices answer in the negative. From Pannenberg's *Jesus: God and Man* to N.T. Wright's *The Resurrection of the Son of God*, impressive attempts have been made in modern theological times to sustain our engagement with the resurrection accounts by deploying historical reason and doing so to positive effect.[34] Speaking generally, I do not for a moment doubt either the validity or the value of these investigations nor, indeed, of their conclusions when they are positive on the historical-critical front. It is eminently reasonable to approach Christianity by considering the affirmations that (a) the credibility of Christian belief in reconciliation in history turns on the historicity of the resurrection of Jesus; (b) investigation of its resurrection claim must be central to the serious investigation of Christianity; (c) an investigation of that claim yields strong grounds for affirming its credibility; and (d) the credibility of

34. Wolfhart Pannenberg, *Jesus: God and Man* (London: SCM, 1968); N.T. Wright, *The Resurrection of the Son of God* (London: SPCK, 2003).

belief in the resurrection accounts lends considerable, if not definitive, weight to the main lines of the testimony of Israel, which culminates not with the last book of the canon of the Hebrew Bible but with the New Testament gospel. If we followed this approach, the gateway to a dogmatic account of reconciliation in history would be opened by an apologetic look at resurrection in history.

It is wrong to omit all reference to this trail, particularly if we are favourably disposed to it. However, to follow it – to whatever conclusion – would be less in keeping with the tenor of this volume than to search out another one more consonant with the background interest that has led to our reflection on the logic of forgiveness. The whole question of theology and apologetics immediately muscles into discussion here, but that discussion is for another time and place. From start to finish in my essay up to this point, interest in moral experience has been hovering in the background. Moral self-sufficiency was there near the beginning; moral self-sacrifice has been here near the end. But what can be ascribed to our moral sense today? It goes without saying that a short answer in relation to the West is designedly and blatantly going to be brutally reductive. Still, we can say that in the West, autonomy persists as a fundamental moral value, rooted in our sensibility. 'Rights' has also surfaced as a fundamental moral demand. But one of the most striking features of the emotional and psychological landscape is the universal presence of shame, sometimes manifest, usually hidden. If shame is not 'the most grievous Punishment in the World', it is certainly a deep, deep wound.[35] Moral values are grafted onto, moral sense grounded in, an experienced selfhood, fragmented more than unitary, shaped by a shame component. Let Dietrich Bonhoeffer set the stage for what follows.

> When . . . a human life is deprived of the conditions that are part of being human, the justification of such a life by grace and faith is at least seriously hindered, if not made impossible. Concretely stated, slaves who have been so deprived of control over their time that they can no longer hear the proclamation of God's word cannot be led by that word of God to a justifying faith. . . . There is a depth of human bondage, of human poverty, and of human ignorance that hinders the gracious coming of Christ. . . . There is a degree of distortion and self-entrapment in lying, in guilt, in one's own occupation, one's own work . . . and in self-love that makes the coming of grace especially difficult.

---

35. The phrase is that of Henry Fielding in his classic, *The History of Tom Jones: A Foundling*, vol. ii (Oxford: Clarendon, 1974) 673.

So the way must be made straight on which Christ is to come to
humanity. . . . It is hard for those thrust into extreme disgrace,
desolation, poverty, and helplessness to believe in God's justice
and goodness. It becomes hard for those whose lives have fallen
into disorder and a lack of discipline to hear the commandments
of God in faith. . . . It is hard for those disappointed by a false
faith and who have lost self-control to find the simplicity of
surrendering their hearts to Christ.[36]

To be sure, this is not all. Bonhoeffer is emphatic: 'Christ comes,
to be sure, clearing the way for this coming, whether one is ready for
it or not'.[37] The last theologian that one will find advocating a kind
of anthropocentric preparation for receiving the gospel is Dietrich
Bonhoeffer. We cannot trace here the contours of his theological
construction in detail. It suffices to take his words to heart. Experience
of shame is an obstacle of the kind Bonhoeffer has in mind.

It is beyond my competence, let alone my remit, to marshal here the
evidence for the centrality of the experience of shame in Western culture,
let alone outside the West. As Bonhoeffer says, 'the forms of the feeling
of shame are various and malleable'.[38] Let me seize on the word 'deprive'
in Bonhoeffer's description, while giving it a specific twist that he does
not. Emotional deprivation amongst children and adults is extremely
widespread today. Doubtless, it has always and everywhere been so but
it particularly comes to light when mental health issues are publicly
profiled as they are today in Western countries. Emotional deprivation
is felt in the body even when the body is otherwise unharmed. Both the
physical and psychological conditions for the well-being of a child –
safety for the body and the experience of love – are tragically absent in
a huge number of instances. The child then constructs defences to cope
with the situation. In the short term, they are necessary for survival. In
the longer term, they psychologically imprison the individual, inhibiting
spiritual and emotional growth, just as long as the occasion for and cause
of the operations of the defence mechanism are not brought to light.
In the complex underground of the human subconscious, shame can
be largely or partially hidden because people are ashamed of their own

---

36. *Ethics*, *Works*, volume 6 (Minneapolis, MN: Fortress, 2009) 160-3. Bonhoeffer's
     allusion to the 'coming of Christ' takes up Luke's reference to the ministry of
     John the Baptist and his preparation of the way of the Lord in line with the
     prophecy of Isaiah.
37. *Ethics*, 162.
38. *Ethics*, 214.

unmet need for love and safety. This is a double sadness: it is sad that the need has not been met, and sad that people are ashamed of the unmet need. The need for love and safety is an entirely and properly human need for which no one should be ashamed. Largely hidden shame generates less hidden self-loathing for the individual I am or have become. In this situation, talk of all things theological, as of all things whatsoever, is heard and apprehended through the emotional and intellectual filters of the shamed estate. It obviously applies to hearing talk of reconciliation in history.[39]

If our two horizons are those of contemporary Western experience and the Christian Scriptures, particularly the New Testament, talk of human shame recalls the New Testament depiction of the cross of Christ as a scene of utter shame. The depiction is faintly recognised even when we are untutored in the world of the first century, when we read of betrayal, denial, ridicule, beating and stripping before the final and painful humiliation of public execution on a cross. The depiction will be rather less faint when we then read the account after probing the nature of shame and honour as understood or experienced in the culture of the Ancient Near East. Finally, the shame of the cross becomes a blinding reality when viewed within the framework of a Jewish culture whose constituent and formative elements included such a pronouncement as: 'Cursed is everyone who is hanged on a tree.'[40] If there has been any place in history where deprivation of bodily safety and of love were exhibited, it was Golgotha. Some humans at the foot of the cross loved Jesus still and, however small their number, they were more than many people have in their hour of need. But what was the love of family for Jesus compared to the love of the Father? Faced with the judgment of his family that he was insane and the judgment of the scribes that he was demon-possessed, Jesus is informed that his mother and brothers have turned up to have him taken away. 'Who are my mother and my brothers? . . . Whoever does the will of God, he is my brother and sister and mother' (Mark 3:33-35). No father turns up with the family to get Jesus committed for insanity and he mentions no father in connection with the family who does the will of God. There is one father and Jesus' food is to do his will (John 6: 34). Doing it, he goes to the cross and experiences the ultimate in adult emotional deprivation as a consequence. Theologies of the cross variously understand the relationship of Jesus to God or

39. See Stephen N. & Susan L. Williams, 'Trauma, Abuse and Christian Faith', Christ on Campus Initiative, Trinity Evangelical Divinity School, 2018, available on the internet.
40. When we read Galatians 3:13, we must think of shame and not just atonement.

Son to the Father, yet there seems little doubt that the cry of dereliction gives agonized voice to the experience of abandonment. At the moment of supreme shame, not to mention pain, the love that, as Jesus alone knew from experience, sustains the world and had also defined his divine being, was apparently blotted out from the realm of experience.

If the earthly story of Christ ended in shame of one kind, the story of fallen humanity began in shame of a different kind. Christologies and soteriologies have contrasted Jesus Christ with pre-lapsarian Adam. Before the fall of Adam and after the death of Christ, 'the first man Adam became a living being; the last Adam became a life-giving spirit' (1 Corinthians 15:45). The act of Adam was one of disobedience, which incurred guilt and entailed death; the act of Christ was one of obedience, which established righteousness and brought life. Obviously, theological reflection on this account is mandatory. What has received less theological attention is the immediate human effect of the primal sin. As Eve led Adam in that sin, so she joins Adam in reaction to its commission. The first thing that Eve did after hearing the serpent's words was to see: she 'saw that the tree was good for food, and that it was a delight to the eyes, and that the tree was desired to make one wise' (3:6). As mentioned in the first chapter of this volume, what Eve saw before partaking of the fruit was, in part, an illusion. The first thing that she and Adam did after the transgression was also to see, but now it was a reality and no illusion: 'Then the eyes of both were opened, and they knew that they were naked' (3:7). After seeing what she did and in the way that she did – that the tree was good for food – Eve reached out for what was not her own and was meant to be alien. Eve and Adam's reactions after eating its fruit was to cover what was their own and was meant to be familiar: 'And they sewed fig leaves together and made themselves loincloths' (3:7).

If two words capture the immediate consequence of transgression, they are guilt and shame, though fear is close on their heels (3:10). In ordinary language, guilt and shame customarily differ, although neither word is undifferentiated in meaning. Standardly, from a legal point of view, you plead guilty if you have violated objective law. To feel shame is different, as is feeling guilty. Speaking generally, these psychological or emotional states are the morally healthy and appropriate accompaniment to the guilt of wrongdoing, at least if the wrongdoing is conscious or intentional. Eve and Adam do not first plead their guilt after their transgression, however guilty they may have felt. Nor does the absence of the Lord, before whom they are guilty, from the scene explain the absence of the plea, because when he does arrive they do not explicitly plead guilt then either. From a psychological and emotional point of view, as revealed in their behaviour, shame seems to be the first psychologically manifested consequence of knowledge. Deprived of communion with God, the first humans discover that the body has become the site of self-alienation, ground of incipient mutual, inter-personal alienation. Later humans who experience emotional deprivation discover that the body is the site of peril or lack of safety. Thus, one shame is grafted onto another if Adam and Eve's transgression and response has a humanly representative character. The reason for their shame is obviously distinguished from subsequent reasons for shame in the experience of the emotionally deprived, but it all makes for one sad and seething morass of shame. The intrusion of alienation amongst and between the wider social company of humans adds evil to primal alienation. Other humans are usually not kind enough to sow garments for us in order to mitigate our sense of self-alienation (3:20).[41]

Of course, I am asserting and not arguing the propriety of theologically using as I have the Genesis narrative, so let the unconvinced reader take it as simply speculation. If we could earlier connect cross and forgiveness with human experience without adverting to the fall, those disposed to suspend theological speculation about the fall in relation to shame may want to concentrate on cross and emotional deprivation, which, after all, is my chief concern. Anyway, connecting the shame brought on in Eden by responsible individuals, the shame brought about in many lives by the conduct of others, and the shame of the cross would make for a hefty project. Our interest is in connecting the experience of shame with reconciliation in history. Eden intimates that the objective guilt of transgression has as its correlate an opaque innate shame about the human condition, which is apparently a substratum of human life. One way or another – and in more ways than one – the human body is the site of a restlessness that defies swift analysis. This characteristic feature of the body is typically something we both conceal and deny, as we do with pride, which is often picked out in the theological tradition as the cause of Adam's transgression, whatever is made of Eve's. The shame that results from emotional deprivation, entirely the fault of others and not our own, is lodged in a human existence in which shame apparently has its strange habitation at the best of times. We need not theorise theologically about connections between Adam and the human race in order to believe and accept that. A constellation of factors – shame,

---

41.   I am no longer as confident as I was in my volume on Nietzsche that Blake was
       near the mark in speaking of shame as 'Prides cloke', quoted in *Shadow*, 259, n.
       60. More precisely, I find it true in a more restricted range of cases than I did
       then.

restlessness, anxiety – attend characteristic human reactions to the body that constitutes my material selfhood, and study of the cultural presuppositions of radical biotechnology leads us into a fertile area for studying these phenomena.

The resurrection of Jesus Christ is relevant to this, with its assurance to us that what is sown in weakness is raised in power (1 Corinthians 15:43). But, grafted onto the shame of Eden, the shame of emotional deprivation is immediately connected with the shame of the cross, not with the re-conquest of the body Christ achieves in his resurrection. This immediate spiritual meeting-point of those shamed on account of emotional deprivation and the crucified figure can be described, though perhaps not exhaustively, under a single rubric: Identification. Here, on the cross, is the profound concretization of the identification with us by the Son of God in his incarnation, which I conceptually touched on earlier in this chapter. Jesus shares with the shamed the knowledge of shame. The causes and form of his shame may be different from those of others but difference does not abolish a slither of shared experience. Jesus has been in the same place. When Jesus identified himself with our human condition, he did not thereby directly experience everything humans experience, for no one human being can do that. The particularity of each human and of human circumstances is a sufficient condition for such a limitation. Nonetheless, even in the realm of normal human relationships, not only can empathy be real and deep on the part of the one empathizing but it can also be recognized as real and deep by the one who is the 'recipient' of empathy, even when the sufferings have not been identical.[42] This obtains in the case of shame. It obtains supremely in the case of Jesus' relationship to suffering humans. He enters into the shame of both those who are godforsaken in their guilt and those forsaken by humans in their deprivation.

How is Jesus' identification with and shared experience of shame meant to contribute to the credibility of reconciliation in history? One way that it does so is that identification highlights the significance of revelation in history. If the life, death and shame of Jesus tell us anything about God that we should not otherwise have known, history has obviously become the scene of revelation. It is life-transforming revelation for those who receive it. The point to be made in relation specifically to reconciliation is comparable to that made earlier in relation to forgiveness, although the conceptual connection between forgiveness and reconciliation is tighter or more immediately conspicuous than the connection between

42. I use 'empathy' in an ordinary-language not in a psychologically technical sense here.

identification and reconciliation.[43] As with forgiveness, the point is that human experience opens out the prospect of reconciliation in history as a prospect aglow with light and not darkly minatory. Jesus' identification with us encompasses the form of shame experienced by those who are emotionally deprived at the cruel hands of human agents. If his identification is in the service of reconciliation, a prospect opens out of reconciliation being a benediction to my soul.

Prima facie, if theological reference to Eden means that reconciliation in history is needed on account of self-incurred guilt, this may appear to bar, and not to open, the way for those shamed in emotional deprivation.[44] Is it not of the first importance for them to receive assurance that they are precisely *not* responsible for their shame, *not* replaying Eden? Yes, it is – and there is no doubt that humanly insensitive proclamation of the universal need for reconciliation and its form in history can erect cruel barriers between the God proclaimed and the human to whom God is proclaimed. But when he who endured shame becomes the object of miraculous trust for those who have hitherto not learned to trust – more, learned not to trust – then trust in the name of Jesus begins to heal the fragmented and re-orient the disoriented life. If what we have before us is not, first and foremost, a *theology* of reconciliation in history, but a reconciling *person* and *presence*, we become open to a theology built on the person.[45] I can even less explore a theology of atonement in relation to shame than I properly could earlier in relation to forgiveness. Yet, I emphasised then that experience of human forgiveness should dispose people to be open to talk of taking sin on oneself, paying the price, even substitution. Just so, attribution of the work of reconciliation to him who was shamed will dispose the shamed to heed talk of a reconciliation through him who identified so deeply with them. If the hand extended to us in the shame of emotional deprivation is a gentle hand, we shall be disposed to trust its gentleness when we are also taken by that hand to view other things beside emotional deprivation. Bonhoeffer thought

43. Admittedly, this is open to challenge from the point of view that incarnation should be viewed as reconciliation in an identification that is rooted in the fact that the unassumed is the unhealed.

44. In putting it like that, I am assuming no specific position on original sin or original guilt. Those who take Adam and Eve literally have long pondered the complicity of the human race in their transgression; those who do not take them literally, take them as portraying universal existential failure.

45. John McLeod Campbell pointed out the importance of the formulation in 1 John 2:2 that it is the person of Christ who is the propitiation for our sins, *The Nature of the Atonement and its Relation to the Remission of Sins*, 3rd edition (London: Macmillan, 1869) 197.

that '[s]hame can be overcome only by being put to shame through the forgiveness of sin', but that can only be true as it stands if he was thinking of the shame involved in personal sin and its consequences.[46] If it is at all right to think of atonement as the cost of forgiveness, it is certainly right to think of shame as the cost of atonement.[47]

Conclusion

It does not follow from the portrayal of human culpability in Scripture that every intellectual manifestation of opposition to reconciliation in history should be traced to nothing but moral resistance. In this volume I have not touched on, let alone explored, the relationship between the historical form in which its detractors encountered the Christian claim about reconciliation and the forms of culpable sinfulness surveyed in the Bible, on whose testimony to human resistance to God I have been drawing. I have not mapped the engagement of the thinkers who have featured in my account, who wrestled with reason and revelation, autonomy and reconciliation, onto the specifics of the biblical story and its theology. I do not question the fact that the historical forms in which its detractors encountered the Christian claim about reconciliation were intertwined with epistemological questions any more than I doubt the intrinsic significance of those epistemological questions.

However, just as the shame of emotionally deprived individuals is grafted onto a generic humanity, which needs the message of reconciliation, so the detail of epistemological challenge to Christianity must be taken seriously without forgetting that it is grafted onto a generic resistance to the message of reconciliation. That is the angle on modernity which I have sought to explore in this volume.

---

46. *Ethics*, 306. On the range of meanings borne by the German word, *Scham*, see 303 [16].
47. Westcott's observation on Hebrews 12:2 surely has to be qualified: 'But what men count shame was seen by Christ in another light. From his position, raised infinitely above them, He could disregard their judgment', B.F. Westcott, *The Epistle to the Hebrews: The Greek Text With Notes And Essays*, 2nd edition (London/New York: NY: Macmillan, 1892) 396. 'Seen in another light', yes, but did Christ feel infinitely above anyone on the cross?

Bibliography

The following is not a list of every title cited in the book, still less of the range of relevant literature on its subject, but of all the most important works cited.

Allison, H.E. *Lessing and the Enlightenment*. Ann Arbor, MI: University of Michigan Press, 1966

Ansell-Pearson, Keith. *Nietzsche contra Rousseau: A Study of Nietzsche's Moral and Political Thought*. Cambridge: Cambridge University Press, 1991

Ansell-Pearson, Keith. 'Nietzsche on Autonomy and Morality: the Challenge to Political Theory', *Political Studies* 39.2, 1991

Ashcraft, Richard. 'Faith and Knowledge in Locke's Philosophy'. In *John Locke: Problems and Perspectives,* edited by John Yolton. Cambridge: Cambridge University Press, 1969

Baillie, John. *The Interpretation of Religion*. Edinburgh: T & T Clark, 1929

Baillie, John, ed. *Natural Theology*. London: Bles, 1934

Barth, Karl. *Church Dogmatics*, I/1. Edinburgh: T & T Clark, 1975

Barth, Karl. *Church Dogmatics*, I/2. Edinburgh: T & T Clark, 1956

Barth, Karl. *Church Dogmatics*, III/2. Edinburgh: T & T Clark, 1960

Barth, Karl. *Protestant Theology in the Nineteenth Century: Its Background and History*. London: SCM, 1972

Beck, Lewis White. *Early German Philosophy*. Cambridge, MA: Belknap, 1969

Bonhoeffer, Dietrich. *Ethics, Works*, volume 6. Minneapolis, MN: Fortress, 2009

Broome, J.H. *Pascal*. London: Arnold, 1965

Brunner, Emil. *The Mediator: A Study Of The Central Doctrine Of The Christian Faith*. Cambridge: The Lutterworth Press, 2003

Brunner, Emil. *Man in Revolt: A Christian Anthropology*. Cambridge: The Lutterworth Press, 2003

Brunner, Emil. *Dogmatics: The Christian Doctrine of Creation and Redemption: volume II*. Cambridge: James Clarke & Co, 2003

Buckley, Michael. *At the Origins of Modern Atheism*. New Haven, CT/London: Yale University Press, 1987

Buddeus, J.F. *Institutiones theologiae dogmaticae*. 1723-24

Bushnell, Horace. *The Vicarious Sacrifice, Grounded in Principles of Universal Obligation*. New York, NY: Scribner, 1866

Bushnell, Horace. *Forgiveness and Law*. London: Hodder & Stoughton, 1875

Byrne, Peter. *Natural Religion and the Nature of Religion: the Legacy of Deism*. London: Routledge, 1989

Cassirer, Ernst. *The Philosophy of the Enlightenment*. Princeton, NJ: Princeton University Press, 1951

Clarke, Desmond. *Descartes: A Biography*. Cambridge: Cambridge University Press, 2006

Clarke, Samuel. *A Demonstration of the Being and Attributes of God*. London, 1728

Cochrane, C.N. *Christianity and Classical Culture: a study of thought and action from Augustus to Augustine*. London: Oxford University Press, 1994

de Condorcet, Nicolas. *Sketch for a Historical Picture of the Progress of the Human Mind*. Translated by J. Barraclough. London: Weidenfeld & Nicolson, 1955

Craig, Edward. *The Mind of God and the Works of Man*. Oxford: Clarendon, 1987

Cranston, Maurice. *John Locke: A Biography*. Oxford: Oxford University Press, 1985

Descartes, René. *The Philosophical Writings of Descartes*. Translated by John Cottingham, Robert Stoothoff and Dugald Murdoch, volume I. Cambridge: Cambridge University Press, 1985; volume II, 1984

Dooyeweerd, Herman. *In the Twilight of Western Christendom*. Nutley, NJ: Craig Press, 1972

Frame, Donald M. *Montaigne: A Biography*. London: Hamilton, 1965

Frei, Hans. *The Eclipse of the Biblical Narrative*. New Haven, CT/London: Yale University Press, 1974

Gaukroger, Stephen. *Descartes: An Intellectual Biography*. Oxford: Clarendon, 1995

Gaukroger, Stephen. *The Emergence of a Scientific Culture: Science and the Shaping of Modernity, 1210-1685*. Oxford: Clarendon, 2006

Gillespie, Michael Allen. *Nihilism Before Nietzsche*. Chicago, IL: University of Chicago Press, 1995

Gorringe, Timothy J. *Karl Barth: Against Hegemony*. Oxford: Oxford University Press, 1999

Green, Bradley G. *Colin Gunton and the Failure of Augustine: The Theology of Colin Gunton in Light of Augustine*. Eugene, OR: Pickwick, 2011

Grimsley, Ronald. *Jean-Jacques Rousseau*. Brighton: Harvester, 1983

Gunton, Colin. 'The Truth of Christology'. In *Belief in Science and in Christian Life: The Relevance of Michael Polanyi's Thought For Christian Faith and Life*, edited by T.F. Torrance. Edinburgh: Handsel, 1980

Gunton, Colin. *Enlightenment and Alienation: An Essay towards a Trinitarian Theology* Basingstoke: Marshall, Morgan & Scott, 1985

Gunton, Colin. *The One, The Three And The Many: An Inaugural Lecture in the Chair of Chrisian Doctrine*. London: King's College, 1985

Gunton, Colin. 'Barth on the Western Intellectual Tradition'. In *Theology Beyond Christendom*, edited by John Thompson. Allison Park, PA: Pickwick, 1986

Gunton, Colin. *The Actuality of the Atonement: a Study in Metaphor, Rationality and the Christian Tradition*. Edinburgh: T & T Clark, 1988

Gunton, Colin. 'The History. Augustine, the Trinity, and the Theological Crisis of the West'. In *The Promise of Trinitarian Theology*. Edinburgh: T & T Clark, 1991

Gunton, Colin. 'Knowledge and Culture: towards and epistemology of the concrete'. In *The Gospel and Contemporary Culture*, edited by Hugh Montefiore. London: Mowbray, 1992

Gunton, Colin. *The One, The Three and the Many: God, Creation and the Culture of Modernity*. Cambridge: Cambridge University Press, 1993

Gunton, Colin. *A Brief Theology of Revelation*. Edinburgh: T & T Clark, 1995

Gunton, Colin. 'Christ, the Wisdom of God: A Study in Divine and Human Action'. In *Where Shall Wisdom be Found? Wisdom in the Bible, the Church and the Contemporary World*, edited by Stephen C. Barton. Edinburgh: T & T Clark, 1999

Gunton, Colin. *Intellect and Action: Elucidations on Christian Theology and the Life of Faith*. Edinburgh: T & T Clark, 2000

Gunton, Colin. 'Towards a Theology of Reconciliation'. In *The Theology of Reconciliation*. London: T & T Clark, 2003

Gunton, Colin. *The Barth Lectures*. Edited by P.H. Brazier. London: T & T Clark, 2007

Gunton, Colin. *Revelation and Reason: Prolegomena to Systematic Theology*. Edited by P. H. Brazier. London: T & T Clark, 2008

Harrison, Peter. *'Religion' and the Religions in the English Enlightenment*. Cambridge: Cambridge University Press, 1990

Harrison, Peter. *The Fall of Man and the Foundations of Science*. Cambridge: Cambridge University Press, 2007

Harvey, Lincoln, ed. *The Theology of Colin Gunton*. London: T & T Clark, 2010

Hayman, Ronald. *Nietzsche: A Critical Life*. London: Weidenfeld & Nicolson, 1980

Hazard, Paul. *The European Mind, 1680-1715*. New Haven, CT: Yale University Press, 1953

Hefelbower, S.G. *The Relation of John Locke to English Deism*. Chicago, IL: University of Chicago Press, 1918

Heidegger, Martin. 'The Word of Nietzsche: "God is Dead"'. In *The Question Concerning Technology and Other Essays*. New York, NY: Harper & Row, 1977

Helm, Paul. 'Locke on Faith and Knowledge'. *Philosophical Quarterly*, January 1973

Höhne, David A. *Spirit and Sonship: Colin Gunton's Theology of Particularity and the Holy Spirit*. Burlington, VT/Farnham: Ashgate, 2010

Hölderlin, F. *Hyperion and Selected Poems*. Edited by E. L. Santner. New York, NY: Continuum, 1994

Hudson, Wayne. *The English Deists: Studies in Early Enlightenment*. London: Pickering & Chatto, 2009

Jüngel, Eberhard. *God as the Mystery of the World*. Edinburgh: T & T Clark, 1983

Kant, Immanuel. *Critique of Pure Reason*. Translated by Norman Kemp Smith. London: Macmillan, 1933

Kant, Immanuel. 'What is Enlightenment?' In *Critique of Practical Reason and Other Writings in Moral Philosophy*, edited by Lewis White Beck. Chicago, IL: University of Chicago Press, 1949

Kant, Immanuel. *Religion Within the Boundaries of Mere Reason* in *Religion and Rational Theology*. Translated by Allen W. Wood and George Di Giovanni. Cambridge: Cambridge University Press, 1996

Kierkegaard, S. *Works of Love*. Translated by Howard and Edna Hong. New York, NY: Harper & Row, 1962

Kierkegaard, S. *Sickness Unto Death: a psychological exposition for upbuilding and awakening*. Translated by Howard and Edna Hong. Princeton, NJ: Princeton University Press, 1980

Kierkegaard, S. *The Concept of Anxiety*. Introduced by Reidar Thomte. Princeton, NJ: Princeton University Press, 1980

Lampert, Laurence. *Nietzsche and Modern Times: A Study of Bacon, Descartes and Nietzsche*. New Haven, CT/London: Yale University Press, 1993

Leibniz, G.W. *New Essays on Human Understanding*. Edited by J. Bennett and Peter Remnant. Cambridge: Cambridge University Press, 1981

Locke, John. *Works*. London, 1824

Locke, John. *Two Treatises of Government*, 2nd edition. Cambridge: Cambridge University Press, 1967

Locke, John. *An Essay Concerning Human Understanding*. Edited by Peter Nidditch. Oxford: Clarendon, 1975

Locke, John. *A Paraphrase and Notes On The Epistles of Saint Paul To The Galatians, 1 and 2 Corinthians, Romans, Ephesians*, volume 1. Edited by A.W. Wainwright. Oxford: Clarendon, 1987

Locke, John. *The Reasonableness of Christianity as delivered in the Scriptures*. Edited by John C. Higgins-Biddle. Oxford: Clarendon, 1999

Locke, John. *Vindications of the Reasonableness of Christianity*. Edited by Victor Nuovo. Oxford: Clarendon, 2012

McGilchrist, Iain. *The Divided Brain and the Making of the Western World*. New Haven, CT/London: Yale University Press, 2012

Mackintosh, H.R. *The Christian Experience of Forgiveness*. London: Nisbet, 1927

Magee, Bryan. *Wagner and Philosophy*. London: Penguin, 2000

Mandrou, Robert. *From Humanism to Science: 1480-1700*. Harmondsworth: Penguin, 1978

Manuel, Frank E. and Fritzie P. *Utopian Thought in the Western World*. Oxford: Blackwell, 1979

Mesnard, J. *Pascal: His Life and Works*. London: Harvill, 1952

Michalson, Gordon E. *Fallen Freedom: Kant on Radical Evil and Moral Regeneration*. Cambridge: Cambridge University Press, 1990

Mitchell, Mark T. *Michael Polanyi: The Art of Knowing*. Wilmington, DE: ISI Books, 2006

de Montaigne, Michel. *An Apology for Raymond Sebond*. Edited by Maurice Screech. London: Penguin, 1993

Mossner, E.C. *Bishop Butler and the Age of Reason*. New York, NY: Macmillan, 1936

Mullin, Bruce. *The Puritan as Yankee: a Life of Horace Bushnell*. Grand Rapids, MI: Eerdmans, 2002

Newbigin, Lesslie. *The Other Side of 1984*. London: World Council of Churches, 1983

Newbigin, Lesslie. *Foolishness to the Greeks*. London: SPCK, 1986

Newbigin, Lesslie. *The Gospel in a Pluralist Society*. London: SPCK, 1989

Newbigin, Lesslie. *Truth to Tell: the Gospel as Public Truth*. London: SPCK, 1991

Nietzsche, Friedrich. *Beyond Good and Evil/On the Genealogy of Morality*. Edited by Adrian Del Carro. Stanford, CA: Stanford University Press, 2014

Nietzsche, Friedrich. *The Birth of Tragedy and the Case of Wagner*. Translated by Walter Kaufmann. New York, NY: Random House, 1967

Nietzsche, Friedrich. *The Birth of Tragedy and Other Writings*. Edited by Raymond Geuss and Ronald Speirs. Cambridge: Cambridge University Press, 1999

Nietzsche, Friedrich. *Daybreak: Thoughts on the Prejudices of Morality*. Translated by R.J. Hollingdale. Cambridge: Cambridge University Press, 1997

Nietzsche, Friedrich. *Ecce Homo: How One Becomes What One Is*. Translated by R.J. Hollingdale. Cambridge: Cambridge University Press, 1996

Nietzsche, Friedrich. *The Gay Science*. Translated by Josefine Nauckhoff. Cambridge: Cambridge University Press, 2001

Nietzsche, Friedrich. *Human, All Too Human: A Book for Free Spirits*. Translated by R.J. Hollingdale. Cambridge: Cambridge University Press, 1996

Nietzsche, Friedrich. *Philosophy in the Tragic Age of the Greeks*. Translated by Marianne Cowan. South Bend, IN: Gateway, 1962

Nietzsche, Friedrich. *The Portable Nietzsche*. Translated by Walter Kaufmann. New York, NY: Viking, 1954

Nietzsche, Friedrich. *Selected Letters*. Translated by Christopher Middleton. Chicago, IL: University of Chicago Press, 1969

Nietzsche, Friedrich. *Thus Spoke Zarathustra*. Translated by Graham Parkes. Oxford: Oxford University Press, 2005

Nietzsche, Friedrich. *Twilight of the Idols*. Translated by Duncan Large. Oxford: Oxford University Press, 1998

Nietzsche, Friedrich. *Twilight of the Idols and The Antichrist*. Translated by R.J. Hollingdale. London: Penguin, 1990

Nietzsche, Friedrich. *Unfashionable Observations*. Translated by Richard Gray. Stanford, CA: Stanford University Press, 1995

Nietzsche, Friedrich. *The Will to Power*. Translated by Walter Kaufmann and R.J. Hollingdale. New York, NY: Vintage, 1968

Nietzsche, Friedrich. *Writings from the Late Notebooks*. Edited by Rüdiger Bittner. Cambridge: Cambridge University Press, 2003

Oman, John. *The Problem of Faith and Freedom*. London: Hodder & Stoughton, 1906

Orr, James. *Sidelights on Christian Doctrine*. London: Marshall, 1909

Pannenberg, Wolfhart. 'Types of Atheism and Their Theological Significance'. In *Basic Questions in Theology*, volume II. London: SCM, 1971

Pannenberg, Wolfhart. *Christianity in a Secularized World*. London: SCM, 1988

Pascal, Blaise. *Pensées*. Translaed by A. J. Krailsheimer. London: Penguin, 1966

Pippin, Robert P. *Modernism as a Philosophical Problem: On the Dissatisfactions of European High Culture*, 2nd edition. Oxford: Blackwell, 1999

Polanyi, Michael. *The Logic of Liberty: Reflections and Rejoinders*. Chicago, IL: University of Chicago Press, 1951

Polanyi, Michael. *Personal Knowledge: Towards a Post-Critical Philosophy*. London: Routledge & Kegan Paul, 1958

Polanyi, Michael. *The Study of Man*. Chicago, IL: University of Chicago Press, 1958

Polanyi, Michael. *The Tacit Dimension*. New York, NY: Anchor, 1967

Polanyi, Michael. *Knowing and Being: Essays by Michael Polanyi*. Edited by M. Grene. London: Routledge & Kegan Paul, 1969

Polanyi, Michael. *Science, Faith and Society*. Chicago, IL: University of Chicago Press, 1964

Polanyi, Michael with Harry Prosch. *Meaning*. Chicago, IL: University of Chicago Press, 1975

Popkin, Richard H. *The History of Scepticism: From Savonarola to Bayle*. Oxford: Oxford University Press, 2003

Rempel, *Nietzsche, Psychohistory and the Birth of Christianity*. Westport, CT: Greenwood Press, 2002

Reventlow, H.-G. *The Authority of the Bible and the Rise of the Modern World*. London: SCM, 1984

Roberts, Tyler. *Contesting Spirit: Nietzsche, Affirmation, Religion*. Princeton, NJ: Princeton University Press, 1998

Sartre, J.-P. *Descartes*. Paris: Trois Collines, 1949

Schouls, Peter. *The Imposition of Method: A Study of Descartes and Locke*. Oxford: Clarendon, 1980

Schouls, Peter. *Descartes and the Enlightenment*. Edinburgh: Edinburgh University Press, 1989

Sell, Alan P. F. *John Locke and the Eighteenth Century Divines*. Cardiff: University of Wales Press, 1997

Spellman, W.M. *John Locke and the Problem of Depravity*. Oxford: Clarendon, 1988

Spink, J.S. *French Free-Thought from Gassendi to Voltaire*. London: Athlone, 1960

Stephen, Leslie. *History of English Thought in the Eighteenth Century*, volume I. New York, NY: Harcourt, Brace and World, 1962

Stout, Jeffrey. *The Flight from Authority: Religion, Morality and the Quest for Autonomy*. Notre Dame, IN: University of Notre Dame Press, 1987

Sullivan, R.E. *John Toland and the Deist Controversy: A Study in Adaptations*. Cambridge, MA: Harvard University Press, 1988

Taylor, Charles. *Sources of the Self: The Making of Modern Identity*. Cambridge: Cambridge University Press, 1989

Temple, William. *Nature, Man and God*. London: Macmillan, 1953

Tindal, Matthew. *Christianity as Old as Creation*. London, 1930

Toland, John. *Christianity Not Mysterious*. London, 1696

Torrance, T.F. *Belief in Science and in Christian Life: The Relevance of Michael Polanyi's Thought For Christian Faith and Life*. Edinburgh: Handsel, 1980

Torrance, T.F. *Transformation and Convergence in the Frame of Knowledge*. Belfast: Christian Journals, 1984

Toulmin, Stephen. *Cosmopolis: The Hidden Agenda of Modernity*. Chicago, IL: University of Chicago Press, 1990

Velkley, Richard L. *Freedom and the End of Reason: On the Moral Foundations of Kant's Critical Philosophy*. Chicago, IL: University of Chicago Press, 1989

von Hügel, F. 'On the Preliminaries to Religious Belief and on the Facts of Suffering, Faith and Love'. In *Essays and Addresses on the Philosophy of Religion*. London: Dent, 1921

Williams, Charles. 'Descent Into Hell'. In *Charles Williams Omnibus*. Oxford: Oxford City Press, 2012

Williams, Stephen. 'Matthew Tindal on Perfection, Positivity and the Life Divine'. *Enlightenment and Dissent* 5, 1986

Williams, Stephen. *Revelation and Reconciliation: a Window on Modernity*. Cambridge: Cambridge University Press, 1995

Williams, Stephen N. *The Shadow of the Antichrist: Nietzsche's Critique of Christianity*. Grand Rapids, MI: Baker Academic Press, 2006

Wolterstorff, Nicholas. *John Locke and the Ethics of Belief*. Cambridge: Cambridge University Press, 1996

Woolhouse, Roger. *Locke: a Biography*. Cambridge: Cambridge University Press, 2007

Yolton, John. *John Locke and the Way of Ideas*. Oxford: Oxford University Press, 1956

Young, J.Z. *Philosophy and the Brain*. Oxford: Oxford University Press, 1988

Index

Aaron, Richard, 41
Allison, Dale, 28
Allison, H.E., 57
Ansell-Pearson, Keith, 101, 114, 117
Ashcraft, Richard, 33, 42, 54
Augustine, x, xii, xiv, xvi-xvii, 6, 14, 63, 123, 127-129, 133-141
Bacon, Francis, xi, 7, 9, 56
Baillie, John, 70, 167
Barth, Karl, viii-ix, 62-92, 98, 100, 106, 115-116, 118-120, 132-133, 150, 155, 169
Barton, Stephen, 147
Bayle, Pierre, 60
Beck, Lewis White, 79
Berry, R.J., 152
Bertonneau, Thomas, 98
Blake, William, 175
Bloom, Allan, 13
Blount, Charles, 55, 75
Blumenberg, Hans, 127, 134-135
Bodin, Jean, 15
Bolingbroke, Henry St. John, Viscount, 55
Bonhoeffer, Dietrich, 15, 139, 171-172, 177
Brazier, Paul, 124, 132

Breukelman, Frans, 69
Brobjer, Thomas, 95
Brock, Brian, 11
Broome, J.H., 10
Brunner, Emil, 65, 70-71, 154-155
Buckley, Michael, 140
Buddeus, J.-F., 69-75, 78, 90
Buddha, 98
Bushnell, Horace, 51, 160-161, 165-170
Butler, Joseph, 45, 57
Byrne, Peter, 56-57
Calvin, John, xvii, 141-142
Campbell, John McLeod, 177
Cassirer, Ernst, 59
Caton, Hiram, 19, 30
Chesterton, G.K., 158
Christina, Queen of Sweden, 29
Cicero, 66
Clarke, Desmond, 9, 16-17, 19, 30
Clarke, Samuel, 55, 58, 60
Cochrane, C.N., xvi-xvii, 133, 139
Coleridge, S.T., 125, 130, 164
Collins, Anthony, 55, 75
de Condorcet, Nicolas, 17
Craig, Edward, xviii, 128
Cranston, Maurice, 33-35

Crous, Ernst, 75
Cunningham, David, 140
Cupitt, Don, viii, x
Damasio, Antonio, 32
Darwin, Charles, 9, 152-153
Descartes, René, viii-xiii, xvii, 1-2,
    6-32, 62, 120, 123-126, 135, 139,
    142-144, 149-150
Diderot, Denis, 17
Doddridge, Philip, 47
Dooyweerd, Herman, 141
Dryden, John, 60
Dumarsais, C.C., 88
Dunn, J., 40
Edwards, Jonathan, 148-149
Elizabeth, Princess of Bohemia, 29
Epictetus, 12
Ferguson, Robert, 54
Feuerbach, Ludwig, xiii, 72, 89-90,
    134
Fichte, J.G., xiii, 60
Fielding, Henry, 171
Frame, D.M., 10
Frei, Hans, 56
Freud, Sigmund, 146
Funkenstein, Amos, 140
Gassendi, Pierre, 8
Gaukroger, Stephen, xi, 6, 16, 23
Gillespie, Michael Allen, 135
von Goethe, J.W., 21, 68, 83, 88
Gorringe, Timothy J, 67
Green, Bradley, 123, 133, 135-136,
    140
Green, Garrett, 59-60
Gregory, Bradley, xviii
Grene, M., 4
Grimsley, Ronald, 88
Gunton, Colin, vii-x, xii-xiv, xvii-xviii,
    2-3, 5, 37, 54, 62-66, 82, 86, 88-
    89, 121-144, 147, 150, 152
Halifax, George Savile, Marquess of,
    60
Harrison, Peter, xviii, 8, 56, 135
Harvey, Lincoln, 122, 133, 135-136
Hayman, Ronald, 92
Hazard, Paul, 60
Hefelbower, S.G., 75

Hegel, G.W.F., xviii, 18-19, 22, 65, 83,
    86-89, 113
Heidegger, Martin, 11, 106
Heller, Erich, 105
Helm, Paul, 34, 36
Heraclitus, 23
Herbert of Cherbury, xv, 53, 55, 81
Herder, J.G., 83
Herrmann, Wilhelm, 168
Higgins-Biddle, John, 46, 51
Hobbes, Thomas, 53, 120
Höhne, David, 122, 139
Hölderlin, Friedrich, 104
Homer, 92, 111
Hudson, Wayne, 55
Huët, Pierre-Daniel, 14
Hume, David, 120
Inge, W.R. (Dean), 169
Irenaeus, 127-129, 136
Irving, Washington, 31
Jüngel, Eberhard, xiii-xiv, 124
Kafka, Franz, 166
Kant, Immanuel, xiii, xvi, 59, 65, 74,
    83, 88, 100-101, 104, 106-117,
    119, 123-125, 139, 143, 145
Kemp, Kenneth, 154
Kierkegaard, S., xvii, 18, 138, 144
Koyré, Alexandre, 31
de Lagarde, Paul, 74-75
Lampert, Lawrence, 17, 19, 30
Laslett, Peter, 52
Leibniz, G.W., 19, 40, 66-68, 83, 88-
    90, 100-101, 104, 106-107, 110
Leiter, Brian, 12
Lessing, G.E., 70, 83
Levin, David, 24-25
Lewis, Hywel D., 25
Locke, John, viii-ix, xi-xiii, xvii, 1-8,
    16-17, 21, 28-29, 31-32, 33-55,
    57, 60, 62, 64, 73, 75-78, 120-
    125, 132-133, 145, 148-150
Louth, Andrew, xv
Luther, Martin, xvii, 100, 103, 105-
    107, 110
McGilchrist, Iain, xviii, 25-26, 28, 32
McGrath, Alister, 132
Mackintosh, H.R., 166-169

Madueme, Hans, 152
Magee, Bryan, 94
Mandrou, Robert, 23
Manuel, Frank, 120
Manuel, Fritzie, 120
Marx, Karl, 146
Mesnard, J., 10
Michalson, Gordon, 114
Middleton, Conyers, 55
Mijuskovic, Ben, 25
Mill, J.S., 120
Mitchell, Mark, 4-8, 17, 22-23, 31
de Montaigne, Michel, 7-16, 20-22, 26, 142, 150
Montefiore, H., xii
Morris, William, 133
Mossner, E.C., 59
Musil, Robert, 25
Newbigin, Lesslie, viii-xvii
Niebuhr, Reinhold, 159
Nietzsche, Friedrich, vii-viii, x, xiii, 11-15, 18-19, 23, 28, 88-120, 124, 135-136, 141, 146, 151-152, 155, 160, 175
Newton, Isaac, xv
Noble, T.A., 152
Novalis, F. von Hardenberg, 83
Nuovo, Victor, 47
Ockham, William of, 35, 126-128, 133-135, 139
Oman, John, 55, 57, 162, 165, 167, 169
Orr, James, 165, 167
Osterwald, J.F., 70-71
Otto, Rudolf, 166
Pannenberg, Wolfhart, 134, 170
Parkes, Graham, 92-93, 119
Pascal, Blaise, xvii, 10-16, 22, 25-26, 28, 31-32, 54, 61-62, 97-98, 113, 147-148, 167
Pattison, Mark, 46
Pfaff, Christian, 70-71
Pippin, Robert, 18, 22, 116, 134
Plato, 120, 127, 135
Plutarch, 9, 12, 66
Polanyi, Michael, viii-ix, xi-xiv, 1-8, 16-18, 21-24, 28-37, 42, 45-46, 51, 53-54, 62, 65, 89, 117, 121-125, 139, 141-142
Popkin, Richard, 8, 23
Prigogine, Ilya, 131
Prosch, H., 4, 142
Protagoras, 142
Reeves, Michael, 152
Rempel, Morgan, 103
Reventlow, H.-G., xiv-xvii, 60, 69, 75, 147
Rice-Davies, Mandy, 147
Richardson, Alan, 46
Ritschl, A., 72
Roberts, Tyler, 111
Rousseau, Jean-Jacques, 13, 21, 82-87, 90, 115-120
Ryle, Gilbert, 54
Sand, George, 118
Santaniello, Weaver, 95
Sartre, J.-P., 18, 124
Schacht, Richard, 12
Schleiermacher, Friedrich, 63, 65, 69-74, 83, 85, 89-90
Schopenhauer, Arthur, 12, 98, 106, 113, 117-118
Schouls, Peter, 16-18, 20, 22, 31, 52, 54
Scotus, Duns, 134
Screech, Maurice, 7, 9, 11, 14
Sell, Alan, 47
Semler, J.S., 70
Seneca, 9, 12
Sextus Empiricus, 7
Simpson, Peter, 35
Spellman, W.M., 51
Spink, J.S., 23
Spinoza, B., 120
Stengers, Isabelle, 131
Stephen, Leslie, 59
Sterne, Laurence, 112
Stillingfleet, Edward, 36-37, 77
Stout, Jeffrey, 61
Strauss, D.F., 72
Sullivan, R.E., 61
Swamidass, S.J., 154
Tacitus, 102
Tanner, Michael, 92

Taylor, Charles, xviii, 17, 20-22, 25,
    126, 142-143
Temple, William, 7, 60
Thielicke, Helmut, 98
Tholuck, August, 90
Tillich, Paul, 81
Tindal, Matthew, 55-60, 77-78, 80-81
Toland, John, 55-56, 61, 76-77
Torrance, T.F., 2-3, 37-38, 54, 62,
    64-65
Toulmin, Stephen, 8, 21-22, 26
Troeltsch, E., 53, 72
Turretini, Jean Alphonse, 70-71
Van Til, Salomon, 71-72
Varro, 10
Velkley, Richard, 114, 116
Voegelin, Eric, 5, 17
Voltaire, F.-M. Arouet, 105
von Hügel, Friedrich, 166-167
von Rad, Gerhard, 144
Vrooman, J.R., 16, 29
Wagner, Richard, 94-95, 104
Wainwright, A.W., 52

Walaeus, 82
Weber, Max, xviii
Webster, John, 133
Wendelin, M. F, 82
Werenfels, Samuel, 70-71
Wesley, John, 53
Westcott, B.F., 178
Westermann, Claus, 144
Willey, Basil, 15, 60
Williams, Charles, 27, 165
Williams, Stephen N., vii, x, xv, 13, 38,
    55, 77, 97-98, 118, 135, 173
Williams, Susan L, 173
Wittgenstein, Ludwig, 156
Wolff, Christian, 70, 72-73, 77, 84, 90
Wollaston, William, 55
Wolterstorff, Nicholas, 34
Woolhouse, Roger, 33
Wordsworth, William, 21
Wright, N.T., 170
Yolton, John, 40, 42, 57
Young, J.Z., 28
Zuboff, Shoshana, xviii

You may also be interested in:

Dogmatics:
Volume I: The Christian Doctrine of God
Volume II: The Christian Doctrine of Creation and Redemption
Volume III: The Christian Doctrine of the Church,
Faith and the Consummation
By Emil Brunner

Available in three volumes, this is one of the great works of 20th Century theology. Brunner presents a profoundly biblical systematic theology, finding a path between the ideas of Barth and Bultmann.

Volume I: Hardback ISBN: 978 0 227 17216 2 / Paperback ISBN: 978 0 227 17215 5
              Specifications: 216x140mm (8.5x5.5in), 372pp / Published: March 2003
Volume II: Hardback ISBN: 978 0 227 17218 6 / Paperback ISBN: 978 0 227 17217 9
              Specifications: 216x140mm (8.5x5.5in), 402pp / Published: March 2003
Volume III: Hardback ISBN: 978 0 227 17220 9 / Paperback ISBN: 978 0 227 17219 3
              Specifications: 216x140mm (8.5x5.5in), 472pp / Published: March 2003

Man in Revolt:
A Christian Anthropology
By Emil Brunner

A wide-ranging discussion of human nature seeing the relationship between God and humanity as the key to the contradiction between what we are and ought to be.

Hardback ISBN: 978 0 7188 9044 5 / Paperback ISBN: 978 0 7188 9043 8
Specifications: 229x153mm (9x6in), 574pp / Published: March 2003

The Mediator:
A Study of the Central Doctrine of the Christian Faith
By Emil Brunner

A thorough and provocative analysis of the biblical doctrine of the Person and the Work of Christ, establishing Jesus as the mediator between God and man.

Hardback ISBN: 978 0 7188 9050 6 / Paperback ISBN: 978 0 7188 9049 0
Specifications: 229x153mm (9x6in), 628pp / Published: April 2003

BV - #0001 - 020321 - C0 - 234/156/11 - CC - 9780227177389 - Gloss Lamination